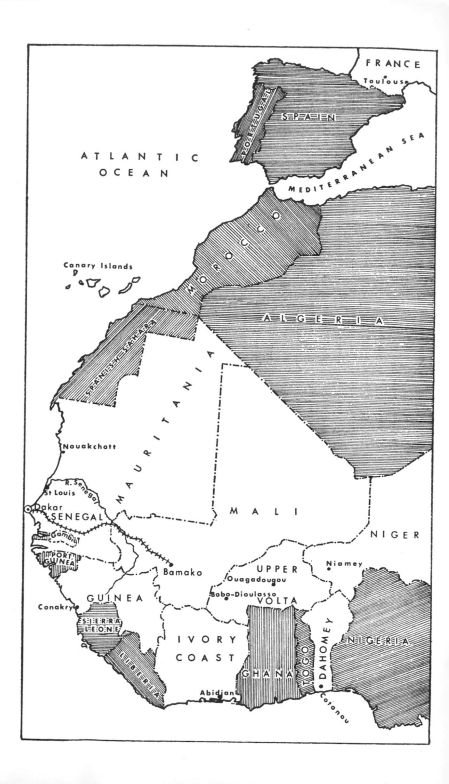

The Foreign Policy of Senegal

The Foreign Policy of Senegal

W. A. E. Skurnik

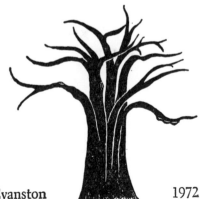

Northwestern University Press Evanston   1972

The material in chapter four on culture and international
relations is partially based on an article by the author
that appeared in *African Forum*, Vol. III, no. 2 (1970),
entitled "Senghor on Culture: The African and International Context."

W. A. E. Skurnik is associate professor of political science
at the University of Colorado.

To my parents, with gratitude

Contents

Tables and Charts

Introduction

THE RECENT IRRUPTION of the new African states into the international arena will have far-reaching consequences for the international state system. It may not yet be possible to ascertain the specific dimensions of this event. But it is possible to take a close look at the motivations, priorities, and policy orientation of African states and to speculate about likely future trends. A glance at the foreign policy of such states as Senegal indicates that the international community must become more responsive to at least three major factors. One is the continued growth of nationalism, meaning both the pursuit of national interests, however defined, and the desire to be a subject rather than an object of contemporary history. Another is the dedication to ending the decolonization process, whatever the means selected or advocated. A third is a demand for restructuring some aspects of international relations to allow for the full participation of the newcomers.

Given their relative novelty, the foreign relations of developing countries are not yet well understood, and this is particularly true of the states of black Africa. Texts on international relations, usually written by generalists, are only beginning to devote some space to Third World countries and to shed some of the bipolar focus which resulted from the cold war.

An understanding of the foreign policy of African states suffers from a variety of simplistic images: of a continent whose volatile and somewhat naïve leaders are choice prey for Communist duplicity, of incessant tribal warfare, of intemperate slogans and rhetoric, and of quaint elites in European dress who play both ends against the middle and open secret Swiss bank accounts. At a time when Americans are reexamining their own foreign policy priorities, it is important that they shed false images and appreciate the immense foreign relations problems inherited by African countries from the colonial era. In the years to come, America's dependence on access to the Third World is bound to increase and so will the need for sympathetic understanding.

American students of Africa have in the main shown deep sympathy for the new African states. At times their sympathy has tended to make heroes of "radicals" and villains of "moderates." Some have suggested that a revolutionary, radical foreign relations stance is the only position which African states ought to pursue. There is something odd about the notion that only the radicals should be allowed to speak for Africa, and that therefore Africans can be separated into the enlightened—presumably those who follow freely the right kind of leader—and the duped —those who are somehow coerced into electing traitors to their best interests. Many Africans reply that this amounts to a new kind of arrogance, of misguided paternalism. They suggest that Africa is not a place of violence and radicalism, but the home of wisdom inherent in balanced judgment, in perspective, in moderation, in reasoned discourse.

Both these views, taken by themselves, are oversimplifications. One of my objectives in preparing this study was to attempt to tell the story of the foreign policy behavior of a "moderate" African state. My concern with the need to redress the balance may have caused me to emphasize justifications of moderate behavior more than would otherwise have been the case; the reader may find traces of my own sympathies for the kind of humanitarianism expressed by Léopold Sédar Senghor. But it should be remembered that many African leaders contend that no one, not even Africans, has a monopoly of wisdom on what is best for Africa.

This book is addressed to students. It is intended as a supplement to more general works on international affairs and on the foreign relations behavior of the new African states, and to materials normally presented by instructors.[1] It is designed to present the student with a sample of foreign relations behavior that provides specific data which make generalizations more meaningful. I have assumed that the foreign relations behavior of Senegal is fairly typical of that of many other African states, which tend to react in similar ways to like problems. Hence, it is intended also as a useful ingredient in the comparative study of African foreign relations. One of the dangers of highly theoretical comparative materials is that they divorce theory and reality; another is that they leave the student with a temptation to link concepts directly with preconceptions without the intermediary of factual background and analysis. The world then becomes an amalgam of commitments and theory, not the best preparation for effective and judicious understanding of African foreign relations.

The material is presented with the help of several overlapping analytical categories: chronological review and reconstruction; aspects of the structure and process of the foreign policy machinery; and economic, philosophical, and political elements of foreign relations. These categories provide data for a focus on the relative potency of domestic, external, and individual variables as seen through representative issue-areas. The discussion

1. The few books dealing with the international relations of African states include Vernon McKay, ed., *African Diplomacy: Studies in the Determinants of Foreign Policy* (New York: Praeger, 1966); Abdul A. Said, *The African Phenomenon* (Boston: Allyn and Bacon, 1966); I. William Zartman, *International Relations in the New Africa* (Englewood Cliffs, N.J.: Prentice-Hall, 1966); and to some extent J. D. B. Miller, *The Politics of the Third World* (New York: Oxford University Press, 1967).

addresses itself also to the concept of nonalignment and seeks to use the notions of adaptation and innovation and to highlight elements of continuity and change. I have assumed that President Senghor is the most important single foreign policy decision-maker in Senegal because such authority is concentrated in his office, because empirical data tend to corroborate the assumption, and, perhaps most important, because influential Senegalese officials believe that this is so.

Chapter one reviews salient aspects of the preindependence foreign relations behavior of Senegal. It concentrates on the dynamics of transformation of Senegal's ties with France and the federation of French West Africa, expressed in the twin themes of autonomy/independence and inter-African unity. It begins with the 1945 attempt to create a "nonpolitical" African federal structure, the Comité d'Etudes Franco-Africaines, and ends with Senegal's ill-fated readiness to give up important elements of political sovereignty to a larger inter-African ensemble. The discussion highlights Senegal's motivations and style, found to correspond closely to the period following independence.

Chapter two, after a brief discussion of the constitutional framework for foreign affairs, focuses on select aspects and problems of the Foreign Ministry. The discussion treats organizational, financial, and personnel policy, as well as the motives for establishing diplomatic missions abroad, and it concludes with a profile of Senegal's ambassadors in an attempt to understand recruitment policy at that level and to speculate about ambassadors' attitudes concerning foreign affairs.

Chapter three presents Senegal's foreign economic links from the point of view of the country's motivations, opportunities, and the structure of heavy dependence on extra-African support and on the inter-African hinterland. The chapter discusses also the trend toward diversification of economic relations encouraged by external and domestic developments.

Chapter four addresses itself to three important components of Senegal's foreign affairs position: policy guidelines, the cultural components of President Senghor's perceptions about international affairs, and the country's inter-African policies within the group of French-speaking African states. This chapter is intended as a descriptive account of, and preparation for, the analysis in the conclusion. To that end, the three specific case studies of the events and motivations surrounding policy decisions seem particularly useful.

Chapter five focuses first on the concept of nonalignment and concludes that it is too imprecise an analytical handle. Consequently, it seeks to use concepts with lower emotional content and suggests the usefulness of such orienting devices as adaptation and innovation, and particularly of James N. Rosenau's "pretheory" adapted for studying the foreign relations behavior of Third World countries.[2] It examines the proposition that the foreign policy decisions of African states can be explained primarily through the idiosyncrasies of individual decision-makers. The evidence in this case suggests that this is not so and that this expectation may be shown to be erroneous in other African states as well. Finally, an attempt is made to project the direction of Senegal's foreign policy after the eventual retirement of President Senghor.

I owe thanks to many people who have helped me in the preparation and writing of this study. I wish to single out Messrs. Simon Kiba, Justin Mendy, and J.-B. Adotévi of *Afrique nouvelle*; Doudou Thiam, Omar Vélé, and other government officials in Senegal; students and professors at the University of Dakar; as well as M. J.-F. Maurel, the much-burdened head of Senegal's archives. I am particularly grateful also to Messrs. Ernest Milcent, Jacques Hubert, and Robert Cornevin for stimulating discussions. Professors William J. Foltz, Kenneth W. Grundy, Claude E. Welch, and I. William Zartman have read a previous draft and offered comments and criticisms; they must be credited with removing obscurities, although I claim responsibility for any remaining errors of fact and interpretation. I wish to acknowledge also financial assistance from the Social Science Council/Graduate School of International Studies of the University of Denver, which made possible a field trip to Senegal

2. "Pre-Theories and Theories of Foreign Policy," in *Approaches to Comparative and International Politics*, ed. R. Barry Farrell (Evanston: Northwestern University Press, 1966).

in the summer of 1967, and assistance by the University of Dakar. To my wife, Peggy, belongs my deep gratitude for editorial criticisms and for her generous understanding and encouragement.

The Foreign Policy of Senegal

CHAPTER ONE

Antecedents of Independence

GENERAL BACKGROUND

Profile of a small state

By most conventional standards, Senegal is a small and poor country. In an area approximately the size of South Dakota, Senegal contains over five times the population recorded for that state in 1967. Her 1968 Gross National Product was estimated at $820 million, and her national budget at $150 million for 1969/70; per capita income was in the neighborhood of $170. These statistics suggest that, among the new states of Africa, she is a medium power at some distance from either extreme.[1]

Senegal's location at the western tip of the African continent places her in a strategically favorable position, at the crossroads of the shortest route from Africa to Brazil, a convenient spot for ocean traffic around the Cape of Good Hope, and of the sea route from black Africa to Europe. These natural advantages

1. For more detailed statistics, consult *Situation économique du Sénégal* (1965) (Dakar: Service de la Statistique, 1966); *Mémento de l'économie africaine, 1967* (Paris: Ediafric, 1967); and *Europe France-Outremer*, Vol. CDLXXX–I (January–February, 1970).

tend to be vitiated, however, by technological develo
which shorten air and sea routes and make it increasing
nomical to bypass Dakar. Within West Africa, economic
alism pushes other countries to develop their own harbor
transport facilities, although Dakar still remains a con
stop for aircraft originating in the United States.

The country's 1,060 miles of land borders, which separ
from Mauritania in the north, Mali in the east, and the
lic of Guinea as well as Portuguese Guinea in the south, a
delineated although highly permeable. Her coastline on
lantic Ocean is generally shallow but also treacherous in
places because of cliffs; the shoreline is nevertheless suita
maritime fishing. The Gambia, a narrow, 200-mile-long s
land inside Senegal on both banks of the Gambia River
irritant: it encourages smuggling and thus deprives Sen
revenue and of a river navigable some 200 miles inlan
requires patient diplomacy with a view to harmonious re
among French- and English-language governments.

Senegal is a poor country from the point of view of av
natural resources. Sandbars obstruct the mouth of the 1,05
long Senegal River, which is navigable only for 150 miles
most of the year, except for shallow craft, which can doub
distance. The climate is arid save for a narrow strip alo
coast, and agricultural development depends mostly on t
which can be made of the Senegal River. There is no
barrier to trade—except for distance. Partly as a result
concentration on one cash crop—the peanut—and par
cause of population pressure, Senegal must import food. N
resources do not appear to forecast a brilliant future. T
some phosphate, iron, and as yet unexploited titaniferou
But the search for oil, natural gas, and coal has so far b
vain; there is some prospect of finding oil, but proba b
enough to provide the basis for any heavy industry. The
est prospects for improving agriculture, and some manu
ing, are through investments in the Senegal River basin. I
the dearth of the country's own resources makes it neces
let foreign capital exploit—and thus control—major d
ment schemes.

It is difficult at best to assess what contribution Senegal

ulation can make to her welfare, and hence to her influence in interstate relations as measured by conventional methods. In terms of numbers, her population is not large enough to be considered a threat to others. Although Senegal has a higher proportion of educated people in the modern sense than have her neighbors, her population at large is as little technologically oriented. Any consideration of national morale must remain speculative since it is largely untested. The government has been able to mobilize rapid, large-scale, and apparently enthusiastic support in connection with a few crises; but it is difficult to extract any generalization from such events, except that, as in most African states, the people will tend to support their government if they perceive a national crisis, especially a foreign threat. Another generalization may be ventured in that the Senegalese regard themselves as proud, honorable, and the equal of any other people. No doubt in an attempt to popularize this facet of national morale, President Senghor has repeatedly underlined the qualitative, as opposed to the quantitative, aspects of his country's virtues.

Senegal's African population is relatively homogeneous, primarily because most important ethnic groups share similar social and political structures and are distinguished chiefly by languages and dialects. The Wolof tongue, that of the largest single ethnic group (37 per cent of the African population), is understood by most Senegalese and tends to be an indigenous lingua franca. Other important ethnic groups include the Serer (20 per cent); the Toucouleur (14 per cent); the Soudanese group, which comprises Mandé, Malinké, Sarakolé, and some Bambara (8.5 per cent); the Foula and Diola (7 per cent each); the Moors (1.6 per cent); and the Lébou (1.3 per cent). The southern region of Casamance is the exception to this relative unity; the region borders on Portuguese Guinea and is geographically isolated from the rest of Senegal by The Gambia.

In 1969, the total population of Senegal was estimated at slightly over 3.8 million. The average density is 30 inhabitants per square mile, with variations from 2 per square mile in the eastern desert area to some 700 in the built-up Cap Vert area in the west. The urban population has increased from 6 per cent of the total in 1900 to some 30 per cent in the mid-nineteen sixties. The African population has more than tripled since about 1900; the city of Dakar has nearly 500,000 people, who are increasing at an annual rate of about 6 per cent.

Senegal's non-African population has decreased since independence. As a result of the africanization of personnel, of the withdrawal of large business firms from the country to urban centers, of the decrease in French armed forces, and of the fewer opportunities perceived by small business, foreigners number about 50,000—there were some 62,000 in 1961. Most foreigners are French, but there are also about 15,000 Lebanese engaged in retail trade along with Mauritanians in urban centers and Diolas as itinerant traders.

The vast majority of Senegalese are Muslim. Only about 500,000 are classified as animist, and some 160,000 as Christian. Both Islam and Christianity are influences of long standing and have made considerable impact on the population. Islam was introduced from the north, first as an elite religion, but in time it was adapted for the masses. Christianity, mostly Roman Catholicism, accompanied the European presence and has in fact become the religion of many business, social, and political elites. Like Islam, the Christian creed was adapted and its meaning has taken on a significance derived from the social context and needs of the inhabitants. Islam, however, is on the ascendancy, as it is elsewhere in West Africa, whereas Christianity is fighting a holding operation at best. Muslims divide their allegiance among three brotherhoods: the Qadiriyya, the Tijaniyya—numerically the largest—with strong attachments in Morocco, and the peculiarly Senegalese phenomenon of the Mourides, who make up the most politically potent Muslim community, look to their khalifa-general as a temporal as well as spiritual savior, and derive their income from peanut cultivation.

Since independence, population movement has been chiefly internal. Before 1960, Soudanese and Guineans came to Senegal during the peanut harvest and returned home afterward. Except for a general movement from country to city, internal migration tends to be seasonal and connected with agriculture. Further, some twenty thousand Senegalese are working in unskilled and semiskilled jobs in France.

Traditional, that is, pre-European, Senegal does not loom large in foreign relations. With one exception, Senegal tended to remain outside the area of the great West African empires and kingdoms; only Tekrour, along the upper Senegal River, had some gold and was subordinated to the Gana Empire and its successor states. As in the case of most of the new African states, elements of Senegal's ethnic groups overlap into other states. Senegal contains some thirty thousand people of Guinean origin, and Toucouleur inhabit the Mauritanian bank of the Senegal River. Problems arising from this distribution have been minimal, primarily because of the government's strict adherence to the integrity of the new states' territory. The most serious potential problem concerns the southern district of Casamance. This is inhabited chiefly by animists, who, partly because they are relatively isolated from the rest of Senegal by The Gambia, have retained very strong ties with their families across the borders with independent Guinea and Portuguese Guinea and still speak of going to Senegal when they contemplate a trip to Dakar. Senegal can make few claims to influence inter-African relations on the basis of historical argument.

Because of her location at the westernmost tip of the African continent, on the Atlantic Ocean, Senegal had early contact with Europeans. Dinis Dias is believed to have been the first European to sail his Portuguese ship to the area in 1444. A French merchant is credited with having established a post in 1639 near Saint-Louis south of the present Mauritanian border and thus laid the basis for subsequent French penetration. French merchants, in fact, more or less controlled much of the Senegal River as well as the coast for two hundred years, from the middle of the seventeenth to the middle of the nineteenth century. The interior of Senegal was brought under French control beginning in the 1850s under Governor Louis Faidherbe, an irascible Frenchman interested in administration, education, and political efficiency. The French push into the interior continued after the Franco-Prussian War chiefly for reasons of prestige, enabling the French to substitute the glory of conquering African territory for the humiliation of losing a war in Europe. The present political boundaries of Senegal were set by 1895, at which time the French government created the Federation of French West Africa (AOF—Afrique Occidentale Française) to streamline

French administrative control and to insure that the burden of colonial administration not be borne by the French taxpayer.[2] In view of the "balkanization" issue popularized by Senegal in the 1950s, it is important to note at this time that AOF was created by the French to serve primarily French, not African, interests.

There are few places in black Africa where French influence has been so potent as in Senegal. French educational facilities were implanted near the turn of the last century; secondary and higher education facilities were created to serve not only Senegal but also other colonies of AOF. French education, and intermarriage, resulted in a social elite among Senegalese centered in Saint-Louis, whose descendants still play an important social and political role in Senegal today. Many Saint-Louisiens, and other Senegalese as well, pride themselves on having been conversant with French language, literature, and culture for several generations.

Senegal was permitted to begin an embryonic, local political life and tradition after the 1870s. Many Senegalese, in fact, derive a vicarious sense of participation in the French Revolution since the colony sent a representative to Paris in 1789 to present grievances as did other parts of France. Four townships (Saint-Louis, Rufisque, Dakar, and Gorée) became as autonomous as other French communes in the late nineteenth century. Their inhabitants—and later their descendants—became French citizens, in contrast to the "subjects" of the rest of Senegal.

One important by-product of this early association with France was the growth of a dual consciousness of being Senegalese as well as being oriented toward France. Senegalese were employed in other colonies in the federal French administration since only they had the required educational qualifications. Senegalese tirailleurs, colonial soldiers in the service of France, helped the metropole to subdue and "pacify" other Africans (although most tirailleurs were not Senegalese). As a result,

2. For details, see Georges Hardy, *Histoire sociale de la colonisation française* (Paris: Larose, 1953); Colin Newbury, "The Formation of the Government-General of French West Africa," *Journal of African History*, Vol. I (1960); and W. A. E. Skurnik, "France and Fragmentation in West Africa: 1945–1960," *Journal of African History*, Vol. VIII (1967).

Senegalese acquired a reputation for arrogance toward other "natives," a sentiment which has survived at least in the popular mind of former AOF states. Shortly after Senegal's independence, President Léopold Sédar Senghor reminded his countrymen to beware of their endemic attitude of superiority, which he termed "Senegalitis." French influence thus served to reinforce a Senegalese consciousness; but from the point of view of inter-African relations, it also introduced an irritant which many Senegalese, until recently, were reluctant to discuss openly.

Because of the politically unitary mentality and the structure of things French, all aspects of African autonomy took place within the political system existing in the metropolitan country. Local autonomy, such as it was until independence, was conditioned by the central authority residing in Paris. The French legislature not being constitutionally empowered to delegate its authority to other legislative bodies, Senegal was first represented in the French parliament in 1848—nearly one hundred years before the same policy was extended to other AOF territories. African quasi-legislatures were introduced in AOF, at the federal and territorial levels, following World War II, for the purpose of allowing Africans to exercise some administrative and financial autonomy. But the seat of political decision-making remained in Paris.

Political background

Senegal's domestic political history has followed a pluralistic pattern, which probably reinforced the present leadership's taste for conciliation as a method for settling conflict. The factions of Senegalese politics include local clans (small groups dominated by individual leaders), religious sects, regional particularisms, and, to a lesser extent, smaller political parties, labor unions, and outstanding personalities capable at times of mobilizing considerable support for specific issues. Since 1951, politics has been dominated by the party created and led by Léopold Sédar Senghor, who became president of the Republic in 1960 and is thus one of Africa's longest officeholders. The methods used by the dominant party to overcome internal opposition have revolved around the concept of compromise: dialogue, symbolic deference, absorption of key leaders, financial and other types of subsidies, and, in only a few cases, reluctant force.

Foreign influence on the domestic politics of Senegal—chiefly French—has been indirect and, on the whole, negligible and unsuccessful. Examples include the extension of the French Socialist party, the services of the Communists in creating or solidifying, or both, Communist-oriented African parties, and traditional religious leaders responding to material and other advantages they received from France. Only the Socialist party succeeded in building a Senegalese base until it was eclipsed by Senghor. In the long run, Senghor was able to insulate Senegal's domestic politics from these influences relatively well.

A Socialist party was created in Senegal around 1930 under the leadership of Amadou Lamine Guèye, a lawyer who represented the interests of French citizens and came to control the country's important municipalities, including the strongholds of Saint-Louis and Dakar. With the help of resident Frenchmen, Guèye became the president of a Senegalese branch of the French Socialist party in 1936 and later led Senegal into a kind of alliance with a French political party, of which he subsequently became a director. Senghor was at first elected to the French constituent and legislative assemblies in 1945 and 1946 under the Socialist banner as a bright young lieutenant of Guèye. This affiliation was at least partly responsible for Senghor's refusal to join an international African party, the Rassemblement Démocratique Africain (RDA), created in 1946 under the leadership of Félix Houphouet-Boigny of the Ivory Coast to protest a resurgence of conservatism in France. As he later explained, he did not attend the meeting "because I obeyed orders from the metropole too blindly." [3]

The RDA later created two branches in Senegal, neither able to secure widespread popular support. One was led by Gabriel d'Arboussier, secretary-general of the interterritorial RDA, whose headquarters were in Dakar; the other was an offshoot whose

3. *Condition humaine* (September 10, 1954). Senghor had signed a joint manifesto protesting French conservatism and planned to attend the meeting.

leadership refused to follow a policy orientation sympathetic to the Communists after the interterritorial RDA ended its tactical affiliation with the French Communist party in Paris.

Other politically overt opposition groups include the Marxist-oriented Parti Africain de l'Indépendance (PAI); because it calls for revolution, if necessary violent, its appeal is restricted to a few intellectuals among whom students at the University of Dakar are prominent. The PAI was declared illegal in 1960 after using forecful methods during an election. Another group, the Parti du Regroupement Africain—Sénégal (PRA—Sénégal), was formed in 1958 by dissidents who wanted to reject the new French constitution and thus lead Senegal into immediate political independence. PRA—Sénégal support is concentrated in the Casamance district, where it amounts to about one-third of that of the dominant party led by Senghor. Following a long series of discussions, PRA—Sénégal leaders decided in 1967 to accept Senghor's invitation to join him, and they secured high party and government offices.[4]

Senghor has been particularly careful to cultivate Muslim religious leaders who control the political votes of their adherents. To judge from his frequent encounters with them, the outward deference he pays them, and the easy access which he grants to their representatives, these religious leaders are not without influence. They have not, however, been independently active politically save for a few occasions; their role is more negative than positive in the sense that they are a conservative force, usually follow Senghor's policy leadership, and only occasionally have opposed him—without success. In 1958, for example, they created a short-lived party, the Parti de Solidarité Sénégalaise (PSS); the PSS acted as a counterweight to the PRA—Sénégal in connection with the independence issue, possibly because they were influenced by the French administration but largely to protect

4. For details, consult William J. Foltz, "Senegal," in *Political Parties and National Integration in Tropical Africa*, ed. James S. Coleman and Carl G. Rosberg (Berkeley and Los Angeles: University of California Press, 1964); Ernest Milcent, *L'A.O.F. entre en scène*, Bibliothèque de l'Homme d'Action (Paris: Editions Témoignage Chrétien, 1958); and Milcent, "Senegal," in *African One-Party States*, ed. Gwendolen M. Carter (Ithaca: Cornell University Press, 1962).

their interests in continued beneficial relations with France. Two years later, Senghor was able to secure their active support against Soudanese encroachments on Senegal's sovereignty at the time the Mali Federation broke up; this was not difficult since they had, along with many French colonial officials, opposed the federation from its inception.

Senghor's predominance in Senegal's politics dates back to 1951. By 1947, Senghor was disillusioned with the French and Senegalese Socialists, partly because the metropolitan party was unconcerned about Africa and because Lamine Guèye, who represented the urban bourgeoisie, would not—or could not—adapt to new political circumstances. At a time when the franchise was extended to ever-increasing numbers of Senegalese "subjects," whose outlook toward French policy was apt to be critical and who asked for their equality with the citizens represented by Lamine Guèye, the Senegalese Socialists failed to adapt themselves to the subjects' rising consciousness. Senghor resigned from the party in 1948 to create his own, the Bloc Démocratique Sénégalais (BDS). Since Senghor had been elected in order to represent the subjects, he capitalized on their defense; and the first electoral test, the 1951 election of deputies for the French legislature, resulted in a crushing BDS victory in the countryside, although Guèye retained control over Saint-Louis and Dakar for some years. Many of the younger Senegalese Socialists joined Senghor in 1956, and the Socialist party itself, still led by Guèye, merged with Senghor's party in 1958 to form the Union Progressiste Sénégalaise (UPS), which has since dominated the country's political life.

Senegal's privileged position

During the preindependence period, Senegal derived substantial material benefits from her geographic location, her long association with France, and her role as the center of the Federation of French West Africa (AOF). Senegal became the largest single beneficiary of French public assistance after the Second World War. Prior to 1945, French investment in AOF remained mostly private; but after the war, the French government recognized the relationship between political and economic development and used public funds to create the preconditions for further economic growth in her Overseas Territories. These public funds were administered by special agencies created for that purpose. Between 1947, when the public assistance program got off the ground, and 1958, the French government granted $542,500,-000 to AOF. Senegal, one of eight AOF territories, received 23 per cent of the total; over 90 per cent of Senegal's share was earmarked for social and economic infrastructure, and the Dakar area received about 75 per cent of the total for Senegal in view of the city's importance as the capital of the federation. The importance of Senegal's role within AOF, from the point of view of French assistance, was highlighted in 1959 when AOF ceased to exist. During that year, Senegal's share of French public funds decreased to 9 per cent since the other AOF states were able to press their claims directly to Paris as autonomous states rather than as members of the federation.

Senegal's export earnings are dependent largely on a single product, the peanut. This was introduced in the middle of the last century and, since the soil proved to be favorable for its cultivation, expanded rapidly. Peanuts are refined into cooking oil, and its by-products include oil cake, which contains from 40 to 50 per cent nitrogen and is therefore useful as animal fodder, as well as shells suitable for burning as fuel. Peanuts are grown mostly in small farm plots with low yields. According to one French study, the peanut provides "only mediocre revenue to the Senegalese farmer and also constitutes a serious threat to the fertility of soils." [5]

The introduction of the peanut into Senegal connected that country's economy with the world, but at the price of French intermediation. Its cultivation was dependent on artificial price supports as a result of which it could not compete outside this restrictive framework. The price paid to the farmer was set by the French government in Paris, although the system attempted to avoid fluctuations. The French government also established quotas to make sure that Senegal could sell the bulk of her annual harvest and production. The primary purpose of encourag-

5. *La République du Sénégal* (Paris: La Documentation Française, no. 2754, February 22, 1961), p. 12.

ing production was the French government's concern that Senegal derive the revenue needed to pay for colonial administration costs from her own resources.

A similar concentration was reflected in French private investment. In 1946, for instance, of the 600 private commercial enterprises in AOF, 393 had their headquarters in Senegal. Ten years later, Senegal accounted for 1,267 of such firms out of an AOF total of 2,298.[6]

The relative economic importance of Senegal within AOF is shown also in regard to foreign trade. Most of Senegal's inter-African trade took place with the Soudan and Mauritania; the three countries were, in fact, treated as a unit in foreign statistics. Prior to national independence, that unit's foreign commerce was AOF's largest for imports and was overtaken by the Ivory Coast–Upper Volta unit for exports only in 1951—reflecting the growth of the Ivory Coast's economy and accentuating that country's increasing discomfort with the federation. In 1947, the Senegal-Mauritania-Soudan unit accounted for over 70 per cent of AOF's total imports, a percentage which decreased to 52.1 in 1956; regarding exports, the corresponding figures were 53.5 per cent in 1947 and 35.1 per cent nine years later.[7] Much of Senegal's economic importance in inter-African trade resulted from the role of the port of Dakar as a center for redistributing goods throughout AOF. That role declined as a function of the development of the economy of the Ivory Coast, especially since the Vridi Canal opened in 1951 and provided access to the capital city of Abidjan; it declined also as a result of the progressive loosening of inter-AOF ties, which set in motion or was accompanied by a nascent economic nationalism in the various territories.

The favorable position Senegal enjoyed as part of AOF may be illustrated also by a few statistical measures for the year 1956. Senegal's more than 5,380 miles of hard-surface roads accounted for only one-sixth of the AOF total, but were used by one-third of AOF's motor vehicles. Senegal had over one-third of AOF's

6. *A.O.F. 1957* (Dakar: Haut Commissariat de la République en Afrique Occidentale Française, 1958), p. 363.
7. *Ibid.*, p. 127.

total railroad mileage and slightly under one-half the total number of rail stations; the major part of Senegal's rail network was the line from Dakar to Koulikoro, an outskirt of Bamako, capital city of the Soudan. Further, Senegal had over half the telephones, and produced more than half the electric power, of the AOF total. The port of Dakar loomed even larger within the federation. It handled nearly three times the number of ships stopping at the other two major ports, Abidjan and Conakry (capital of Guinea), more than the combined tonnage of merchandise of these two other ports, and nearly double the number of arriving passengers.[8]

SENEGALO-FRENCH TIES, 1945–1957

Between 1945 and the gaining of national independence in 1960, Senegal pursued two interrelated goals: to increase her internal political and administrative autonomy, and to insure the continuation of French economic support and African economic space.

The first of these objectives was achieved with the transfer of international sovereignty from French to Senegalese authority. This was the result in part of the general movement toward independence, in part of Senegal's conscious policy, and in part of the fortuitous end of the French Fourth Republic, which allowed African-French ties to be altered substantially. The movement toward independence was a psychological ground swell, a sign of the age, to which Senegal reacted with some caution because of the need to conciliate it with material welfare highly dependent on continued French help.

From the end of World War II, Senghor, Senegal's most prominent political leader, consistently advocated a fundamental transformation of African-French constitutional ties. His policy was anchored in a desire for equality, expressed in the self-determination of peoples derived from the notion of equality of individuals. He succeeded in leading his country into what he believed was premature political independence from France to

8. *Ibid., passim.*

a large extent through the adroit manipulation of symbols eliciting favorable responses in Africa and in France. In Africa, he became a champion of unity by consciously exploiting an inherent receptivity to that concept. In France, he became a symbol of the very finest product of French civilization and of French-generated universal, interracial friendship.

Senegal's economic goals may be divided into two parts. One was economic support from France, the other economic space in Africa. Senegal's preindependence policy toward the first was successful, whereas her policy toward the second was a failure. The reasons for both success and failure lie in events and factors more external than internal to Senegal. For her own reasons, France decided to continue such economic support; Senghor contributed to that decision by treading softly on the issue of political independence and by insisting that political independence meant continued cooperation rather than a break.

Economic space in Africa meant the retention of the Federation of French West Africa, one of the Senghor's major concerns in preindependence inter-African relations. The goal was expressed in Senghor's creation of the mystique of African unity and in various pressures on French governments. It was also expressed in the ill-fated attempt to create an all-African federation, which failed chiefly because of the territorial base of post–World War II political development, the diversity among the economic interests of the territories, political struggles which pitted two interterritorial organizations against one another, and because AOF had been created as a convenience for the French rather than as an instrument of the Africans.

Senegal's preindependence political and economic objectives suffered from tensions inherent in the colonial situation. Political autonomy was directed against the very nature of the colonial relationship, whereas economic assistance aimed at the continuation of at least part of the penetration of the colonial power. The primary political goal aimed at independence, whereas the economic goal aimed at continued dependence—at least in the short run. Although both can be said to have been achieved, Senegal's leaders placed the material welfare of their people above the psychological benefits of political independence.

There was no clear-cut choice between the two goals; it was merely a question of deciding which was more important or less fraught with untoward consequences. The pursuit of the political objective alone would have jeopardized the economic goal. Hence, Senegal's policy was a compromise which tended to tone down political independence in order to retain economic support.

Political liberalization

The context of France's liberation from German occupation seemed at first favorable toward the liberalization of some African-French institutional ties. Africans had participated in that liberation, and many Frenchmen were painfully aware of the excesses of the Vichy regime toward Africans. General de Gaulle, during a press conference in Washington, D.C., on July 10, 1944, had committed himself to a *système à forme fédérale* for future Franco-African relations.[9] René Pléven, as colonial commissioner of the Comité Français de Libération Nationale, encouraged the search for a federal system by declaring to the Provisional Consultative Assembly meeting in Algiers in January, 1944, that "the time has come to expose, to probe the federal conception."[10] But the prospects of changing France's traditional unitary system into a novel, federal institution tended to recede as Allied victory came closer. During his 1944 Brazzaville speech, de Gaulle recognized that African territories must be "associated" with the management of their own affairs but emphatically rejected future self-government, which could lead only to secession from the Franco-African ensemble and to eventual independence. It is true that the French Socialist party remained committed to the federal ideal, but it is also the case that partisans of the indivisibility of a unitary France reasserted themselves.

French fears of African independence permeated the discus-

9. Quoted in P.-F. Gonidec, *Droit d'Outre-Mer: De l'empire colonial de la France à la Communauté* (Paris: Montchrestien, 1959), p. 348.
10. *Ibid.*

sions of the two Constituent Assemblies in 1945 and 1946. Senghor's objectives, as defined and refined over several years, were (1) to alter the economic and social disparities between Africa and France by giving the territories more political leverage in Paris, and (2) to satisfy Africans' psychological and material demands for more local autonomy. Given the somewhat uncertain context, Senghor—and other Africans participating in the Constituent Assemblies—advocated a partially federal system. They asked for a "freely consented" union between France and the territories, as the embryo of a future federation, a union which would formally recognize, at least in principle, the Overseas Territories and metropolitan France as separate entities. As an intermediary solution, they were satisfied with African representation in the French legislature in the hope that their influence would tend to offset that of the colonial and other bureaucracies known for their conservative views and readiness to accommodate colonial interest groups. On the local level, they asked for African political participation through elections and local assemblies.

France's first postwar constitution went a long way to meet these demands. The French Empire was officially changed into the French Union, a consultative proto-federal device with African participation, and the constitution provided for local, quasi-legislative assemblies elected by universal suffrage, and for African participation also in France's political institutions. Moreover, the French government's representative in the territories was to be responsible to the French National Assembly—on which African deputies sat—rather than to the bureaucracy.

But that constitution was rejected by French voters fearful of the proposed unicameral legislature—not by African voters—and the political context changed drastically. Not only was the new Constituent Assembly more conservative than the first, but colonial interests organized a drive to oppose liberal reforms. Edouard Herriot, French elder statesman, quipped that federalism would transform France into a colony of her colonies. More important, influential colonial interest groups formed the Estates General of Colonization and emphasized a paternalist concern for law and order and the need for what they saw as slow, gradual reforms. As Senghor expressed it,

We can presently see an offensive of colonial trusts; the Dakar Chamber of Commerce recently took a position in favor of the suppression of citizenship and advocated that the overseas deputies be reduced to a consultative role [in the French legislature].[11]

Faced with the prospect of losing all or nearly all the gains embodied in the first constitution, the African members of the second Constituent Assembly tried to salvage what they could. Senghor deplored the fact that the previous agreement was but a "scrap of paper, a simple soap bubble," and declared:

We who have fought against the racism of Hitler and of the Vichy government accept entrance into the French Union with open heart, but we intend to enter it on a basis of equality with the . . . metropole.[12]

In concert with other African members of the second French Constituent Assembly, Senghor took a number of steps designed to dramatize the importance of not taking away reforms already granted. He temporarily resigned his elected mandate to protest the introduction of a constitutional amendment reintroducing the double electoral college in Senegal; the amendment was defeated. He suggested that the territories be empowered to decide the kind of association they wanted with France—prior to a decision in Paris. He declared that "we must not make the French Union . . . into a cage which no one wants to enter." [13] And he signed a petition asking that the rights granted by the first constitution be maintained in the second.

Given the changed context, however, Senghor—along with other African deputies—decided to postpone the realization of a federation further and, in the meantime, to participate in the

11. Cited in Lamine Guèye, *Itinéraire africain* (Paris: Présence Africaine, 1966), p. 158.

12. France, *Séances de la Commission de la Constitution: Comptes rendus analytiques* (Paris: Imprimerie de l'Assemblée Nationale Constituante élue le 2 juin 1946, 1946), p. 31.

13. "Recueil des interventions faites à l'assemblée nationale française par le Président Léopold Sédar Senghor de 1946 à 1958 en sa qualité de Député du Sénégal," mimeographed (Dakar, n.d. [1967?]), p. 19.

work of future French legislatures during a period of political
"apprenticeship." "We must," he said, "take realities into account." But, he added,

> in ten years, in twenty years, there must be a constituent
> assembly where populations are really represented, and
> which will finally write the . . . constitution of the French
> Union, with a federal assembly controlling a responsible
> government.[14]

As it emerged from the second French constitution, the framework of the new French Union was clearly unitary, although
with a superimposed consultative assembly in which Africans
participated. The Union was based not on "free consent" but on
"equal rights and duties." The Overseas Territories unambiguously remained an integral part of the French Republic, and the
preamble indicated the intention to "associate" Africans in the
management of their affairs without "arbitrary" colonization. Authority to modify this structure was vested in the French legislature and was thus dependent on the composition and mood of
that body. Moreover, universal suffrage was replaced by a more
restrictive system, and the agents of the French government in
the territories—the governors, and the governors-general for the
African federations—remained under the direct control of the
French executive.

African frustrations

Between 1946 and 1956, the substance of Senghor's views concerning territorial autonomy and relations with France did not
change; he gave them varying emphases as the situation seemed
to require or permit but altered them only in some details. His
first decision was to accept the new French Union as an inevitable development, at least in the short run, and to concentrate on improving the material welfare of his constituents. "The

14. France, *Séances de la Commission*, p. 114. As a member of the committee, he said, "We remain federalists, but believe that presently it is not
possible to create a federation." *Ibid.*, p. 119.

future of the French Union," he declared in 1949, "is dominated by economic and social development." [15]

Yet during that same period his demands for political reforms became increasingly outspoken; they began with impatience at bureaucratic sluggishness in implementing authorized reforms and ended by calling for basic structural changes in the French Union. Two principal motives underlay his increasing militancy. One was rooted in domestic politics and resulted in his dissociation from the French Socialist party. As noted above, after about one year of serving as the chief lieutenant to Lamine Guèye, Senegal's Socialist elder statesman, Senghor believed that Guèye was no longer sufficiently flexible to adapt himself and his political machine to changing conditions. Taking advantage of a threefold increase in the electorate, he successfully appealed to the rural population to unseat Guèye, whose support remained concentrated in several cities. Senghor's growing support was based mainly on the fact that he—unlike Guèye but like the rural population—was not a "native" French citizen.

Having failed to convince the Senegalese Socialists of the need to attract the new voters, Senghor resigned from the party in late 1948 to create a party of his own. Coincidentally, this resignation brought to a head the second principal motive for his greater militancy: his disenchantment with the postwar behavior of French politics. Colonial bureaucrats failed to implement reforms, political parties tended to consider their African allies as mere voting devices, French parliamentary immobilism prevented the resolution of important issues, and conservative pressures threatened some gains Africans had made.[16]

The second motive for the shift in Senghor's attitude developed from the fact that, in France, the euphoria of liberation from German occupation had given way to more pedestrian con-

15. *Condition humaine* (January 11, 1949).

16. One example of such conservative pressures will illustrate. In 1952, the government appointed a French official to "share" the authority of a secretary of state representing Cameroun, Dr. Louis Paul Aujoulat. Aujoulat resigned in protest, and Senghor declared that he had "preferred freedom to the alms of a post . . . which a feeling of elementary dignity forbade one to accept." *Afrique nouvelle* (January 14, 1953). This statement anticipated by five years a like phrase used by Sékou Touré of Guinea.

cerns. Legislators had become absorbed, once more, by narrow factionalism and power struggles. Senghor expressed his disillusionment in the following terms:

> The Africans have realized that the [metropolitan] political parties, preoccupied with their own problems, find it impossible to interest themselves completely in overseas territories which they easily turn into currency for internal [French] politics.[17]

The French Socialist party had rejected several measures of great importance to Africans, and Senghor, as a member of that party's board of directors, was keenly aware of the Africans' bruised hopes. Moreover, his resignation coincided with the beginning of the ideological cold war between the United States and the Soviet Union; the Socialists wanted to play a mediation role between the two antagonists. In theory, Senghor favored the idea, perhaps an early version of a policy of "buffer" nonalignment. He explained that this policy should not be interpreted as either anti-Soviet or anti-American but could be useful if such a party, belonging to neither camp, could help prevent another world war. But in practice Senghor feared the further extension of French political party influence into Africa, with the consequent loss of autonomy for separate, African parties. Hence, he turned down the "third force" proposal and instead emphasized his African commitment: "What concerns us is . . . the Primary Force of black Africa which must again become the first force. This is, in the end, the *sine qua non* of any efficient struggle." [18]

By the early 1950s, Africans were so frustrated at the slow pace of reforms that Senghor questioned the usefulness of the French Union.[19] Around 1953, he became convinced that the most effective way out of the impasse was another structural

17. *Condition humaine* (January 11, 1949).
18. *Ibid.* (February 11, 1948).
19. "As the great year of Liberation recedes," he said, "as the remembrance of our common sacrifices becomes blurred in the fog of specific interests, the government forgets. . . . The government returns to previous errors." *Ibid.* (February 10, 1953).

change in Franco-African relations. As the head of a loose coalition of African deputies in Paris, the Indépendants d'Outre-Mer (IOM), he took the lead in demanding a revision of the French constitution. He was careful to avoid antagonizing powerful French conservatives and pointed out that both nationalism and independence were anachronistic. In opposition to some Africans who favored closer integration with France, Senghor advocated "active federalism," which would eventually transform the French Union into a federation "one and divisible." [20] His impatience with French lethargy increased, and two years later he envisaged "even a confederation," should a federation not be feasible.[21] A structural change ought to take place by 1970, with federal authority confined to foreign affairs, defense, and financial and economic coordination. In the meantime, the local African quasi-legislatures should be complemented by African executives responsible to real legislatures.

Senghor defined the purpose of the desired structural changes as an increase in local autonomy and in African influence over decisions affecting their welfare:

> We want, on one hand, the autonomous administration of local affairs by legitimate representatives in each territory and each group of territories and, on the other hand, the coordination of the economies of the French Union by an executive [organ] which would not be entirely metropolitan in composition and goals.[22]

At the same time, Senghor issued a number of public warnings in France in order to exert moral pressure on French consciences. In 1954, for instance, he declared:

> The truth is that the present system does not answer the needs of the hour . . . that in the Overseas Territories the formula of the "one and indivisible" Republic is hypocrisy.

20. See *ibid.* (February 25, 1953); *Paris-Dakar* (February 17, 1953); and *Afrique nouvelle* (February 18, 1953).
21. *Condition humaine* (April 22, 1955).
22. "Recueil," p. 161.

Thus I say that if France continues in blindness, before 10 years you shall have other Tunisias, other Moroccos in black Africa, and I hope that there will be no other Indochinas.[23]

Yielding to the persistent pressures by Africans, and to fears lest black Africa become the scene of violence, the French government induced the legislature to delegate to it authority to undertake at least some reforms in the territories. This was accomplished through a *loi cadre* (enabling act) approved by the French legislature in June, 1956; it did not concern the much-discussed federal or unitary question at the level of African-French relations since it was not a revision of the 1946 French constitution. But it was another step toward the political and administrative autonomy of the African territories. Three specific measures reinforced this autonomy. First, future elections would be in a single college and by universal suffrage. Second, it increased the authority of the territorial assemblies. These became responsible for running government services hitherto operated by AOF, received regulatory powers, and obtained political leverage through a reorganization of the civil service. Last, the assemblies were authorized to elect a territorial executive consisting of ministers and a vice-president, responsible for running one or more public services.

All these measures were welcome and had been asked for by African leaders for several years. Universal suffrage strengthened the leaders' bargaining position with France since they were now presumed to represent their people more fully than before. Public services transferred from the jurisdiction of the Federal Council at Dakar to the Overseas Territories included those for agricultural education, lighthouses, the archives of Mauritania, Senegal, and the Ivory Coast, the federal pharmacies, and the territorial components of the Institut Français de l'Afrique Noire. The civil service for overseas France had been divided horizontally and, in order of descending importance, into "general," "superior," and "local" components. The 1956 reform consisted in drawing a vertical line through the pyramid, thus separating

23. "L'Avenir de la France dans l'Outre-Mer," *Politique étrangère*, XIX, no. 4 (October, 1954), 420.

the state (French) service from the newly created territorial services, while retaining the horizontal divisions. At the same time, the state services agreed to open their doors to qualified Africans, who began to apply by the hundreds after this became known. The urgency of these reforms may be measured by the fact that they did, in fact, violate the French constitution in that executive or parliamentary—or regulatory—authority could not legally be abandoned to regional or territorial elements of the unitary Republic.

Senghor was less than completely satisfied with the *loi cadre*. For one thing, it had no effect on his major concern—increased African influence on matters related to economic development. For another, the reforms were to be implemented by the French bureaucracy, not outstanding for its sympathy for the Africans' cause. As he put it:

> Our first reaction . . . was to reject it. The government asks us for full powers in political and administrative matters. In other words, it asks us to renounce, in its favor, our right to legislate.
> What is serious . . . is that the government substitutes, for the "valid partners" which we are . . . partners which are the bureaus, which do not represent us and which are not particularly revolutionary. In the end, a mediocre law . . . is preferable to the absence of law.[24]

Another reason underlying Senghor's dissatisfaction was the government's refusal to give the territories authority over such services as customs, postal and radio communications, and higher education, which remained under French control although the Africans had been almost unanimous in asking for their transfer to the territories. As Senghor put it in a widely quoted phrase: "The government . . . leaves us only toys and lollipops." Finally, Senghor was beginning to become concerned about the consequences for Senegal of the French refusal to maintain AOF. At the time of the passage of the enabling act, he was preoccu-

---

24. France, *Journal officiel de la république française, débats parlementaires—assemblée nationale*, March 20, 1956, pp. 1069, 1070 (hereafter cited as *JORF, DP-AN*).

pied mainly by what the act could do for the territories. But the law also foreshadowed the eventual demise of the federations of French West and Equatorial Africa. Article One stipulated that "administrative decentralization and deconcentration measures shall be taken in . . . the groups of territories." The second paragraph further indicated that the French government was authorized to "modify the role and the administrative . . . powers of the Governments-General in order to transform them into organs of coordination." In consequence, the text added, the government could also "modify the composition and authority of the Federal Councils." The French legislature's debates on the *loi cadre* contain only three passages in which Senghor expressed a "warning" that AOF would probably not survive its French sponsorship, and Senghor appears to have waited until he could appeal directly to Africans in Africa as the most useful technique to attempt to safeguard Senegal's economic interests by maintaining the federation. To dramatize their discontent, Senghor and Mamadou Dia abstained from the final vote on the *loi cadre*—whereas most other Africans, including Sékou Touré and Modibo Keita, voted in favor.[25]

By the beginning of 1957, when the *loi cadre* reforms were being translated from paper to reality, Senghor had nonetheless accomplished at least part of his goals. The French Union was being transformed and Senegal—with the rest of AOF—was moving along the road to political self-determination. Through their participation in the central decision-making process in Paris, African leaders were successful in overcoming conservative, bureaucratic, and sluggish political forces in the metropole, which had a strong, traditional commitment to the unitary political structure of the Republic and were therefore opposed to the devolution of political authority to the African territories. They had, also, successfully appealed to many French consciences by pointing to the egregious examples of French policy in Indochina and Algeria and by raising the specter of violence

25. The list of the African deputies' votes is printed in *ibid.*, March 22, 1956, p. 1222. For the text of the *loi cadre* and its implementation decrees, see *Réforme Outre-Mer: Loi no. 56–619 du 23 juin 1956 et décrets d'application* (Paris: Imprimerie des Journaux Officiels, 1957). The "lollipop" phrase is found in *JORF, DP-AN*, March 20, 1956, p. 485.

spreading to black Africa. In view of their token representation in French decision-making bodies, to have convinced the French that they must make some concessions—despite the spirit and letter of the constitution—was no small achievement. The Africans remained disenchanted and frustrated, but their partial success no doubt reinforced their determination to remain within the system, especially since Senghor envisaged the same kind of success regarding the allocation of French aid and the closer integration of the economies of territories and metropole.

INTER-AFRICAN TIES, 1945–1960

The preindependence relations among the components of AOF are frequently presented as a series of efforts toward a variant of African unity. As discussed below, Senghor in fact championed African unity within the AOF context and contributed to the rapid and widespread popularity of the concept. Long before the unity issue moved into the foreground in 1956, Senghor had been active in maneuvers to regroup various interterritorial political forces in Africa as well as in Paris. All these efforts failed, however, to unite AOF political leaders and to translate such unity into successful policy.

A variety of factors account for continued failure, and it is useful to break them down into two parts by using the potency of the stakes for Senegal as a distinguishing criterion. The first period covers the years from 1945 to about 1956. That period witnessed, initially, attempts to spread the influence of the Socialist party to other areas besides Senegal, and later to find a way to use the common interests of the two African interterritorial political structures to gain desired ends. Unity attempts during this period failed essentially for two reasons. First, they ran counter to the nascent territorial nationalism which followed World War II. Second, both interterritorial parties sought to use "unity" to strengthen their electoral support and weaken that of their competitors, at both the local territorial and international levels.

The second period followed the 1956 French reforms, which weakened AOF bonds and thus presented a danger for Senegal's economic interests. This period was marked by the slogan of balkanization and also witnessed the use of the slogans internal autonomy, independence, and African unity as pressures on the French government designed, from the vantage point of Senegal, to salvage necessary African economic breathing space. The slogans were used also to bolster the interterritorial African alliance of which Senghor was the leader. These efforts also ended in failure, despite the clear africanization of political issues, and despite the fact that they produced a profound cleavage in the interterritorial alliance headed by Houphouet-Boigny of the Ivory Coast.

Although the issue of African unity as an abstraction and as a demand for retaining the AOF framework shifted African popular support away from Houphouet-Boigny toward Senghor, that support was not reflected in the formal political process and structures which rested on partisan elections. Territorial nationalism and rivalries between the two international "parties" contributed to the failure to translate support into successful policy. The affective ties of adherents of Houphouet-Boigny's organization seem to have been a major factor in that failure. There were also other compelling reasons. One was the reluctance of the government of the French Fifth Republic to allow AOF to survive. Of greater consequence was the fortuitous combination of events over which Senghor had no influence: on one hand, the advent of the French Fifth Republic, which transferred the power center from the legislature to the executive and deprived Senghor, as a deputy in the National Assembly, of an effective voice; on the other hand, the selection of Houphouet-Boigny as the French government's chief African adviser, which practically insured the defeat of Senghor's African unity goals in view of Houphouet-Boigny's adamant opposition to them.

The second period witnessed also the short-lived Mali Federation, an experiment which for Senegal represented a last-ditch effort to save the position which she owed to the colonial power. In this case, the failure must be ascribed chiefly to the incompatibility of leaders and elites in the Soudan and Senegal. Despite the sound constitutional balance which the African federal partners carefully worked out, the appeal of Soudanese political programs to some segments of Senegal's elite and the political style of the Soudanese eventually posed a threat to Senghor's power base and caused Senegal, ironically, to declare her independence from the very African ensemble she had worked so hard to establish.

International political structures

An attempt was made to create an interterritorial African political organization early in 1945. Given the previous implantation in Senegal of a branch of the French Socialist party, it was an effort to extend that influence into three other territories and was calculated to fill the political vacuum in those areas. The Senegalese Socialist party had been founded under the leadership of Amadou Lamine Guèye in the late 1920s and transformed into the Senegalese Federation of the French parent party in 1936 at the time of the French Popular Front. Three years later, the federation merged with a local French counterpart, with Guèye as the new president. In 1945, the new French government agreed to allow Africans to organize politically to elect representatives to the Constituent Assembly; since Senegal had a head start in political structure, Lamine Guèye no doubt counted on this—and on friendly French governors in other territories—to help fill the relative political void.

The organization created for that purpose in Dakar, the Comité d'Etudes Franco-Africaines (CEFA), was ephemeral, and it all but disappeared by the end of 1946. It failed partly because of the militant orientation of the young cadres sent out to build local branches, but mostly because it conflicted with nascent territorial nationalism outside Senegal.

Under the leadership of Guèye, Senghor, and Houphouet-Boigny, CEFA was to serve as an electoral machine for Socialist candidates more or less controlled from Dakar. To conform to French administrative control, CEFA officially presented itself as an inoffensive cultural organization; it projected an image of future equality designed to appeal to Senegalese "subjects" yearning for citizenship and to other Africans moved by apparently imminent possibilities of improving their lot. In other words, CEFA aimed at taking advantage of African hopes for a better future following the Allied victory after World War II. This hope was noted by one French governor, for instance, in the following terms: "No one is satisfied. A kind of demand psychosis has been created. One wishes to become assimilated to the Europeans in salary, in indemnities, in medical care. . . . [Africans] believe that they are as competent as Europeans and demand 'equal pay for equal work,' assuming as a fact the equality of the work performed. But they never speak of professional responsibility, of efficiency." The governor-general in Dakar insisted on changing the CEFA constitution to include the requirement to develop the French language, "which must be considered and remain the first preoccupation of the comité." [26]

Two CEFA agents, Amara Soumah and Kane N'Diaye, were sent to Conakry. They sought the support of two different ethnic groups and quickly were at odds. Although CEFA headquarters replaced them with a Socialist friend of Guèye, Yacine Diallo, the Guinean CEFA branch does not seem to have survived these early quarrels. Another CEFA agent, Massène Sène, was sent to the Soudan. Sène was arrested by the French authorities twice in 1943 for "outrages, threats, and rebellion." Later he was committed to psychiatric institutions in Marseilles and Dakar and pronounced mentally unbalanced. In 1944, he visited the Soudan with the intention of creating a newspaper to be called L'Humanité. The Soudanese governor was "good enough" to advise him to leave that territory, which Sène did "suddenly." The tenor of his speeches, once mandated by CEFA, in which he appealed to fellow Africans to "close their fists and threaten the usurper who feeds on our flesh and drinks our blood," commended itself to neither Lamine Guèye nor the French. He was quickly replaced as the CEFA agent in the Soudan by another of Guèye's friends, Fily Dabo Sissoko.

In Sikasso, another Soudanese city, the CEFA section was taken over by a militant teacher calling himself Modibo Keita, who used that organization and the established Socialist party unit to further his own political ambitions. By the end of 1946, Keita had infiltrated the French administration—the governor

26. Report of the Soudan governor to Dakar, July 7, 1945; governor-general to French overseas minister, 4359:AP/I, July 20, 1945.

called him the "occult administrator of the district"—and secured the support of Soudanese veterans of the French armed forces. The Soudanese governor reported to his superiors that Keita was dangerous, had turned the area into his personal fief, and had succeeded in "gaining absolute authority . . . over the former *tirailleurs*, a portion of the civil service, and of an important part of the population." A delegation of European women went to Bamako and demanded from the governor "either their evacuation, or arms" to defend themselves and their children. On the occasion of the visit of an African elected dignitary, Keita met him "in a superb automobile decorated with a magnificent flag" and presented to his guest "his small army of 200 to 300 *pétards* made up of *tirailleurs* entirely devoted to him." [27]

CEFA's greatest success occurred among the Bobo of Upper Volta, where membership grew from 6,500 at the end of 1945 to some 13,000 at the beginning of 1946. Although that CEFA branch ostensibly supported Houphouet-Boigny, its strategic location between the Mossi majority in Upper Volta, whose domination they resented, and the upper Ivory Coast courted by Houphouet-Boigny resulted in antagonism rather than cooperation. The CEFA agent was a Senegalese, Aboukane Diop, who as a French citizen was immune from much administrative interference and collaborated with other Senegalese resident among the Bobo. But Houphouet-Boigny, with the help of the Ivory Coast's Communist governor, André Latrille, discredited Diop by denouncing him as a "foreign" agent collecting money for Dakar, and maneuvered to absorb the CEFA branch into his own political party. After learning that Diop represented an "instrument for the exploitation of the natives," the CEFA membership was persuaded to dissolve that organization and to join Houphouet-Boigny's Parti Démocratique. Latrille had previously dissolved CEFA, and conveniently recalled it into being for the internal, "voluntary" dissolution. In so doing, Latrille apparently acted against orders from Dakar. The governor-general wrote him, "I do not think that, except in the case of new infor-

27. Security officer at Bamako to his superior in Dakar, in a report from the Guinea governor to Dakar, A/R, June, 1945; Soudan governor to Dakar, 1320/APA/I, July, 1946, and 765/C, December 1, 1946.

mation which I may ignore since your correspondence on that subject has always been brief, there is good reason to prevent the constitution of a local CEFA section in Bobo." [28]

In late 1948 Senghor joined a group of African deputies at the French National Assembly, the Indépendants d'Outre-Mer (IOM). Shortly thereafter he became the IOM president, partly because of his prominence and partly because he was the only IOM member who controlled politics in his home territory. The IOM was a loose association of African representatives in Paris, created chiefly as a defensive device against the challenge arising from another interterritorial party, the Rassemblement Démocratique Africain (RDA), which was gaining support in several territories at the expense of local elites. The RDA was an outgrowth of the 1946 common African protest against the second French constitution, when some deputies, including Houphouet-Boigny, decided to create an African party instead of relying on alliances with French political parties in Paris. Initially, Senghor favored the initiative and signed a written protest; but he and other Africans withdrew their support under French pressure.

The second reason for creating the IOM was that their founders were uncomfortable with the RDA's affiliation, in the French lower house, with the French Communist party. The final reason was the realization that French parties welcomed the votes of their African affiliates but remained timid in their actions on behalf of their African colleagues. For Senghor, there was an additional reason: he had severed his ties with the French Socialists and was in need of allies.

In 1950, the RDA approached the IOM and proposed a merger into a new African organization which could presumably have a greater impact on French politics. At the time, the RDA was in the process of disengaging itself from the French Communists, and on the surface it looked as though chances for a measure

28. Telegram Abidjan to Dakar, 111/APS/I, March 13, 1946; Abidjan to Governor-general Cournarie, 334/APS, August 27, 1946; Latrille letter to the governor-general, 20/AP, January 22, 1946; and transcript of the governor-general's director-general for political, administrative, and social affairs, 380/AP/2, December 3, 1946.

of African unity were good. Elections for a new National Assembly were scheduled for June, 1951, and a new, more powerful alliance among Africans could be useful in stirring up French legislators to pay attention to their joint demands.

Although Senghor reacted favorably, the attempt to find a way to unify the IOM and the RDA failed. The failure was the result of three factors: (1) the doubtful value of RDA support for the IOM, which was already an autonomous parliamentary group, (2) internal political struggles in several territories, and (3) Houphouet-Boigny's insistence on an organizational merger rather than less binding common action, "affiliation," or other devices. First, the RDA had reached a low point in influence both in Paris and in the territories. The French Communists had not belonged to French governments, and Governor André Latrille was replaced by a Socialist in 1947. Severe repressive measures against the RDA, especially in the Ivory Coast, reduced its influence further. The RDA proposal for a rapprochement with the IOM, therefore, was a device to acquire respectability by association. Hence, the IOM would have gained little by accepting the offer. Second, a merger raised questions regarding the least painful method for cooperation, on the territorial level, among local political antagonists; since the RDA was much better organized than its local opponents, territorial leaders feared absorption and eclipse by a potentially stronger opponent. Senghor, as president of the IOM, explained:

> We needed proof of the sincerity of our [RDA] partners: not, specifically, we Senegalese, but our friends from Upper Volta, inasmuch as they had, for years, led an almost inexplicable fight against the RDA.[29]

Finally, Senghor's attempts to compromise by suggesting that unity be achieved by steps, beginning with IOM-RDA affiliation in the National Assembly, met with a curt RDA refusal. Perhaps Houphouet-Boigny counted on the support of a French politician, François Mitterand, with whom he had just had long

29. *Condition humaine* (April 10, 1951).

discussions and with whose party the RDA subsequently affiliated itself (Mitterand having become minister for Overseas France).

At the time, the search for inter-African alliances continued until four months before the National Assembly election. Houphouet-Boigny took the initiative and sought to enlarge the group originally proposed by including all African deputies. Lamine Guèye responded with alacrity, attempted to reassert his authority as the African elder statesman, and talked about the common defense of the "vital interests of the French Union." [30] Guèye called together a meeting of some thirty leaders of IOM, RDA, and Socialist parties during the inauguration of new harbor facilities at Abidjan and proposed the formation of an all-African group which would act in concert but retain the members' individualities. The participants were interested in unity only to the extent that it would help them and be detrimental to their opponents. Consequently, the meeting merely served to underline sources of friction and to make the participants conscious of their disunity. Their eyes were cast on the forthcoming elections, and that meant struggle, not compromise. Moreover, Guèye used the potential group to embarrass Senghor, against whom he was still fighting a political rearguard action in Senegal. Everyone apparently abandoned these unity efforts after the June, 1951, election.

Another attempt at inter-African unity was made in 1956 at the time of new elections for the French National Assembly. This time the initiative came from Senghor, when the IOM electoral position had deteriorated both in Africa and in Paris.[31] Senghor proposed regrouping the African deputies in Paris on the basis of a minimum program for common action, but Houphouet-Boigny countered by insisting on a merger of all local, territorial parties. Such a merger would have all but eclipsed the IOM as an inter-African political force: it would have insured RDA control in four territories (the Soudan, the

30. *Ibid.* (March 6, 1951).
31. In the new French lower house, the IOM had seven deputies, the RDA seven, the Socialists four; in the African legislatures, the RDA obtained the largest single number of deputies.

Ivory Coast, Guinea, and Niger) and promoted RDA domination in two more (Upper Volta and Dahomey), leaving only Senegal as the IOM stronghold and Mauritania, which stood aloof from inter-African alliances. Given the consequences of Houphouet-Boigny's terms, Senghor abandoned his effort.

Senghor's tactics derived from the weakened electoral support for the IOM as well as from his concern for a revision of the French constitution. He had served in the cabinet of French Premier Edgar Faure since early 1955 and had been entrusted with drafting a constitutional revision; following the RDA's renewed political strength, the post of African adviser in the French executive went to Houphouet-Boigny as RDA president. Senghor then decided to try to work through Houphouet-Boigny in order to continue to influence the direction of the impending constitutional revision.

The symbolism of African unity

As shown above, efforts to bring about inter-African party unity failed, essentially because they conflicted with the territorial base of postwar politics. The reinforcement of territorial autonomy which followed the 1956 French enabling act brought in its wake widespread support for another aspect of African unity: a call for the maintenance and reinforcement of the Federation of French West Africa. That federation had been created at the turn of the last century as a temporary administrative device serving chiefly French, not African, interests.[32] From the French point of view, it was no longer useful by 1956 and consequently was slowly allowed to expire as a French-created institution, although the Africans were legally free to maintain AOF on their own accord. The French government stripped AOF of much authority by transferring responsibility for most federal services elsewhere and by interposing an interterritorial conference of Africa and French executive leaders between the territories and a weakened French Government-General to coordinate "common interests." Symbolically, the new regulations

32. See Skurnik, "France and Fragmentation in West Africa."

regarding AOF substituted "group of territories" for "federation."

Léopold Senghor rose to save the federation and in the process became a champion of African unity, created a strong current of enthusiasm for his cause, and split the ranks of the RDA. He had sounded the alarm during the discussions of the *loi cadre*, and an IOM delegation went to the French government warning that

> The dislocation and the disintegration of the federation would lead to the suppression of the spirit of solidarity in the federation. . . . The Federal Council not being able to play its regulatory role, conflicts would arise between the territories.[33]

Being removed from the seat of French executive authority, he could not hope to influence the decision-makers directly. He attempted, instead, to influence them indirectly. One way to do this was to manipulate Africans' emotions, by condemning the colonial power for balkanizing an African institution which many had come to take for granted and by launching a rallying cry of unity. During the discussion of the implementation decrees of the 1956 *loi cadre*, he said, "I warned the National Assembly . . . that the immediate consequence of this balkanization would be the birth of a mystique of unity. This mystique undeniably exists today." [34]

Senghor's motives in seeking to retain, and strengthen, AOF were economic as well as political. As was shown earlier, much of Senegal's economic progress was the result of the location of the federal capital in Dakar, of that port city's role as an entrepôt for Franco-African trade, and of the creation in Senegal of processing industries catering to the needs of the vast AOF hinterland. Maintaining the federation was for Senegal a vital economic necessity since without her privileged status she would face serious problems of underemployment, receding business activity, and loss of income and prestige, perhaps accompanied

33. *JORF, DP-AN*, March 20, 1956, p. 1070.
34. *Afrique nouvelle* (April 3, 1959).

by social and political domestic disturbances. Political motivations were marginal compared to the prospect of economic distress, but they were not without importance. The theme of African unity could provide the IOM with a much-needed injection of support in the face of recent RDA political successes. Such support was welcome not only for its own sake but because it was vital in demonstrating to the French decision-makers that the IOM, and not the RDA, was the authentic representative of the Africans' yearning for unity.

Senghor shrewdly realized that the mystique of African unity could be exploited easily. In fact, support for the concept mushroomed almost overnight. It came from the IOM, from neutrals, from the ranks of the RDA, and from federal, institutional vested interests.

Leaders of Niger and Mauritania favored retention of the federation because of the economic advantages they derived from the federal budget: as poorer, landlocked territories, they received federal subsidies far in excess of their contributions.[35] Additional support came from two RDA strongholds, the Soudan and Guinea, whose leaders were commited to AOF on a matter of principle. African executives were created in the territories, and so the development toward the Africans' political autonomy required that such an executive also be created in Dakar for the federation. As Sékou Touré put it,

> Our pride demands that we should designate democratically those who will administer the common inheritance, instead of being forced to accept the decisions of a high commissioner, human as he may be.[36]

Thus the African unity issue produced a deep cleavage within the RDA leadership, at a time when its president, Houphouet-

35. Thus Mokhtar Ould Daddah, vice-president of Mauritania's Government Council, decided that it was time to "lift the veil of solitude," and that "solidarity is not an empty word; we are members of AOF and shall therefore appeal to the solidarity of all." Another reason for Mauritania's "solidarity" was the Moroccan threat against her existence. *Ibid.* (June 25, 1957).

36. *Ibid.* (October 1, 1957); emphasis added.

Boigny, served in the French cabinet and did what he could, for his own reasons, to weaken AOF. That cleavage became evident in September, 1957, and helped to bring about the demise of the RDA as an effective interterritorial organization. During the second RDA congress, President Houphouet-Boigny suffered the indignity of being told by one of his lieutenants to champion the party's cause rather than his own. The studied vagueness of the final resolution of the congress, to "democratize the existing federal organs" and to transform AOF into a federal state, could not conceal the triumph of the unity thesis.[37]

Finally, support came also from the Federal Council itself, presumably because it was reluctant to underwrite its own disappearance. The council passed several resolutions asking for an African federal executive—the last one being adopted by a large RDA majority.[38]

As a complement of the growing support for the African federal executive, Senghor sought to strengthen organizational support. At first, he sought to reinforce the cohesiveness of the IOM; his next move was to attempt a merger of African political parties, at the same time underlining the chief aim of creating an African federation. In January, 1957, Senghor transformed the IOM into the Convention Africaine (CA). The new interterritorial party enjoyed less electoral support than had its predecessor in the early 1950s. Hence, it devised a vague ideology of a "new overseas man" and confined itself to future integration from the top. The major speaker at the meeting, Mamadou Dia of Senegal, described the CA as a "defensive reaction" and as the only means available to "accomplish our mission," namely, a protest against the threat of balkanization.[39]

From the viewpoint of an African federation, Senghor experi-

37. Ibid.
38. Ibid. (December 28, 1956); Ernest Milcent, L'A.O.F. entre en scène, Bibliothèque de l'Homme d'Action (Paris: Editions Témoignage Chrétien, 1958), p. 123.
39. Afrique nouvelle (January 11, 1957). In addition to Senegal, the CA included local representatives from Upper Volta, Dahomey, and Niger. There were delegates from French Equatorial Africa, Togo, and Cameroun; and observers from the Brazzaville-Congo, Guinea, and the RDA, which sent one of its most prominent leaders, Ouezzin Coulibaly.

enced his finest hour at an inter-African party meeting in Paris in February, 1958. Delegates of the CA, the RDA, and the newly created Mouvement Socialiste Africain (MSA), headed by Lamine Guèye, responded to Senghor's invitation and issued a ringing declaration: "French West Africa shall be a federation, constituted democratically by [the] territories, on the basis of voluntary abandonment of territorial sovereignty." [40]

It was clear that the emotional appeal of "African unity" had become nearly irresistible. Moreover, there was general agreement regarding the need to revise the French constitution and to replace it with a federal framework capable of uniting autonomous African states and France on the basis of at least legal equality. The RDA, previously opposed to a constitutional change, had come to accept Senghor's thesis at its congress in Bamako in 1957.[41] Prominent French officials—including the minister for Overseas France—and political leaders—including Pierre Mendès-France and François Mitterand—publicly indicated their support. Senghor's purpose, to put pressure on the French government and to demonstrate quasiunanimous African support for an African federal executive, was achieved with the unambiguous joint declaration.

But other factors, over which he had no control, prevented that pressure from being translated into favorable government action. First, it was Houphouet-Boigny, and not Senghor, who was the government's African adviser. More important, the unity issue, for all the intensity and breadth of the commitments underlying it, was not intense enough to move the RDA toward a new, single African political party on any terms but

40. *Ibid.* (February 21, 1958). The meeting included Houphouet-Boigny, Sékou Touré, Modibo Keita, and Gabriel d'Arboussier for the RDA; Senghor, Mamadou Dia, and Abdoulaye Ly for the CA; Djibo Bakaray and Lamine Guèye for the MSA; as well as representatives of several minor parties.
41. In 1955, Houphouet-Boigny, speaking at a meeting of the RDA Coordination Committee, declared that a constitutional revision was unimportant, that the present one worked well enough, and that it was "not necessary to waste one's time looking for something else." *Ibid.* (July 19, 1955). Two years later, at the RDA congress, he said that the *loi cadre* "will soon permit" a constitutional revision transforming the French Union into a real federation. *Ibid.* (October 1, 1957).

its own. Whereas Senghor and his followers had suggested creating an entirely new party (reflecting in part Senegal's domestic tradition of party fusion, but also concern lest the RDA sweep aside its opponents), RDA leaders insisted that the purpose of any such "regroupment" must be their adversaries' integration into the RDA. Speaking of the CA and the MSA, Houphouet-Boigny defined RDA policy as "that of absorbing them." [42] Thus RDA leaders, split on the federal issue, remained solidary concerning the structure of their party. Party loyalties, and deep emotional attachment to the symbol RDA, were stronger than their loyalties to an African executive symbolic of African autonomy and pride.

Interparty unity among Africans not being possible as a means of pressure on the French government, Senghor altered his strategy so as to circumvent this obstacle. He continued to demand the revision of the constitution, but since France and some Africans were unwilling to maintain the African federation, he proposed that the decision be removed from France to Africa and articulated the demand that France recognize the right of Africans to political independence. Instead of advocating a federation between the French Republic and African autonomous states, he suggested a three-step plan: (1) complete autonomy of the territories, (2) an African constitutional referendum on the question of African federation, and (3) relations with France determined by mutual agreement.

In order to press demands for the realization of step (1), Senghor proposed that France recognize, a priori, the right of the territories to decide for themselves whether or not they wished to become independent at some later date. Thus he hoped to exploit the immense popularity of the African federal, or unity, issue and isolate it from African factionalism revolving around party loyalties and deriving from the postwar territorial-

42. *Ibid.* This position was later endorsed by the Coordination Committee, which declared that the unification of the African parties must rest on the following principles: "The minority parties in each territory must state their readiness to change their name into that of the majority party which retains or takes the name of the section of the RDA." *Ibid.* (November 27, 1957).

ization of political life. The issue of relations with France, thus stated, secured the support of most African leaders and revived the intra-RDA tensions temporarily papered over by party loyalties.[43]

Senghor resumed his campaign shortly after the anguished interlude which followed the fall of the French Fourth Republic, when African leaders feared a military coup d'état à l'algérienne in Dakar. Senghor and other Senegalese leaders feared a military dictatorship and a return of the powerful influence of colonial interests and other right-wing opponents of the freedoms Africans had so far gained. In Dakar, French paratroops circulated tracts asking for the creation of committees on public safety and talked of assaulting the governor-general's palace. Although the governor-general, Gaston Cusin, forbade public demonstrations, such a committee was created illegally by restless paratroops wanting to "do something." Senegalese leaders immediately created a Committee on Republican Defense and appealed to the people "to be vigilant, ready to defend democratic liberties." [44] At the inter-African level, Senghor transformed the CA into a new interterritorial party, the Parti du Regroupement Africain (PRA), which now included most leaders of the MSA, and used it as a platform from which to publicize his objectives. The PRA decided to establish, first, a "solid African community before free and equal cooperation with any other community," and then to

> adopt the slogan of immediate independence . . . , to call for the rapid meeting of the Constituent Assembly of Black Africa . . . to organize the new nation, a federation based on equality and on voluntary abandonment of sovereignty by the present territories.[45]

43. Sékou Touré, for instance, declared that "public opinion has become agitated. . . . What is evident is that the Africans of all territories (Mauritania and the Ivory Coast included) favor the safeguarding of African unity and would opt, if a referendum were presently organized, for the creation of a federal organism, of a federal executive." *Ibid.* (June 6, 1958).

44. See Georges Chaffard, *Les Carnets secrets de la décolonisation* (Paris: Calmann-Lévy, 1965), pp. 331–46.

45. *Afrique nouvelle* (August 1, 1958).

African unity and independence

During the next few months, the African unity issue was none-theless overshadowed by the demand for French official recognition of the Africans' right to independence. By mid-1958, that demand was made by most African leaders, who had lost some of their confidence that France would willingly give up its unitary conception of the Republic and its sovereignty over her African territories. The right-to-independence issue, moreover, assumed added importance for its own sake in the minds of some Africans who, like Senghor, regarded independence as an inalienable right but added that it must be granted regardless of consequences.[46] Recognition of that right therefore became a cornerstone of African strategy to obtain the desired constitutional revision. Senghor, as one of black Africa's outstanding leaders and head of the PRA, was called on to help draft the part of the new constitution that dealt with the Overseas Territories. Political independence was his ultimate goal,[47] but he was also aware of powerful French opposition—reinforced by that of Houphouet-Boigny, whose dissidence revealed the Africans' disunity and whose position in the French cabinet wielded considerable influence.[48]

46. Sékou Touré, for instance, told the French Overseas minister, "Our heart, our reason, in addition to our most evident interests, led us to choose, without hesitation, interdependence and liberty in this union, rather than a future without France. In the face of the despair which would result from failure [to recognize that right], the peoples of Africa . . . would take the only road open which would remain: that of independence, corresponding, it is true, to a leap into the unknown." *Ibid.* (March 7, 1958).

47. During his report to the PRA congress, he explained, "We do not refuse independence. We have proclaimed its right for all. Nominal independence shall inevitably be the ultimate form of our political evolution." *Ibid.* (August 1, 1958).

48. Houphouet-Boigny later claimed responsibility for influencing de Gaulle. "General de Gaulle," he said, "and this is perhaps the only time I was not in agreement with him, told me, after learning the intentions of certain members of the Consultative Constitutional Committee, that he would propose independence with the possibility of a revision of the constitution every five years. This I opposed, and fiercely, . . . this periodic rendezvous with blackmail and distrust. Faced with my insistence, de Gaulle consented to accept . . . that distrust not be constitutionalized."

For Senghor, the possibility of an African decision concerning an African federation hinged on the recognition of the right to independence. As one of four African members of the Consultative Constitutional Committee (CCC), which prepared a draft constitution, Senghor advocated that the constitution allow Africans to choose independence within a five-year period beginning with the promulgation of the constitution. That stipulation was retained in the final draft submitted to the government.[49]

With the arrival of General de Gaulle as the head of the new French government, however, decision-making influence shifted away from the legislature—and from the CCC—to the executive. What influence Senghor could have brought to bear under "normal," Fourth Republic, circumstances was thereby curtailed drastically since he operated through the legislature, whereas Houphouet-Boigny was a member of the French executive and, as minister of state, was one of four officials who had prepared the initial constitutional draft submitted to the CCC. It is likely that, had the legislature retained its preponderant influence, Senghor's thesis concerning the issues surrounding the right to independence would have prevailed; the CCC endorsed that right and embodied it in the draft which it submitted to the executive. In the process, Senghor's strategy became the victim of a shift in executive-legislative relations over which he had no control.

The French government rejected the CCC proposal and substituted a provision according to which independence was possible only by rejecting the constitution, which would mean the end of French assistance. Lest there be any doubt about the consequence of this kind of independence, de Gaulle explained that he saw it as voluntary secession from the Franco-African ensemble: "Never, personally, shall I take the responsibility of imposing burdens on the Community for the benefit of a terri-

---

Ivory Coast, *Discours prononcé par M. le Ministre Houphouet-Boigny au Stade Géo André à Abidjan le 7 septembre 1958* (Abidjan: Imprimerie de la Côte d'Ivoire, 1958), p. 10.

49. France, *Travaux préparatoires de la constitution: Avis et débats du comité consultatif constitutionnel* (Paris: La Documentation Française, 1960), p. 219.

tory which shall have opted for secession." [50] In one of the most dramatic exchanges in colonial history, Senghor declared,

> We reject this [false] dilemma. Our desire for independence can accommodate a strong association with France, [a country] which we need. If France tells us that there will be no marriage, then we shall have complete independence. . . . Were the Bretons told that, if they voted "no," they would be separatists? Then why are we told so? I regret that Frenchmen, who have a sense of honor, disregard its existence among the peoples of Africa.
>
> Beware: if you do not give us the choice which we ask, then we shall . . . vote against the constitution.[51]

The advent of the Community, and of internal autonomy for the territories, set into motion the final stages of complete territorial nationalism generated by the beginning of political activity in 1945. In general, political leaders were concerned primarily with the retention or strengthening of their domestic power base and with continued external economic rewards from the only really important source—France. They yielded, although reluctantly and only temporarily, to de Gaulle's "secession" blackmail. The exception was Guinea, which chose independence without continued French aid. However, Guinea's leaders, in contrast to their like-minded counterparts, already fully controlled the politics of their country and did not believe de Gaulle's warnings about the economic consequences of "secession"; they therefore yielded to the potency of such abstractions as freedom and dignity as they interpreted them.

Territories such as Senegal and the Soudan accepted the novel framework for African-French ties but interpreted it as a move toward independence; a rejection of the 1958 constitution would have threatened their political support sufficiently to bring about widespread turmoil and disruption and, given strong French pressures, a decrease, rather than an increase, of

50. *Ibid.*, p. 133.
51. *Ibid.*, p. 157. Senghor was so incensed that he considered resigning from the committee.

actual autonomy. The strong attachment to France of Senegal's religious leaders, whose political support was crucial for Senghor since they controlled the votes of the essentially rural population, made it impossible for Senghor to recommend rejecting the new constitution. He decided to accept it, but as another step toward nominal independence.

The Community, to which the African territories adhered by virtue of approving the new French constitution, was a hybrid containing unitary and federal elements. It may be described as a one-sided quasi-federation. Structurally, it was unitary in the sense that its basic law was the French constitution, which contained a special title outlining the Community relationship, and because only France could amend the document. It was federal in the sense that authority was divided among the central and component governments, that there was a special arbitration mechanism, and that Africans were given some electoral participation and representation in Community organs.

Despite these structural elements, France was preponderant in functional terms.[52] The executive of the Community consisted of its president, assisted by a cabinet called the Secretariat-General. The president derived his mandate largely from the French electorate since the constitution stipulated that he be the president of France, ex officio. The participation of the member states in the election of Charles de Gaulle, one of three candidates for the office in 1958, was only symbolic. With over 30 per cent of the population, they contributed only 4.4 per cent of the votes of the electoral college, and the states of West Africa accounted for only slightly over 2 per cent of the vote. The Community president presided over and represented the ensemble, "formulated" its decisions, appointed all admin-

52. Elements of central authority were broken down into three categories: (a) those which must remain "common" interests, including foreign affairs, defense, common monetary, fiscal, and economic policy, and strategic raw materials; (b) those which could revert to member states, including higher education, justice, and external and internal transportation and telecommunications; and (c) those which could be created by mutual agreement. *Journal officiel de la Communauté* (January 15, 1959) (hereafter cited as *JOC*). Since the Community's authority was limited, other areas were residual by implication and exercised by the member states.

istrative personnel, and enjoyed wide emergency powers.[53] The Secretariat-General replaced the defunct Ministry for Overseas France and was made responsible for coordinating the activities of the member states. The aggressive incumbent rapidly transcended his coordination role and tacitly acted in the name of the French prime minister regarding France's political relations with the African states.

Both the Senate, whose members were elected by state legislatures, and the Executive Council, made up of the member states' chief executives and the common ministers, were advisory bodies; they served chiefly as sounding boards and, on occasion, as a platform to further French foreign policy objectives.[54] Finally, an Arbitration Court was empowered to make decisions interpreting the constitution if requested to do so by the Community president; even so, these "decisions" were secret and were communicated only to President de Gaulle.

Senegal—like other member states—looked on membership in the Community as transitory. The new framework had increased local autonomy and assured continued material aid from France through structural political links. But it had, for all practical purposes, removed African influence from the decisions concerning such aid; the Executive Council could discuss and make recommendations about French aid, but the instrument of French assistance became wholly French. Moreover, the Community removed the previous African "federal" framework and shifted the burden of African unity to the Africans.

Once the Community was established and the continuation of Senegalo-French ties secure, Senghor returned his attention

53. On April 14, 1959, President de Gaulle "decided" that he could declare a state of emergency in any part of the Community either on request by the chief executive of a member state or "in case of trouble preventing the regular functioning of the public powers." Such a state of emergency would automatically signify the transfer of responsibility for public order to the representative of the president of the Community. *Ibid.* (April 15, 1959).

54. This was the case, for example, when the Executive Council approved the explosion of a French atomic device and expressed its solidarity concerning the "great international issues to be discussed in Geneva." See *ibid.* (April 15, 1960, and May 15, 1959).

to inter-African relations, this time to create an African primary federation as a partial replacement for AOF and an outlet for Senegal's economic activity and potential. The choice of partners was limited. The Ivory Coast, breathing a sigh of relief at the disappearance of AOF, favored direct ties with France without an African federal intermediary; Guinea had become an independent state and was thus outside the framework within which the French-language African states operated; and Mauritania, assured of continued French aid, followed another twist in her policy of the connecting link between black and Arab Africa: she remained aloof from both.

The last example, then, of Senegal's preindependence international behavior was that of the Mali Federation experiment. Modibo Keita, the Soudanese leader, first had sought to use RDA ties to promote the African federation proposed by Senghor; he responded to Senghor's invitation only after these attempts failed. The new federation was set into motion in December, 1958, among Senegal, the Soudan, Upper Volta, and Dahomey. The last two states soon withdrew because of internal political struggles, the strength of their economic ties with France and the Ivory Coast, and political influence on the part of Houphouet-Boigny and French officials. Senegal and the Soudan then decided to join into a federation consisting of only two of the eight AOF states. The Mali Federation was created in June, 1959, became independent in June, 1960, and collapsed two months later when Senegal withdrew.

The substance of mutual cooperation of the Mali Federation was limited because much of it was already preempted by the Community. The common interests of the new federation fell into three categories for which authority was assigned to federal organs. First there was cultural solidarity, which included lower and secondary education, and information. The second concerned the rights and liberties of citizens, a category interpreted liberally to cover problems affecting the civil service; work rules; and civil, commercial, and penal activities. The most important common interest was "economic and financial solidarity." This referred, first, to federal services and, second, to a federal solidarity fund intended to decrease two of the original four states' dependence on French budgetary subsidies; since most of the funds would come from Senegal, this was an inducement by that country to secure the adherence of other states.

The federal leaders had to contend with the tensions between the ideal of African unity from which followed a theoretical willingness to give up "sovereignty" and the practical interests of the states jealous of their novel autonomy. They worked out a careful structural balance in the federal organs. "The major worry of the Commission on Institutions," said its rapporteur, "was the preservation of the personality of the states which compose the federation." [55]

The first federal constitution, written by the initial four partners, provided for a legislature including twelve members per state and empowered to approve the head of the federal executive and his cabinet (and sharing legislative initiative with the federal government). There was no arbiter to decide conflicts since the federal court dealt only with administrative and constitutional problems. At the same time, an effort was made to create a strong executive in view of the familiar, uninviting example of the French Fourth Republic. Neither the federal legislature nor the premier could dismiss the other, although the latter could initiate the confidence question—a negative vote resulting in the resignation of government and legislature.

After the withdrawal of Dahomey and Upper Volta, the second constitution worked out a new balance between Senegal and the Soudan, resulting in a dual executive. This was accomplished through the creation, at the insistence of Senegal, of an additional office: that of the president of the federation. The federal president was to be elected by a college consisting of the members of the federal assembly and of the states' legislatures. The president was given authority to nominate the federal premier, to preside over the cabinet, and to promulgate laws. He was also the chief of the federal armed forces. The

55. Federation of Mali, Procès verbaux des séances des 14 et 17 janvier 1959 de l'assemblée fédérale constituante (Dakar: Grande Imprimerie Africaine, 1959), p. 45 (hereafter cited as Procès). For an excellent discussion of the Mali Federation, consult William J. Foltz, From French West Africa to the Mali Federation (New Haven: Yale University Press, 1965).

federal premier, in turn, was given the authority to choose and dismiss his cabinet (subject to the *agrément* of the appropriate delegation in the assembly) and to define and conduct federal policy. Moreover, he was made responsible for national defense.

Another outstanding feature of the revised constitution was an arbitration mechanism consisting of three elements: first, a federal supreme court with independent authority to rule on the constitutionality of federal and state legislation and of international agreements; second, a conference of the heads of the state governments, meeting semiannually to "harmonize" policies; and third, the authority of the federal president to arbitrate disputes between the states or between the federation and the states.[56] In view of the federal president's arbitration role, much would depend on the incumbent. Although that post seems to have been tailor-made for Senghor, whose conciliatory outlook was a guarantee of his impartiality, a bitter dispute arose between Senegal and the Soudan, each of which wanted to man the post. The crucial importance each side attached to the office came to light as the date for the election neared: it never took place, and the federation ended one week before the election was scheduled.

Unaccustomed, intimate contact between Senegalese and Soudanese leaders brought to the surface differences of substance and style. Senegalo-Soudanese divergences were rooted in different domestic political settings and experience as well as individual leaders' personal preferences. Perhaps the most important contrasts concerned political style and consequent false expectations. The Soudanese, following their political experience of RDA methods of organization to combat a relatively harsh colonial administration, favored centralization and authoritarian methods fortified by their conviction that only their path was the correct one. "We have always endeavored," explained Modibo Keita,

56. The two countries also agreed on a formula for the distribution of federal posts. One country would supply the federal president, the president of the federal assembly, and the vice-president of the federal government, for whom a new, ambiguous post was created for the occasion. The other country would supply the federal premier, who would also have charge of foreign affairs and national defense.

to bend . . . the policy of the [Senegalese] leaders toward a better understanding of African problems, be they political, economic, or social. The rest is only pretext [and] misleads, alas, the good faith of numerous citizens, but shall disappear in smoke, sooner or later, inevitably.[57]

The Senegalese, with a political tradition of party fusion and compromise among divergent elements, expected that the good sense of the Soudanese would make them recognize the virtue of Senegal's style. Whereas Soudanese, after the failure of the federation, placed the blame squarely on Senegal, Léopold Senghor spoke of profound sociological differences and told his people:

> Mr. Modibo Keita—I speak of him without rancor, but not without sadness—guided by ill-boding counsel, dreamed of leaning on the Mali army, even on the French army, to subdue the Senegalese people. [But] the reasons for the crisis are political and sociological. They go beyond quarrels about posts; they surely go beyond personal ambitions, although these have played—this is human—a certain role.[58]

Every important issue discussed by the Senegalese and the Soudanese revealed a deep cleavage. They clashed, for instance, on the question of independence for the new federation. The Soudanese pressed for immediate independence, which they regarded as a precondition for further progress and from which they expected the rapid disappearance of the colonial era. Senghor, by contrast, took a more moderate, long-range view, which distinguished between real and nominal independence:

> When independence is solely nominal, it is false. It can satisfy national pride; but it does not abolish the consciousness of alienation, the feeling of frustration, the inferiority complex, since it does not solve the concrete problems that

57. *L'Essor hebdomadaire* (August 29, 1960).
58. Senegal, *Conférence de presse du 23 août 1960 par Léopold Sédar Senghor* (Dakar: Ministère de l'Information, 1960), p. 7.

face underdeveloped countries: to house, clothe, feed, heal, educate the masses.

As we develop economically and socially, as we have the cadres necessary to the state, as we shall have elevated, with the level of education, the standard of living of our people, then we shall negotiate . . . in friendship, the transfers of powers. . . .

Let us seek real independence, and the rest will follow.[59]

They also clashed on the proper method to build the federal nation. Keita regarded the unification of the two countries' political parties as the key to success. The joint federal party should be used to obliterate national and subnational particularisms, to force the nation to grow, and to control the federal decision-making process. Senghor looked on nation-building as a slow, sociological maturation process which required, in addition to time, a complementary view of different partners willing to cooperate and, if need be, compromise. The new nation was, for Senghor, an artificial, ideal concept; to realize it would require "centuries of effort and patience" so that it could mature internally, "like a fruit." [60]

Senghor persisted in supporting the Mali Federation long after other Senegalese were convinced that it would never work. Several factors help account for his obstinacy. First was the consideration of the high stakes for his country's economic progress. The loss of the Soudan as a trading partner threatened to bring about the very isolation in Africa which Senghor had worked to prevent. A second factor was the general euphoria which accompanied every institutional step marking the birth

59. *Congrès constitutif du parti de la fédération africaine* (Dakar, 1959), p. 24.

60. *Ibid.*, p. 59. Other differences concerned economic development; the Soudanese, hardly modernized but self-sufficient in staples, were anxious to experiment and to change social and economic structures rapidly. The Senegalese, with a better infrastructure and a highly developed consumer sector, favored complementary development. Similarly, replacing Europeans with Africans was, for the Soudanese, a pressing political problem, whereas for Senegal it was a question merely of educating enough Africans to replace European expatriates, thus avoiding the dislocations attendant upon raising political orthodoxy above technical qualifications.

of the new federation. The federation did represent, for Senghor, the crowning achievement of several years' effort, and that achievement tended to overshadow the many warning signs that all was not well. Members of the federal constituent assembly had taken a solemn oath to "become the indefatigable preachers . . . of African political unity" and concluded their work with a sacred promise to lay down their lives if need be.[61] For many, the federation tended to take on an ideal life of its own partly divorced from the realities. It had become a vision to some extent more important than the states on whose practical cooperation it depended. For Senghor, "everything . . . must be subordinated to the consolidation and extension of the federation. It cannot be called into question." [62]

It was not until after the Soudanese were openly criticized by Senegalese elites for alleged arrogance, had violated several agreements to appoint federal officials only with the agrément of Senegal, and had pressured Senegalese trade unions, youth and women's organizations, and, most important, religious leaders, that Senghor reacted. The Senegalese political system, being more liberal than that of Soudan, allowed more or less open and vocal opposition which on occasion sided with Soudanese leaders within the federal structure. Senegal was thus in danger of being placed in a permanent minority in spite of the constitutional balance, and of being "subverted" from within. Reluctantly convinced that he must act to safeguard his country's independence, Senghor warned the Soudanese that they should stop their intervention in the internal affairs of Senegal. "Mali," he said in a public address, "cannot hold fast if Senegal is divided." Senegal's premier, Mamadou Dia, told supporters,

> To have independence is not everything. One must also keep it. Senegal is our mother country. Before creating anything, before solidifying the Mali Federation, one must first think of Senegal.[63]

61. "And if," recited the delegates, "for the Mali Federation, for political unity, for African unity, I must accept the ultimate consequence, I shall not hesitate, I shall not retreat." *Procès*, pp. 82–83.
62. *Congrès constitutif du parti de la fédération africaine*, p. 58.
63. *L'Unité africaine* (August 20, 1960).

The federation experiment ended on August 20, 1960, less than a year after its creation. Technically, the end came when Senegal declared her independence from the Mali Federation; but this followed a series of measures taken by Modibo Keita, interpreted by Senegal as a coup d'état against her sovereignty. Keita dismissed Mamadou Dia as federal defense minister, declared a state of emergency, appealed for French armed support, and asked for an immediate session of the United Nations Security Council. The underlying struggle between Senegal and the Soudan involved control over the federal armed forces, since France refused to intervene. The Soudanese failed essentially because these forces were Senegalese stationed in Senegal who remained loyal to their government, and because Senegal's authorities were able to take effective countermeasures. The Mali experiment, needless to say, impressed on Senegal's leaders a keen consciousness of the dangers of external subversion and of the difficulties in political unification among Africa's new states.

Substance and style

One way to define outstanding aspects of Senghor's preindependence international policies is to examine the limits which confined the pursuit of such policies. Senegal's preindependence foreign policy should be inspected from the points of view of both substance and style for this purpose. Policy substance aimed toward increasing domestic autonomy, to be wrested from the French decision-makers, and toward maintaining economic and other benefits anchored in the existing structure of relations with France and within the framework of AOF.

As discussed earlier, the progressive weakening of African bonds with France, and thus internal autonomy, was achieved in some fifteen years following the end of World War II. Important elements of Senghor's policy contributed to this development. The question which arises in the context of this discussion is: When and why was Senghor willing to limit his pursuit of the general objective sought? Two answers may be suggested, taking into consideration the political context in which limits appeared. First, limits to autonomy were accepted when there appeared no way of going beyond them. This was true especially in the French postliberation period, during the ten years following 1945. Like other African leaders, Senghor yielded to the inevitable obstacles of French conservatism, political immobilism, and unwillingness to contemplate changing a unitary political system.

The second limitation of the autonomy objective derived from comparative economic advantage. The continued economic assistance of France was a necessity, and continued economic cooperation with the African hinterland, which Senegal's modern economic sector was designed to serve, was regarded as only slightly less important. At no time did Senghor seriously envision a political break from France; his views on independence mirror, in large part, the fact that his concern for actual economic benefits loomed larger in his mind than did the simple, superficial transfer of political authority by dint of signatures on a document, solemn and psychologically rewarding though it might be.

Economic needs also underlay his championship of African unity. Fully aware that the existing, French-imposed federation would not outlast French support, he sought at first to pressure France directly into retaining it; it was only after this tactic failed that he mobilized African opinion around the slogan of "unity" to pressure the French indirectly. Because of their limited economic objectives, the various proposals to maintain the African federation did not specify the anticipated political relationship between the territories (or autonomous states) and the federation except in the vague terms of two coexisting levels of government. Further, it was chiefly for economic reasons that Senghor was willing to limit Senegal's sovereignty when entering into an African primary federation. Economic limits of political autonomy testify to a profound understanding of Senegal's economic needs; economic French West African unity, to Senghor, was more important than political independence.

Senghor's preindependence foreign policy style may be described as gradualist and compromising, and several factors help to account for it. First, Senghor had accepted becoming part of the French decision-making machinery. As a result he became sensitized to the need for attuning progress to the difficulties of reaching compromises, and the potency of domestic political struggle, in the French Fourth Republic. No doubt the help and encouragement he received from French friends and allies made the complex rules of the game more palatable than they otherwise would have been. But the rules of the game of French politics required patience, and progress was achieved at the end of long, gradual pressures for change.

Second, compromise as a political style had its roots also in domestic politics. The peculiar nature of Senegal's political clans, as well as tensions between conservative religious and urban bourgeois elites, on one hand, and impatient younger radicals on the other, favored endless compromises manifest in a tradition of political pluralism and party fusions.

A third reason for a gradualist style was the African interterritorial environment. Such interterritorial alliances of which Senghor became the leader in West Africa (the IOM, CA, and PRA) were attempts at integration from the top. Because of the limited following enjoyed by Senghor's allies in other territories, and because of the domestic rivalries between these allies and opposition to the RDA, neither of these parties could be fashioned into a solidly structured political organization. It followed that common action rested on compromise rather than on joint decisions implemented through political organization. To these limitations on interterritorial cooperation must be added those which threatened either Senghor's international parties or his political support at home.

One final aspect of Senegal's preindependence foreign policy style was the result of personal characteristics of Senghor's thought. Two such characteristics may be singled out at this time: one is connected with negritude, another with his occasional tendency to ascribe extraordinary influence to articles of his own faith. If we assume that the Africans' identity crisis is at the root of separation from France, then it is clear that Senghor's own identity crisis antedated postwar political developments. He lived his crisis in the late 1930s and early 1940s; he settled it negatively by rejecting cultural assimilation and positively by championing the African values of negritude. Once this was accomplished,

Senghor reached a maturation point which placed him ahead of most other African leaders who experienced that crisis in connection with later political issues. Having regained his pride, he had no need to become as emotionally involved as did some Africans over such issues as national independence or African unity. In fact, most Africans' enthusiasm for African unity and independence was primarily psychological in origin; but for Senghor, these two themes were different: he manipulated the first—unity —for economic gains and bowed to the second—independence— as inevitable, given the circumstances. It is not surprising, then, that Senghor was able to retain the perspective necessary to emphasize, with relative equanimity, the distinctions between real and nominal independence at a time when that concept monopolized everyone's attention and commitments.

The other personal factor responsible in part for Senegal's policy style is Senghor's faith in the power of his own ideals. This was evident in the unshakable faith which underlay his conceptions of how Franco-African institutional ties ought to be changed, that French governments would allow—indeed welcome—their African partners into the small circle of those who allocate material rewards. Senghor clearly expected that the French Republic could be transformed into a federation which would relinquish, at least in part, such authority to a federal executive including extrametropolitan Frenchmen. Postwar evidence of the allocation of French aid to Africa, notwithstanding the territories' privileged status as recipients, pointed the other way. In spite of the Africans' advisory role in that process, decisions were made by Frenchmen in the national interest of France. Senghor's hopes in that respect appear to have rested on nothing much more than his faith in one version of the brotherhood of mankind, perhaps reinforced by French Socialists' convictions about international solidarity among the less fortunate.

Senghor's faith was evident also in his persistence during the short-lived Mali Federation. To the many warnings and complaints about Soudanese behavior in Senegal, he responded by counseling calm and patience and reiterating his belief in ultimate success. As he wrote in late 1960,

We were naïve to believe that a federation was possible, in 1959, between states disunited in 1957. . . . We neglected to analyze and understand the sociological differences which existed among the territories of former AOF.[64]

64. *Nation et voie africaine du socialisme* (Paris: Présence Africaine), p. 10.

CHAPTER TWO

Structure and Process

THE CONSTITUTIONAL FRAMEWORK

Executive centralization

Before looking at the structure of the Foreign Ministry, it is appropriate to review briefly the constitutional framework in which it operates. The most important aspect of that framework is that formal foreign policy responsibility in Senegal has come to rest in the office of the president of the Republic. The structure of that office has followed the pattern of centralization from the First Republic, which lasted from independence to December, 1962, to the Second Republic, which succeeded it. The subsequent government decentralization of early 1970 appears to have had little, if any, bearing on the foreign policy structure.

As is customary in parliamentary regimes, authority during the First Republic was divided between the president of the Republic and head of state, on one hand, and the prime minister and head of the government, on the other. Responsibility for defining and conducting foreign relations consequently resided in the office of the prime minister as part of his general mandate for national policy.

It is true that, although the president of the Republic was expected to act mostly as an arbiter in the political life of the country, he retained some foreign affairs prerogatives. Thus, as head of state, he performed diplomatic accreditation functions, negotiated international treaties, chaired the High Council on National Defense, and was chief of the armed forces. But the constitution also required that presidential decisions on general policy, as well as on administrative and military appointments, be either countersigned by the premier or made collectively in cabinet sessions. Nonetheless, the premier was solely responsible for national policy, headed the administration, and "disposed of" the armed forces.

Following the end of the First Republic, after Senghor had won reelection as president of the Republic with the telling slogan of "a single hat on a single head," the formal political system was transformed into a presidential regime. Henceforth it was Senghor who, as chief executive, was responsible for defining and implementing all aspects of national policy. As head of the administration with authority to appoint all civil servants, President Senghor was particularly concerned about nepotism and corruption. Consequently, he took a personal interest in the civil service and delegated his appointing authority to cabinet members only in the case of relatively low-ranking officials.[1] Furthermore, the Ecole Nationale d'Administration of the University of Dakar, the most important training ground for higher civil servants, was attached directly to the Presidency of the Republic.

Another aspect of executive centralization is reflected in the nature of emergency powers. In the First Republic, a state of emergency could be declared by the Council of Ministers; the constitution was silent about what constituted such an emergency and stipulated merely that it required legislative approval within twelve days. The 1963 Senegalese constitution, reproducing almost textually the content of article 16 of the constitution of the French Fifth Republic, is much more specific. Article 47 states that the president of the Republic can take "any measure tending . . . to safeguard the nation" if he believes that, inter

1. Dmitri-Georges Lavroff, *La République du Sénégal* (Paris: Librairie Générale de Droit et de Jurisprudence, 1966), p. 112.

alia, the "execution of international agreements, the independence of the nation, or the integrity of its territory" is "threatened in an immediate and grave manner."

After having determined that such a threat exists, the president of the Republic need only inform the nation, but is not required—as is the president of France—to seek anyone's guidance or approval. Any measure "of a legislative nature" must then be approved by the National Assembly within two weeks, failing which it becomes null and void. Assuming that measures of a legislative nature are those falling within the circumscribed domain of legislative responsibility, then, according to article 56, these involve only "regulations concerning . . . the constraints imposed on citizens by national defense . . ." or the "fundamental principles . . . of the general organization of national defense" or both. Assuming further that these issues have been settled by appropriate legislation, then it appears that the president of the Republic has wide discretionary authority—in case of emergency.

The president of the Republic, moreover, is more than a *primus inter pares* among his close collaborators: through a variety of constitutional and administrative devices he controls the cabinet and has at his disposal a powerful servant in the form of the secretary-general of the Presidency of the Republic.

The president appoints, and dismisses, the members of his cabinet, who are responsible to him and have no independent constitutional authority. An effort was made to detach cabinet members from their political or professional base by forbidding them, upon retirement from executive office, to resume either their seat in the legislature if they were drawn from that body, or their prior professional activity, until six months after termination of cabinet service.

The cabinet itself is a relatively weak body. As Professor Dmitri-Georges Lavroff has pointed out, a presidential circular defined its function as a "customary meeting whose consultation is, for me, purely discretionary and without effect on the validity of presidential acts." [2] Meaningful discussion and exchange of opinions take place in the more restricted Joint Minis-

2. *Ibid.*, p. 131.

terial Committees summoned by President Senghor to discuss specific issues. The results of its decisions are subsequently communicated to the cabinet for endorsement.

The secretary-general of the Presidency of the Republic exercises administrative control over the formulation and execution of decisions. The secretary-general is appointed by President Senghor and participates in cabinet meetings as a full equal with the ministers. He checks ministerial proposals for their conformity with general policy and decides, in principle, which are to be submitted for presidential signature. He also convenes the meetings of both the cabinet and the Joint Ministerial Committees and draws up their agendas. Finally, he supervises the implementation of decisions, primarily through ministerial reports routed through his office. The secretary-general may thus be considered a kind of super minister who enjoys, in the administration of national policy, a degree of presidential confidence second to none among the president's close advisers.[3]

Another structural reorganization of the Senegalese government occurred in February, 1970, when the country's voters approved a new constitution. That reorganization followed severe disturbances which began in 1968 when students at Dakar University, and later trade unions, began agitating for reforms. The major innovations of Senegal's "new regime" include creation of the post of prime minister and the cooptation of some younger technocrats and union leaders into an enlarged cabinet. The new premier, thirty-five-year-old Abdou Diouf, is known as an able administrator who has served in a number of government posts, most recently as minister of planning and industry.

It does not seem, however, that the decentralization of government responsibilities which accompanied this latest change has any noticeable effect on foreign policy. For one thing, President Senghor retains the authority to define national policy, to be carried out by the prime minister and his cabinet. Moreover, the new constitution specifically reserves control over foreign affairs, national defense, and the armed forces as the special province of the president of the Republic. It is true that a new post of secretary of state for foreign affairs was created as part of the

3. *Ibid.*, pp. 132–35.

refurbished governmental structure. But the incumbent, a labor leader, appears to owe his promotion to cooptation rather than to any foreign affairs expertise.

Legislative influence

The national legislature has some constitutional prerogatives in foreign affairs. The Assembly must authorize a declaration of war, ratify treaties, and pass the national budget. But in case of conflict, all the legislature can do is to embarrass the executive. It may refuse to approve the budget, which can then be adopted by executive fiat; it may refuse to approve emergency measures, which could result in a constitutional deadlock; it may amend legislation, provided that new expenditures are covered by new revenue; it may ask oral or written questions from the government, either with or without debate—but without vote; and, finally, it may create Commissions of Enquiry.[4]

What influence the legislature's Committee on Foreign Affairs may enjoy is not reflected in plenary sessions. Nonetheless, some members of the Foreign Affairs Committee may exert influence through close contacts with and access to the government and party executive, and most members have direct access to the larger Assembly structure. In 1967, four of the committee members also belonged to the UPS national executive, and two of these were officers: one was a political commissioner and the other was secretary for women's affairs. Sixteen members were either officers or members of legislative committees other than their own. One was a vice-president of the Assembly, while another was president of the Committee on Legislation, Justice, and General Administration and Rules. Yet another was president of the legislature's Parliamentary Group. The Foreign Affairs Committee's second vice-president and its secretary belonged to the Committee on Defense. In addition, members of

4. The president of the Republic may present messages to a silent Assembly; ask for a second, obligatory reading of bills; and place "priority" draft laws on the Assembly's agendum. He may also dissolve the legislature after it has existed for three years; in this case the mandate of the deputies ends, whereas the president of the Republic and the government remain in office until the results of a new presidential election are known.

the Foreign Affairs Committee belonged also to the Assembly's Committees on Legislation and Defense; Finance, Economic Affairs, Development, and Planning; Work, Social Security, Health, and Civil Service; Education, Culture, Information, Arts, Youth, and Sports; Public Works, Transportation, Communication, Mines, and Tourism; and the Committee on Delegations.[5]

The chief executive may occasionally take the initiative in smoothing over difficulties with the legislature. The official in charge of relations with the Assembly makes it a point to study the opinions of that body through informal discussions, and he reports to his superiors any discontent with or opposition to executive policy. Other officials, sometimes the president of the Republic, then invite opponents for discussions in order to reach agreement. But this procedure has, apparently, never involved international policy.

THE FOREIGN MINISTRY

Early problems

Unlike other government departments which had existed officially since about 1957, the Ministry of Foreign Affairs was a postindependence addition. The structure of that ministry, set up a few months after the breakup of the Mali Federation in August, 1960, remained temporary and experimental until the end of 1963.

As constituted in late 1960, the Foreign Ministry included five major agencies: the minister's cabinet, the protocol service, the Office of Political Affairs, the Inspectorate of Diplomatic Posts, and the Secretariat-General. The Secretariat-General was responsible for coordinating the internal services, which consisted of the Office of Chancellery and Administrative Affairs, the Office of Cultural and Social Affairs, the Office of Economic and Financial Agreements and Treaties, the Bureau for Code

5. Ambassadors frequently call on the president of the legislature's Foreign Affairs Committee during their passage through Senegal; hence, it may be assumed that he is kept au courant of late, important developments.

and Correspondence, and the Bureau for Information, Press, and Translation.

A variety of factors affected and determined the temporary nature of the ministry. These included the ambiguity surrounding the new ministry's status, the scarcity of available personnel, coordination problems, and a problem peculiar to the manner in which Senegal became an independent state.

First, conflicting estimates of the need for a Foreign Ministry handicapped its growth. There was a general tendency to welcome the new institution as an attribute of sovereignty, but this was counterbalanced by inertia and concern lest the achievement be at the expense of the establishment. The Foreign Ministry was a symbol of national independence, an object useful for pomp and circumstance, but also a luxury which was desirable but not necessarily essential. As one former Foreign Affairs official who was involved in its creation explained, "No one thought of denying that Senegal should have her own foreign policy, but no one was interested in the instrument of that policy." [6]

Second, the Foreign Ministry had to be built around available qualified personnel. When the Mali Federation's External Relations Bureau was dissolved, it was embryonic and consisted of only a few technical advisers. At the beginning, it proved very difficult for the Foreign Ministry to "raid" other government departments, and the reluctance of other ministries to part with valuable people added another handicap to the fledgling newcomer. Established ministerial departments cannot be said to have been enthusiastic about the prospect of losing some of their authority; they argued that, since their competence in their own technical fields was proved and exceeded that of the Foreign Ministry, shifting responsibilities to a less qualified agency could result only in inefficiency. Moreover, some of the older ministries had been conducting international relations before Senegal became formally independent. For example, the Ministry for Pub-

6. Jacques Hubert, *Les Relations extérieures d'un état nouveau: Le Sénégal* (Dakar: Faculté de Droit et de Sciences Economiques, 1963), p. 20.

lic Health was responsible for relations with such international organizations as the World Health Organization, the United Nations Food and Agriculture Organization, and UNESCO.[7]

Third, and perhaps most important from the point of view of smooth operation, there were problems of coordination. It seems logical that technical competence be the major criterion for assigning responsibilities, and that therefore the "technical" ministries reserve for themselves the technical aspects of foreign relations. But the lack of precision in defining areas of authority created jurisdictional conflicts, rivalries, and unnecessary bitterness.

Some of these conflicts resulted from the strong position of the prime minister, Mamadou Dia. Dia, a student of economics, relied heavily for advice on agencies other than the Foreign Ministry, such as the Ministry of Commerce and Industry and the External Finance Service of the now defunct Ministry for Cooperation and Technical Assistance. The Foreign Ministry remained ignorant of important initiatives affecting international affairs and learned of some, such as in the case of Senegalese delegations to international conferences, through the press.

Premier Dia's position enabled him to bypass the foreign minister—and the president of the Republic as well—and to take a number of foreign policy initiatives which anticipated the debate over the relative importance and speed of industrialization in Senegal's economic growth and led to his subsequent removal in December, 1962. Two specific examples of this coordination problem will serve as illustration. In an effort to secure a trade agreement with the People's Republic of China, the prime minister independently communicated with the Guinean ambassador in Dakar, a move which at the time was not in harmony with the policy of the president of the Republic. At the end of 1961, Dia communicated with the governments of Scandinavia and

7. Hubert reports that one of the reasons that diplomatic affairs were separated from the general coordinating responsibility of the secretary-general was the seniority of the head of the Office of Political Affairs, a Frenchman whose length of service as *administrateur-en-chef de la France d'Outre-Mer* exceeded that of the incumbent secretary-general. See *ibid.*, p. 58.

Yugoslavia prior to his visit to those countries; the Foreign Ministry became involved only after these governments sent their correspondence concerning the planned visit to that agency.[8]

Finally, the ministry was created at a time when political and diplomatic priorities other than structural claimed much of the foreign minister's time and efforts. After the Mali Federation fiasco, Senegal's major foreign affairs concern was a fear of diplomatic isolation; consequently, the foreign minister, Doudou Thiam, became a traveling spokesman to explain and justify Senegal's action leading to her independence. As late as 1962, his duties in foreign countries, as well as his annual vacation, led him abroad for at least seven of twelve months.[9]

Reorganization

Two basic reorganizations took place after the inauguration of the Senegalese Second Republic. The first was the result of the close personal relations between President Senghor and his foreign minister, Thiam, the only person to have held ministerial posts without interruption since independence. In December, 1962, Thiam became one of the president's closest collaborators. Not only was he asked to continue his duties as foreign minister; he was also the only cabinet member promoted to minister of state and entrusted with running the government during the president's absence from the country. Moreover, he was given the additional task of conducting relations between the national executive and the assemblies, that is, the legislature and the Social and Economic Council.

This latter responsibility, however, gave rise to a number of problems. The Foreign Ministry, still in the process of formation, was less than ideally equipped for handling the delicate and time-consuming job of serving as a screen between the Presidency and the National Assembly. The secretary-general of the Presidency of the Republic, moreover, argued that his office did have the required experience and staff. Consequently, executive-legis-

8. *Ibid.*, p. 37.
9. *Ibid.*, p. 26

lative relations were later transferred to a commissioner on relations with the assemblies under the supervision of the secretary-general of the Presidency. The second reorganization, motivated by a desire for efficiency, took place in April, 1965. The foreign minister, in keeping with his increased stature, was charged with the "clarification and implementation of the foreign relations of the state," whereas the 1960 prime minister's ordinance had defined that authority as directing and supervising foreign policy "on behalf of the government." [10]

The earlier jurisdictional problem was remedied by maintaining the division of labor between ministries but improving coordination. The foreign minister was given exclusive authority for contacts and correspondence with foreign states, and the reform stipulated that, whenever possible, his ministry should head delegations abroad. In recognition of the greater technical competence of other ministries, however, these were allowed to correspond directly with foreign countries on technical subjects, "provided that the Ministry of Foreign Affairs be informed." [11]

Other, internal aspects of the Foreign Ministry structure were streamlined to complement the reforms at the top. Most important was the clarification of the respective functions of the ministry's cabinet director and secretary-general. Experience had shown the impracticability of letting the secretary-general coordinate the activities of only some of the central administrative staff, without any responsibility for political affairs or overseas personnel. Moreover, his coordination task had become increasingly difficult because his imprecise mandate encouraged autonomy on the part of offices technically under his jurisdiction. An equally vexing problem was that, again as a result of imprecision, the cabinet director had become burdened with a crushing number

10. See Décret 60–343/PCG, October 13, 1960; Décret 65–264/MAE, April 22, 1965; and the Foreign Ministry's arrêtés 9152, 9153, June 18, 1965, and 15,526, November 3, 1966, defining the authority of the Office of Political, Cultural, and Social Affairs, the Office of Administrative Affairs and Chancelleries, and the Office of International Economic and Technical Cooperation, respectively.
11. Décret 65–264/MAE, April 22, 1965.

of administrative duties, even to the point of his signing "the least important memorandum of transmittal." [12]

To correct these deficiencies, more specific duties were assigned to each office. The cabinet director, chosen by the foreign minister as his personal representative, was given the authority to define department policy, and was made generally responsible for diplomatic and political tasks. The secretary-general, a career administrator appointed by the president of the Republic, was given direct administrative authority for the three major Offices and two minor agencies in the ministry. Chart 1 indicates the new structure of the Foreign Ministry (pp. 70–71).

At this time it may be noted that the structure of the Foreign Ministry reflects a number of priorities which, as will be shown below, correspond to the general thrust of policy orientation. The first priority is clearly for economic affairs, which are the responsibility of one of the two operational offices devoted to a single functional area. Second, the Geographic Sectors Division ranks Africa first, Europe second, America third, and the rest of the world last.[13] Third, one division in each of the two functional offices is also responsible for relations with such organizations as the European Economic Community and the United Nations Economic Commission for Africa. Finally, the protocol service remained in a class by itself, its importance highlighted by the service's chief as the only one with the rank of minister plenipotentiary.

Personnel policy

Foreign service officers may belong to one of three categories, which, in order of descending importance, are called counselors and secretaries of foreign affairs, assistant secretaries of foreign affairs, and chancellery secretaries. The first category provides mission heads, embassy counselors, consuls-general, embassy secretaries, or consuls in the external service, or general leadership

12. Hubert, *Les Relations extérieures*, p. 46.
13. The earlier structure of that division had copied the French breakdown of one bureau for both Africa and the Middle East and had two other bureaus: one for Europe and North America, and another for Latin America, the Far East, Oceania, and other areas.

positions in the internal service. The second category includes bureau chiefs in the central service and embassy secretaries, consuls-general and consuls, and embassy attachés in the external service. The third and lowest category includes general administrative assistants such as code clerks and couriers in the central service; in the external service they may perform similar duties, act as interpreters, archivists, or consular attachés.

In theory, recruitment into the foreign service results from successful completion of annual competitive examinations; either foreign service employees or outsiders are eligible. The level of these examinations is geared to the category for which entry is sought. To enter the service, requirements are as follows: for the first category, graduation from the diplomatic program of the Senegalese École Nationale d'Administration (ENAS); for the second, a degree of bachelor of arts or its equivalent. Regulations for in-service promotions are more lenient and take into account length of service in addition to the requisite examinations. Promotions depend generally on the length of service, which varies between three and fourteen years, and a minimum of two years spent in the rank from which promotion is sought.

In view of the scarcity of competent personnel (when the ministry was established), however, these ideal recruitment standards were modified to permit the lateral entry of outsiders into the service. Thus, for the highest category of officials, requirements included either (1) Senegalese citizenship and the rank of administrateur de la France d'Outre-Mer or counselor of administrative affairs, (2) Senegalese citizenship and graduation from the French Institut des Hautes Etudes d'Outre-Mer with a foreign affairs specialization, (3) a bachelor of laws or of higher education, or (4) where not enough ENAS graduates were available, a doctorate of laws, a bachelor of laws plus one graduate diploma, a state doctorate, or a bachelor's degree in any field plus at least one graduate diploma. For the second category, either former attachés de la France d'Outre-Mer or division chiefs, or ENAS students with lower than average grades, were permitted to compete. The lowest category, likewise, opened its doors to administrative secretaries from the former Civil Service Corps bearing that designation.

The diplomatic section of ENAS turns out only four or five

CHART 1
FOREIGN MINISTRY OF SENEGAL,
ORGANIZATION IN 1967

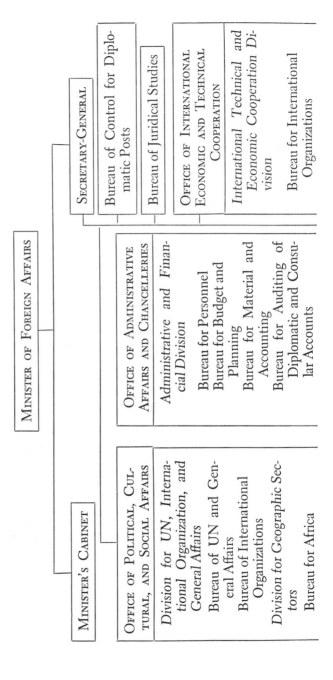

MINISTER OF FOREIGN AFFAIRS

SECRETARY-GENERAL

Bureau of Control for Diplomatic Posts

Bureau of Juridical Studies

OFFICE OF INTERNATIONAL ECONOMIC AND TECHNICAL COOPERATION

International Technical and Economic Cooperation Division

Bureau for International Organizations

OFFICE OF ADMINISTRATIVE AFFAIRS AND CHANCELLERIES

Administrative and Financial Division

Bureau for Personnel
Bureau for Budget and Planning
Bureau for Material and Accounting
Bureau for Auditing of Diplomatic and Consular Accounts

MINISTER'S CABINET

OFFICE OF POLITICAL, CULTURAL, AND SOCIAL AFFAIRS

Division for UN, International Organization, and General Affairs

Bureau of UN and General Affairs
Bureau of International Organizations
Division for Geographic Sectors

Bureau for Africa

Bureau for Foreign Extra-African Relations
Inter-African Economic Co-operation Division
Bureau for African Cooperation
Bureau for Bilateral and Subregional Cooperation

Chancellery Division
Bureau for Consular Affairs
Bureau for Liaison

PROTOCOL SERVICE

Press and Information Bureau

Translation Bureau

Code and Courier Bureau

Bureau for Europe
Bureau for America
Bureau for the Middle East, Asia, and Oceania
Division for Cultural Relations
Bureau for Cultural Relations
Bureau for Social Affairs

graduates each year. Careers in the foreign service have not yet fired the enthusiasm of students, although a top graduate may immediately enter the highest category in the ministry, with the exception, of course, of being named ambassador. One reason for this reluctance on the part of young Senegalese is their apparent lack of interest in foreign affairs careers; another is that ENAS also trains another category of civil servants, the *administrateurs civils*, who have immediate access to high administrative posts throughout the country which bring with them the combined rewards of prestige, command, and perquisites at home.

It is likely that the foreign affairs hierarchy seems unduly conservative to young, ambitious Senegalese and that this acts as a deterrent to recruitment. A candidate with a bachelor's degree, entering the second category, must wait a minimum of eight years before he can hope to reach the fourth, or lowest, rank in the first category in the foreign service. By contrast, a student with a bachelor's degree may enter ENAS and graduate in one year with the coveted title of *administrateur civil*. Moreover, the Foreign Ministry's regulations do not recognize the proper place for such highly specialized individuals as translators and interpreters since these are confined to the lowest category, on a par with couriers and messengers.

By 1967, the Foreign Ministry seemed to have reached its "cruising speed" with approximately one hundred members of the external service, including ambassadors, secretaries, and counselors of embassy, and with some two hundred employees of the central services. If the number of chauffeurs (about thirty for the protocol service alone), janitors, gardeners, and other relatively unskilled employees is deducted from the total, the prospects for access to a position of responsibility are not encouraging to a prospective applicant.

The personnel policy of the Foreign Ministry is based on the assumption of a slow, orderly development of the service's competence. What adaptations were made to attract outside personnel into the foreign service were temporary. But since the device of lateral entry provided most of the officials, and since the size of the agency is not expected to increase drastically in future years, the result is a manpower configuration in which improvements of qualifications can be expected to depend on in-service promotion rather than on the entry of new people whose initial foreign affairs training may be better than that of the present staff.

This situation may tend to place on the Foreign Ministry a stamp of stagnation and inflexibility in viewing and implementing foreign policy. It is likely that, in time, these problems will be solved. There is some evidence of promotion of younger men with the appropriate academic requirements into top positions. In 1967, for instance, the interim director of the Office of Political Affairs was an ENAS graduate whose subsequent on-the-job training included a three-year period as counselor of embassy in Brazil. Nonetheless, present personnel policy, with its cumbersome hierarchical content, limitations on growth, and emphasis on legal training, seems to reflect a French model more than an imaginative adaptation to Senegal's needs.

Information and reporting

Sources of printed information on international events available to the foreign policy makers fall into four general categories. First, both the Presidency of the Republic and the Ministry of Foreign Affairs subscribe to round-the-clock wire services— Agence France Presse and Reuters—and thus receive almost instantaneous news about general major events throughout the world.

Second, both offices regularly receive a number of newspapers and periodicals. Newspapers from Europe and Africa predominate, and include such European dailies as Hamburg's *Die Zeit,* the London *Times,* and an Italian paper, as well as daily, weekly, and occasional papers printed in French-speaking African countries. French papers predominate among those from Europe, including *Le Monde, Le Figaro, Le Nouvel Observateur, L'Express,* and *L'Humanité.* Magazines include *Jeune-Afrique, Paris-Match,* as well as *Newsweek.* By contrast, there are few English-language African newspapers or magazines. In view of President Senghor's longtime interest in social philosophy and association with French and African periodicals, many of these are found in the library of his office. This material, derived mostly from French public and private sources, tends to insert a French point of view into the Senegalese decision-making process. At the lower and middle levels of the Foreign Ministry at least, there is a tendency to accept somewhat uncritically the material contained in French sources. The actual effect of these sources on Senegalese policy is, of course, not apparent or proved merely by identifying this kind of predisposition.

Third, the Ministry of Information also subscribes to the printed matter mentioned and has, because of former Premier Mamadou Dia's policy of centralizing the information function in that ministry and because of the availability of personnel, an impressive collection of printed news media. For a number of years, the Information Ministry has accumulated a file of newspaper and magazine clippings for a morgue, and the Foreign Ministry has been making progress in that direction under the direction of the only Frenchman employed in foreign affairs as head of the Bureau for Press, Information, and Translation. His bureau also employs four translator/interpreters: one for English, one for Arabic, one for Russian and German, and another for Arabic and Spanish.

Fourth, the Foreign Affairs Ministry receives regular and special reports from embassies abroad, of which relevant excerpts are circulated among the staff. The ministry also receives a stream of background materials, such as news releases, pamphlets, and other documents from diplomatic missions in Dakar, and this is supplemented by news and other data supplied by the correspondents of seven foreign news agencies resident in Dakar: Agence France Presse, Italy's ANSAS, West Germany's Deutsche Presse Agentur, the New China News Agency, the Middle East News Agency, Tass, and United Press International. Furthermore, Radio Senegal monitors foreign broadcasts and some of these are communicated to the Foreign Ministry.

Considerable progress appears to have been made in the Foreign Ministry in the past few years in the preparation of background materials for the consideration of upper echelons in the decision-making process.[14] Weekly situation reports are pre-

14. I. William Zartman reported earlier that the Senegalese Foreign Ministry wrote only one background paper on the entire subject of the breakup of the Mali Federation. See his *International Relations in the New Africa* (Englewood Cliffs, N.J.: Prentice-Hall, 1966), p. 61.

pared in the Office of Political Affairs for presentation to the minister. Each of these generally covers three major topics, emphasizes African developments, and is twelve to fifteen pages in length. Among the topics covered in July and August, 1967, for example, were the "little summit" meeting of five African states in Cairo, the situation in Nigeria, the Middle East crisis, the situation in Aden, a meeting of the European Economic Community in Rome, and an important debate in the French National Assembly. Normally, the director of the Office of Political Affairs appears to have sole discretion for selecting topics for these situation reports. Frequently, however, his superiors specify subjects to be covered. These reports serve as the basis for the foreign minister's reports to the cabinet, and portions are usually incorporated in the official announcement of cabinet decisions read to the press by the information minister. This process tends to shield the Foreign Ministry—as well as the president of the Republic—from possible untoward repercussions of decisions since these are attributed to the cabinet collectively; the Foreign Ministry has no official spokesman.

In addition to using regular diplomatic channels, the president of the Republic makes use of personal emissaries to foreign statesmen. A few examples will illustrate. Lamine Guèye, late president of the National Assembly and personal friend of Senghor in spite of past political differences, visited Lagos in January, 1963, ostensibly to extend an invitation to Prime Minister Abubakar Tafawa Balewa for an official visit to Senegal. Mahdi Cissoko, former minister of transport and urbanism as well as assistant political secretary on the party's national executive, was dispatched to Mali and Niger shortly after the Arab-Israeli War in June, 1967, with a personal message from President Senghor. Joseph M'Bengue, political secretary of the national executive of the UPS as well as former justice minister, visited with King Hassan II in Casablanca in mid-1967 to discuss the general Middle East situation.

The general coordination process described above, following the clarification of respective areas of responsibility in 1965, appears to work well and to keep friction to a minimum. Officials in the Foreign Ministry seem to be aware of the need to lean heavily on the expertise of colleagues in other ministries and to have adjusted to it. As one of them explained, the Foreign Ministry has no interest in "inviting opposition" on the part of colleagues who are better qualified than are foreign affairs personnel.[15] The Senegalese justice minister, in fact, has acquired a reputation as a sensitive and successful troubleshooter. His patience, outward calm, and sense of responsibility greatly facilitated the rapprochement between his country and the Mali Republic in 1963, and he seems to have emerged as one of his country's star negotiators.

Budgetary analysis

An examination of budget appropriations for the Foreign Ministry, although imprecise because the figures do not reflect actual expenditures, nonetheless yields information on internal financial trends and priorities. As may be expected in the case of a new government agency, budget appropriations for the Foreign Ministry increased absolutely, from 796,519,000 CFA (Communauté Financière Africaine) francs for fiscal year 1961/62 to 869,377,-000 CFA francs for fiscal year 1967/68. But these sums represent a fairly stable percentage of the total national budget—1.88 per cent for fiscal year 1961/62, 2.27 per cent for fiscal year 1965/66, and again 1.88 per cent for fiscal year 1967/68. Expenses for matériel within the Foreign Ministry have declined in comparison with personnel expenses, starting with a 5:3 ratio, continuing with a steady decline, and reaching a 1:1 ratio in the 1967/68 fiscal year.[16]

The distribution of available funds within the central administrative services of the ministry reflects a hierarchy of priorities that varied only slightly over the years. During fiscal year 1961/62, the allocation of funds ranked the internal services according to the following order of descending importance: the cabinet; the protocol service; the Office of Political, Cultural, and Social Affairs; the Office of Administrative Affairs and Chancelleries; the Secretariat-General; and the Office of Interna-

15. Omar Vélé, secretary-general of the Foreign Ministry, in an interview, June 28, 1967.
16. Senegal, *Budget général* (Rufisque: Imprimerie Nationale).

tional Economic and Technical Cooperation. According to this index, the cabinet is clearly at the center of the ministry's decision-making process, whereas the Secretariat-General is expected to perform routine administrative duties. During the 1967/68 fiscal year, the comparative ranking was as follows: the cabinet maintained its supremacy, followed by the Office of Political, Cultural, and Social Affairs; the protocol service; the Office of Administrative Affairs and Chancelleries; the Office of International Economic and Technical Cooperation; and the Secretariat-General. The relatively low ranking of the Office of International Economic and Technical Cooperation no doubt reflects the fact that the administration of technical assistance is located not in the Foreign Ministry but in the office of the president of the Republic.

The financial trend for Senegal's diplomatic missions abroad has been toward an increase in funds. Both in absolute terms as well as in relation to the total funds placed at the disposal of the Foreign Ministry, appropriations for missions increased, from 272,040,000 CFA francs in fiscal year 1961/62 to 420,915,000 CFA francs in fiscal year 1967/68. Since the appropriations for missions were slightly higher during fiscal years 1964/65 and 1965/66, the figure for fiscal year 1967/68 may indicate an optimum amount which is apt to remain fairly constant in subsequent years.

Among the four geographic areas where Senegal maintains diplomatic missions, Europe ranks first, followed by Africa, the Americas, and the Middle East; the corresponding percentages of funds allocated in fiscal year 1967/68 were 49.2 per cent, 33.3 per cent, 18.9 per cent, and 4.9 per cent. It should be noted that Africa was the only beneficiary of a relative increase in funds appropriated (from 27.1 per cent in fiscal year 1961/62), whereas the relative share of the other three areas has declined over the period discussed.

Among Senegal's missions abroad during the period under consideration, twelve have been given slightly over two-thirds of the total mission funds. Between 1960 and 1969, these have included (in different years) France, the United States, the United Nations, the Soviet Union, Great Britain, West Germany, Belgium, Italy, Switzerland, Saudi Arabia, Yugoslavia, The Gambia,

Egypt, the Vatican, Tunisia, Morocco, the Kinshasa-Congo, Ghana, Lebanon, and Brazil. A number of comments may be made on trends involving the retention or change of certain countries among the twelve over the years. First, some countries have enjoyed a consistent priority, with France, the United States, and the United Nations at the top of the list. (In view of the close interconnection between the missions to the United States and the United Nations, they were considered as one until 1966, and as two separate missions thereafter.) The mission to Great Britain ranked fourth during the entire period. The Soviet Union has ranked fifth ever since a Senegalese embassy was opened in Moscow.

These priorities can be correlated with some elements of Senegal's foreign policy. The priority of France needs no comment here; that of the United States, the United Nations, and the Soviet Union reflects the importance of the two superpowers and of the United Nations for a new, developing country like Senegal. The ranking of Great Britain was initially the result of the location there of the headquarters of the Commonwealth, through which were channeled relations with English-speaking African dependencies; it has been maintained in part because of the hopes—unrealized so far—for increased Senegalo-British trade.

The importance to Senegal of her relations with the European Economic Community is reflected by the inclusion of most EEC countries most of the time. Belgium, host country of the EEC headquarters, was always included, and it has remained in sixth place since 1965. The ranking of a number of other countries has declined. Thus, Yugoslavia was seventh among the first twelve in 1961, tenth in 1964, and no longer on the list afterward; the Vatican appears on the list only the first year; Brazil was eighth in 1963 and eleventh in 1967; Saudi Arabia was fifth in 1961, seventh in 1963, and no longer among the twelve thereafter. These shifts may be attributed to these countries' replacement by others in Senegal's foreign priorities, or to the decreasing cost of embassies once initial fixed costs have been met. Senegalese representation in African countries has become more important over the years. In 1961, Egypt and The Gambia were among the twelve, whereas in 1967 that list also included Morocco and the Kinshasa-Congo.

One final aspect of the Foreign Ministry's finances is Senegal's contribution to international organizations. In fiscal year 1967/ 68, there were at least forty-five such organizations receiving a total of 140.5 million CFA francs from Senegal, an amount comparing favorably with the initial appropriation of a little over 63 million CFA francs for fiscal year 1962/63. (Fifty CFA francs equal 1 French Franc; one million CFA francs equals U.S. $4,000.) It should be noted that more than half (55 per cent) of these contributions go to African organizations. Three of these—the Organization of African Unity, that body's Liberation Committee, and the Organisation Commune Africaine et Malgache—each received more (the first, 22 million, the others 15 million CFA francs each) than any other single international organization during the 1966/67 fiscal year. The United Nations and its various agencies were allocated 32 per cent, and other, general organizations the remainder during that same year.

Diplomatic missions abroad

The number of Senegalese diplomatic missions abroad numbered ten in 1960, shortly after independence; increased to twenty-one in 1967; and further increased to twenty-three in 1969, as follows: in Africa—Algeria, The Gambia, Ghana, Guinea (closed in July, 1967, but subsequently reopened), Egypt, Ethiopia, the Kinshasa-Congo, Nigeria, Mali, Morocco, and Tunisia; in Europe—Belgium, France, Great Britain, Italy, the Soviet Union, the Vatican, and West Germany; in the Middle East—Lebanon and Saudi Arabia; and in the Americas —Brazil, the United Nations, and the United States.

The geographic distribution of Senegalese missions shifted emphasis toward greater interest in inter-African affairs, so that by 1966 there were more missions in Africa than in any other geographical region. In 1960, shortly after independence, there were five in Europe (Belgium, France, Great Britain, the Vatican, and West Germany), four in Africa (Egypt, The Gambia, Morocco, and Tunisia), and one in the United States. Five missions were closed: those in Portuguese Guinea (1964), Switzerland (1964), Yugoslavia (1964), Liberia (1965), and Guinea (1967), although, as was noted, the latter was subsequently reopened. In 1969, missions in Africa broke down into the following geographical regions: five in West Africa, four in North Africa, one in Central Africa, and one in East Africa (the Senegalese government was contemplating opening another embassy in Tanzania). Missions in Africa, past and present, may be broken down as follows by linguistic zones: seven in French-speaking areas (including the Kinshasa-Congo, Morocco, and Tunisia), five in English-speaking areas, one where the language is Arabic (Egypt), and one in Portuguese Guinea.

A variety of criteria has been used to justify the opening, and closing, of Senegalese diplomatic missions resident in foreign countries. Many of these criteria are imprecise; most overlap in the sense that two or more reasons were invoked to open or close missions; some cannot be measured accurately, as when economic desiderata do not correspond with trade or aid statistics. Nonetheless, three sets of criteria may be distinguished for analytical purposes: economic, religious, and political.

The first set is expressed in the importance of either actual or hoped-for economic benefits. Countries in this category include, in Europe, the members of the European Economic Community, Great Britain, and the Soviet Union; and, in the Americas, the United Nations, the United States, and Brazil (because opening the Senegalese embassy in Brasilia in February, 1963, was preceded by the visit of an important Brazilian trade delegation in Dakar, which raised high hopes for mutually beneficial economic intercourse). African countries in this category include the Mali Republic, which values access to the port facilities at Dakar; Morocco, Tunisia, and Algeria, which belong to the franc zone and produce many goods useful to Senegal; Liberia and Nigeria, because of Senegalese hopes for close trade relations and for cooperation with Nigeria as an important peanut producer; and The Gambia, whose economy ought to be better integrated with that of surrounding Senegal.

Second, religious criteria played an important role in the decisions to send missions to Morocco, Saudi Arabia, and the Vatican. Large numbers of Moroccans reside in Senegal; part of the

Senegalese Muslim community belongs to the Tijaniyya brotherhood, which maintains historic ties with Morocco; and many
Senegalese make the annual religious pilgrimage to the Moroccan city of Fez. The same general justification was used for
Saudi Arabia, which includes the holy city of Mecca, the greatest Muslim shrine, which inspires thousands of Senegalese an-
nually to undertake the long and costly voyage and to return
with the coveted title of "el hadj." The Senegalese embassy in
the Vatican is justified by the existence of a small but influential
Roman Catholic minority in Senegal, and on the grounds that
the mission in the Vatican serves to counterbalance the one at
Jedda as well as to look after the interests of Senegalese pil-
grims to the Holy See. No doubt the personal preference of
President Senghor, who has cultivated a strong philosophic attachment to various aspects of Roman Catholic thought, is also
a factor. The pope's repeated forthright statements regarding
the plight of developing nations may be another reason.

A third set of criteria has been political; this includes considerations of nonalignment, the prominence of some countries
in international affairs, the nature of personal relations among
top political leaders, the extension of Senegal's influence abroad,
the attraction of foreign nations' political and social experiments
for possible emulation, suspicions that other states seek a preponderance of influence in a territory contiguous to Senegal, the
usefulness of listening posts, and prestige. Countries in this
category include nearly all those in which Senegal has established diplomatic posts. The great powers, from the vantage
point of Dakar, include France; Great Britain; the Soviet Union;
Switzerland (in the past), as the seat of numerous international
organizations; and the United States, both as a country and as
the seat of the United Nations.

Yugoslavia was important, shortly after independence, because Titoist neutralism and efforts to solve economic and social
problems in a novel fashion promised to have some relevance to
similar Senegalese problems. Former Prime Minister Mamadou
Dia was equally interested in the Scandinavian version of socialism, but that interest did not lead to the establishment of a
Senegalese embassy at least in part because none of the Scandinavian countries was a leader among the nonaligned, whereas

Yugoslavia had the added attraction of serving as an open door to East Europe and the Soviet Union.

African countries fall into various subcategories of political criteria. Ghana, Guinea, Nigeria, the UAR, and Ethiopia were among the most influential on that continent because of the nature of their activities, their potential influence due to size, or their emergence as foci of inter-African dialogue. Senegal's special interest in close and harmonious relations with The Gambia was underlined by sending to Bathurst, in December, 1960, not just an ordinary ambassador, but a special high commissioner.

The Senegalese diplomatic missions in Morocco and Tunisia, particularly the latter, reflect close personal, temperamental affinities among Presidents Senghor and Habib Bourguiba and King Hassan II. Guinea, as a neighboring country, is important, not only because of the inter-African political leadership President Touré has sought to exert, but also because of the history of close ties between the two countries within the framework of the former Federation of French West Africa. Senegal's embassy was closed in July, 1967, ostensibly for reasons of economy, but actually because the maintenance of political relations between these two states had become problematic, to say the least, following a prolonged period of Guinean abuse directed at Senegal. Toward the end of 1967, however, the flow of abuse was stilled, and the Senegalese government decided to reopen its previous embassy in Conakry, after discarding a plan to open a consulate there.

The Senegalese consulate in Bissau, in operation between 1961 and 1964, testified to Senegalese hopes of settling the outstanding colonial question of Portuguese Guinea by negotiations with Portuguese authorities, and to a desire to have a foot in the door of a contiguous territory whose nationalist forces included one element supported by the Republic of Guinea. Closing the consulate resulted from both disappointment of earlier hopes for negotiations and the continued annoyance of having Portuguese troops allegedly violating Senegalese sovereignty when pursuing African nationalists.

Another subcategory of political criteria is prestige. It should be recalled that Senegal, prior to national independence, was accustomed to close relations with other territories of French West and Equatorial Africa and to serving in delegations to international conferences. For historical reasons, the Senegalese have long considered themselves the senior members of French-speaking sub-Saharan Africa. Independence, therefore, carried with it the novelty of complete structural isolation from this tradition. It was understandable, given these circumstances, that Senegal should seek to continue this tradition after formal independence.

Moreover, an embassy abroad is a badge of sovereignty as well as an object of pride. Senegalese Foreign Ministry officials readily agree that some embassies were opened in 1960 and 1961 in haste and because of a simple desire for representation and recognition. This state of mind led Hamet Diaw, rapporteur of the National Assembly's Finance Committee, in one of the very few allusions to foreign affairs ever recorded in the legislature, to warn that "in the future we must be careful that our efforts not be dispersed by opening diplomatic posts inconsiderately." [17]

Subsequent economies were made by adopting the practice of multiple accreditation. In 1967, five Senegalese ambassadors were accredited to twelve countries and one international organization in addition to those countries in which they resided. Thus, the ambassador to France was also accredited to Spain and UNESCO; the one in Germany, to Holland and Switzerland; the one in the United States, to Canada, Mexico, Haiti, and Trinidad/Tobago; the one in Russia, to Poland; and the one in Britain, to Denmark, Norway, Sweden, and Austria (and Portugal until 1961). The trend toward multiple accreditation continued; by 1969, seven ambassadors represented Senegal in twenty-three countries in Africa, Europe, the Middle East, Asia, and the Americas.

One final criterion for establishing a mission abroad was cultural. The establishment of the Senegalese embassy in Brazil was related in part to President Senghor's visit to that country

17. Senegal, *Journal officiel de la République du Sénégal: Débats parlementaires* (February 22, 1962), p. 76.

and to his concern for the cultural affinities between black Africans and black Brazilians, an outgrowth of an aspect of negritude termed "lusitropicology." [18]

The government of Senegal cooperated with other former French African states in efforts to pool manpower and financial resources through common diplomatic representation. These efforts ended in failure, however, as a result in part of the intensity of the new states' attachment to the prerogatives of national independence, in part of divergences among the states' policies, and in part of refusal to entrust other African states with negotiations of vital questions on their behalf.

In September, 1961, the twelve-member Union Africaine et Malgache (UAM) approved the principle of common representation on the initiative of President Houphouet-Boigny of the Ivory Coast. Various organs of the UAM discussed implementation of this principle in several subsequent meetings, but general agreement was reached only on consultation and coordination of aspects of foreign policy.

At first, the UAM states concentrated on the creation of special links between the member states. Debate centered on the accreditation, to the foreign minister of each state, of a permanent representative without diplomatic rank. At the 1962 UAM conference in Libreville, the heads of state decided instead to send a permanent representative to each country, accredited to the appropriate head of state. The Senegalese government, however, was concerned about the additional costs and the unnecessary duplication involved and never sent any permanent representatives to fellow UAM states.

At later UAM meetings, the question of common external UAM representation was discussed further. An agreement subsequently reached embodied a compromise between multilateral and bilateral representation. The UAM decided on a list of twenty prospective foreign countries eligible for common rep-

18. "Lusitropicology" refers to cultural ties between Africa and Portugal, and hence Brazil. See Senegal, *Voyage officiel aux Etats-Unis du Brésil de S. Exec. M. Léopold Sédar Senghor, President de la République du Sénégal, 19 septembre–25 septembre 1964* (Dakar: Grande Imprimerie Africaine, 1964); and Ronald H. Chilcote, *Portuguese Africa* (Englewood Cliffs, N.J.: Prentice-Hall, 1967).

resentation. The list included five posts for Africa, six for Asia (the Middle East included), five for Europe, three for Central and Latin America, and one for Oceania (Australia). Prominently absent from this list were France, the United Nations, and the United States; the UAM countries evidently expected that individual diplomatic missions were more useful at these posts.

In principle, the UAM approved plans for creating three types of representation abroad: individual missions, common missions where UAM states with a post in a foreign country would look after the interests of other UAM states, and general, common UAM diplomatic missions.

In practice, only the first type was used. Common representation was never instituted; it was merely replaced by consultation and coordination efforts. Perhaps the biggest obstacle to common representation was the widely divergent foreign policy interests among the UAM states, plus the loss of influence, collective and individual, which would have resulted from a single UAM vote in the United Nations and other international organizations. The sensitivity of individual heads of state was reflected in sidetracking the UAM secretary-general from any coordination role: this was assumed by the incumbent UAM president, who was given the mandate to "harmonize" the instructions of the UAM states.

In matters of national policy, the Organisation Commune Africaine et Malgache (OCAM), the successor to the UAM, played a secondary role in that its secretary-general, Diakha Dieng, was given responsibility for arranging consultations among OCAM members through foreign ministers rather than heads of state. OCAM consultation, prior to policy decisions and votes in the Organization of African Unity or the United Nations, nonetheless took place, with occasional success. One example is the candidacy of Senegal for a seat in the United Nations Security Council; that candidacy was announced, and support solicited, through OCAM before being taken up—and approved—by the OAU.

It may be asked whether a country the size of South Dakota, with the relatively small, on the world scale, population of 3.8 million, and a per capita annual income of $170, is realistic in maintaining over a score of full-fledged diplomatic missions in foreign lands.

In some areas, such as Europe (seven embassies) and North Africa (four embassies including one in the UAR), the argument of excessive concentration is obvious. If President William Tubman of Liberia "understood" the closing of the Senegalese embassy in Monrovia, then there seems little reason to believe that President Bourguiba or King Hassan II would not likewise understand. Furthermore, if the Senegalese government were to consider closing the embassies in Algiers or Cairo or both as part of a general austerity program, it is not apparent that such a move would meet great resistance in North Africa or have untoward consequences for Senegal.

In many cases, consulates could probably be just as effective as are embassies in looking after Senegal's interests, although a "demotion" of embassies into consulates would present some delicate problems. Aside from attitudes in the host country, consulates are, by definition, a lesser breed of international communications instruments than are embassies. Perhaps the most important problem that the change to consulates would cause concerns recruitment; a consular post is infinitely less attractive to a prospective incumbent than is first-class diplomatic citizenship. This consideration applies not only to present ambassadors, who would resent their downgrading, but also to younger people considering a foreign service career and consequently may harm recruitment policy and the quality of personnel.

Some Foreign Ministry officials favor thinning out overconcentration and opening new embassies elsewhere, because some areas in the world are not covered at all. This raises the question of how important it is for Senegal to be in possession of intimate knowledge about domestic political and economic developments in far-off places. At the end of 1967, Dakar was host to fourteen African, nine American, six Asian, and four Middle Eastern countries as well as eight international organizations, all of which were represented by thirty-seven ambassadors, one apostolic nuncio, one high commissioner, three consuls-general, and eight honorary consuls. At the beginning of 1969, foreign diplomatic representation had increased to a total of forty-two resident ambassadors, while eight countries covered Senegal with ambassadors resident elsewhere, thus giving Senegal direct access to fifty foreign countries. From the point of view of effective contacts with the world, it cannot be said that Senegal is confined to diplomatic isolation. Thus there is no immediately apparent reason why Senegal should attempt to "cover the world" by sending out resident ambassadors.

A number of ways can be suggested to realize economies. Placing Senegal on the map is, by itself, a questionable justification for the expense of an embassy, which should yield some tangible results. Much greater use could be made of foreign missions resident in Senegal, and no doubt a number of Senegalese embassies could be dispensed with on that basis. Greater emphasis could be placed on special envoys. A small number of outstanding troubleshooters in the Foreign Ministry would involve less cost, and yield greater returns, than do resident embassies because of the increment of prestige attached to personal representatives flying into a foreign capital on an ad hoc special mission. Also, a minimum amount of actual and potential trade and aid could be used, in many cases, as the major criterion for the existence of a diplomatic mission. Any such calculation would be arbitrary, but not more so than are present considerations of prestige, culture, religion, or politics. Reducing the number of foreign posts would have the additional advantage of making more funds available to those which remain and render them more productive in "selling" Senegal, in strengthening existing ties through greater penetration of propaganda as well as through the discovery, solidification, and enlargement of economic interests.

Considerations of prestige are, of course, always present in diplomatic representation. In many countries, relatively marginal interests can be represented either by a consulate or by a third country. Another aspect of prestige is that the host country may insist, as Ghana did under President Kwame Nkrumah, that nothing less than a full-fledged embassy would reflect that country's estimate of its own importance; the determining factor was the prestige of Ghana, not that of Senegal. The French government, similarly, was reportedly furious when the Senegalese government sent to Paris a brilliant young career ambassador—the French objected that the ambassador's prestige was not in keeping with the grandeur of France, and he was replaced by a more eminent Senegalese personality.

When all this is said, the impression remains that Senegal has far too many embassies abroad. It is not apparent that the welfare of the country or its foreign interests would be substantially affected by a drastic reduction in the total number of diplomatic missions.

One way to approach this question is to ask what functions can be expected of Senegalese embassies. Two important roles to be served by ambassadors stand out: first, the development of actual and potential tangible economic benefits; second, the task of "selling" Senegal in countries where the prospects of getting concrete returns are good. Literature extolling the beauties of Senegalese culture, foreign appearances by Senegalese artists, exhibitions of Senegalese products, and invitations to influential foreigners could, if well planned, coordinated, and executed, promote interest as well as solidify old and create new economic ties. In the past, available funds were spread so thin that neither of these functions could be performed with any great hope of tangible results. If Senegal were to reduce the number of its diplomatic missions by, say, half, then correspondingly larger sums could be placed at the disposal of the remaining dozen or so embassies, with vastly increased chances for greater effectiveness. Ten or twelve embassies, located in strategic countries and staffed with dedicated specialists, could do more for Senegal than two or three times that number subsisting on relatively meager funds. In this sense, Senegal's diplomatic efforts are too dispersed for effective salesmanship. African embassies tend to be decorative badges of sovereignty whose creative and concrete functions are hard to discern. Some hardheaded thinking by Senegalese party and legislative leaders, who are sometimes puzzled by the diplomatic panoply they are asked to support, could provide a nudge in the direction of a more rational use of diplomatic missions in foreign lands.

There are, of course, important psychological aspects of the diplomatic establishment, particularly in new countries sensitive to—and jealous about—formal and external signs of sovereignty. It is likely, however, that most Senegalese know very little about most of the countries to which their government has accredited diplomatic representatives. To the extent, therefore, that ambassies are badges of independence and objects of national pride, they are so more for the elite than for the general population. Hence, the psychological importance of having two dozen diplomatic missions, complete with official gardeners and janitors, affects only a small number of Senegalese. Moreover, this psychological benefit is a function less of numbers and usefulness than of mere existence. It is difficult to envisage important segments of the Senegalese people and elite arising to overthrow a government intent on reducing drastically the number of diplomatic posts it maintains abroad. It is easy, by contrast, to imagine that such a move would win widespread support as an example of desirable austerity. A serious retrenchment may, in fact, tend to enhance Senegal's prestige abroad in addition to eliciting domestic approval.

It should not be difficult to select those countries in which resident diplomats could be used most effectively in furthering Senegal's moral and material interests. These would include, in Europe, France, Belgium, the Soviet Union, and perhaps Great Britain. In view of the relatively frequent personal contacts among African heads of state and government, it would be economically practical to maintain diplomatic missions in those regions offering the greatest usefulness. One embassy in North Africa, another covering English-speaking countries in West Africa, and perhaps one each in Central and East Africa would suffice. It is not apparent that Senegalese ambassadors resident in Guinea, Mali, and Mauritania have materially contributed to reinforcing mutual ties; they came usually during or after periods when tolerable relations were established. The existing machinery of the Organisation des Etats Riverains du Fleuve Sénégal could be used just as effectively as resident diplomats. The seven Senegalese embassies in Europe could thus be reduced to four, and the dozen in Africa to five if the special high commission in The Gambia is maintained. The fact that Senegal makes greater use of multiple accreditation than do foreign countries in Senegal does not invalidate the soundness of arguments for retrenchment. African leaders' own estimate of the prestige of their countries, evident in demands for a full-fledged

Senegalese embassy, need not be an operating criterion for Senegal. If it were presented as an austerity move, closing a diplomatic mission (or declining to open a new one) in an African country could serve as an example for other African states and lead them to ask like questions about the value of an embassy abroad.

Ambassadorial profile

A variety of biographical information about past Senegalese ambassadors is useful in shedding some light on important aspects and trends in recruitment policy, and in speculating about possible attitudes of ambassadors that pertain to the performance of their diplomatic duties. The available information is broken down into six overlapping, general categories: (1) average age, (2) religious and ethnic affiliation, (3) previous government service, (4) diplomatic experience prior to appointment, (5) professional background, and (6) academic training.[19]

The first category is age at appointment or reappointment. The average age of newly appointed ambassadors has tended to increase until 1965, then to decrease with the appointment of three ambassadors in 1966 whose average age was forty. The average age of previously appointed ambassadors was forty-one in 1960, forty-seven in 1961, forty-eight in 1962, forty-three in 1963, forty-seven in 1964, and fifty in 1965. The average age of incumbent ambassadors transferred to other locations has declined, but only slightly: it was fifty-four in 1962, fifty-one in 1963, forty-six in 1964, but returned to fifty-two for the eight ambassadors transferred to other posts in 1965. Average retirement age for Senegal's ambassadors has increased from forty-five in 1962 to sixty-four in 1966 (for the intervening years, average retirement ages were fifty-one in 1963, forty-nine in 1964, and forty-one in 1965). The apparent trend toward appointment of younger people is evident also in a comparison of the range of ages at appointment: in 1960, ambassadors' ages varied from

19. Biographical information was accumulated from official and private sources; the data remain in the author's personal files

thirty-nine to fifty-four, whereas in 1966 the three newly appointed diplomats were twenty-eight, forty-three, and forty-eight
years old.

Moreover, the younger ambassadors tend to be posted in
Africa and Europe and the older ones in the Middle East and
the Americas. Since both categories include traditional and modern societies, there seems to be no correlation between the age
of ambassadors and the presumed emphasis on ascription or
achievement in the host countries. It may be that African posts
can be staffed with younger people in view of the frequent and
close contacts among government leaders, so that "technicians"
are appointed to implement policies decided at higher levels.

It does not appear that either religious or ethnic affiliation
per se is a significant variable in the Foreign Ministry's appointment policy for ambassadors. Of a total of forty-one ambassadors
appointed between 1960 and 1966, twenty-five were Wolof, six
were métis, four were Toucouleur, two each were Serer and
Diola, and one each were Bambara and Lébou. Wolof and
métis have historically enjoyed the greatest educational opportunities in Senegal, and it is therefore not surprising to find
thirty-one members of these two groups among the forty-one
ambassadors discussed above. It is nonetheless of interest to
point out that new appointees included seven Wolof, three
métis, and one Diola in 1960, but one Wolof, one métis, and
one Toucouleur in 1966.[20]

Some ambassadors are appointed as a result of special circumstances. Thus, one of the métis was appointed because the host
government wanted a career diplomat replaced by a more prominent Senegalese personality. Also, one Toucouleur was named to
an African post partly because of his friendship with the host
country's head of state. But this writer has found no evidence
that internal Senegalese ethnic considerations, as such, are operative in deciding appointments.

Very much the same can be said of religious criteria: they
reflect availability of candidates rather than Senegalese govern-

20. In this context, métis refers to the issue from a black African and
white European marriage.

ment policy. Of the forty-one ambassadors appointed between 1960 and 1966, thirty were Muslim and eleven were Roman Catholic. During that same period, nineteen Muslims and four Roman Catholics were transferred, and twelve Muslims and seven Roman Catholics retired. The relatively large number of Roman Catholics must be attributed to their preeminence among Senegal's elites. In some cases, considerations external to Senegal dictate the religion of an ambassador; it would be awkward at best to send a Muslim to the Vatican or a Roman Catholic to Jedda.

Evidence regarding the third category, previous government service, lends itself to a twofold distinction. The first is geographic and includes three types of service: in French, federal (AOF), and Senegalese organizations. The second is functional and separates executive from legislative experience. The information providing the background for this discussion is variegated and may be summarized as follows. Service in the French government occurred prior to independence; legislative experience includes membership or the holding of an office in either house of the French legislature, the Council of the French Union, the French Economic and Social Council, or the Senate of the Community; executive service includes high administrative posts, ministerial portfolios, and service in the armed forces. In the former AOF, there were members and officers of the Federal Council (*Grand Conseil*), legislative or executive officers in the Mali Federation, and other executive officers in the federation within and outside Senegal. Two ambassadors are former presidents of the Federal Council for French West Africa. Finally, national service in Senegal includes membership in legislatures (either before or after independence), and offices in these bodies; in the national executive, in addition to four cabinet posts, there are ministerial cabinet directorships, headships of government departments, and regional governorships and assistant governorships. Posts in local government include those of mayors and assistant mayors, *cercle* chiefs, and municipal councillors.

Since most ambassadors had served in more than one government post prior to their diplomatic appointment, it is more useful to consider instances of experience than to count heads for the purposes of this discussion. Senegalese ambassadors appointed between 1960 and 1966 had previously served in a total of seventy government posts. As might be expected after independence, Senegalese experience has tended to displace experience in French and AOF bodies. This is apparent from a comparison of the experience of ambassadors in the Foreign Ministry's formative years (1960–62) and the subsequent period (1963–66). During the first period, Senegalese experience accounted for 55 per cent of the total, and French experience for 27 per cent; in the second period, by contrast, Senegalese experience rose to 77 per cent and French experience fell to 19 per cent. The amount of previous government experience among ambassadorial appointees thus merely reflects the fact that there were many candidates available with such experience.

Another trend is the increasing importance of executive experience in Senegal as a springboard to ambassadorial appointment. In 1960, those appointed included nine instances of executive, but nineteen instances of legislative experience. During the formative period, 1960–62, there were thirteen instances of executive and thirty-one instances of legislative experience. This direction was reversed in the period 1963–66, for there were twenty-two instances of executive and only four instances of legislative experience. The initially large number of people with legislative experience was the result of two factors. One is that many politically prominent Senegalese served in French and Senegalese legislative bodies. The other is the government's decision, during the early appointment years, to tap the Senegalese legislature. It was thought at the time that legislators, since they are part of the official government machinery and belong to the dominant political party, would be ideal candidates to represent their country abroad. After a few years, however, it was discovered that the legislators were unhappy at the distance between them and their constituents, and that they tended to be caught between loyalty toward the nation which they represented and defended abroad, and loyalty toward their role as critics of the administration. For these reasons the government no longer appointed Senegalese legislators as ambassadors after 1962.

The fourth category of biographical data, diplomatic experience prior to appointment as ambassador, shows that twenty-two out of forty-one envoys appointed between 1960 and 1966 had had such experience. Breaking down the general category of diplomatic experience into four subcategories discloses a general trend in the direction of service in the Foreign Ministry in appointment policy. The first subcategory, that of service in the ministry, clearly ranks first with twenty-three instances of such service; it includes service in that government department, either abroad as attaché or embassy counselor, or in Senegal as division head or chief of the protocol service of the Foreign Ministry. The second subcategory, that of "missions," includes fourteen instances and refers to miscellaneous diplomatic missions performed as part of government negotiating teams, to service in consular posts, and in one case to a former ambassadorial post for another African country. The third subcategory, of which there were four examples, indicates a post of member or head of a Senegalese mission to the United Nations General Assembly or to its specialized agencies. Finally, the fourth subcategory, "training," trails the others with three instances, and denotes on-the-job diplomatic training either in the French Foreign Ministry or in a French diplomatic post.

This discussion suggests that actual experience in the Foreign Ministry may have been the most important criterion for appointing Senegal's ambassadors. This impression is reinforced in a comparison of the early period (1960–62) with the later years of foreign service appointments. In the first period, the criterion of "missions" abroad was first with eight posts, followed by Foreign Ministry and United Nations samples with four each. This composition was reversed during the second period, when Foreign Ministry posts numbered nineteen out of a total of twenty-six appointments.

The fifth category, professional background, indicates that there were more civil service (twenty-eight) than private professional posts (twenty-one) in the background of the ambassadorial appointees selected from 1960 to 1966. Law clearly predominates in occupational samples, with fourteen of the total, both in and out of government; the next most important subcategories of professional background are education (seven), medicine and administration (six each), and business and diplomacy (four each). These were followed by trade union leaders and religious chiefs and scholars (three each), and one military officer and one professional writer. The overall trend is toward more civil servants and fewer private citizens; the ratio of civil service posts to professions changed from 12:15 during the first period (1960–62) to 16:6 in the second period. This may indicate that, during the first period, there were not yet enough men with appropriate experience in government available for ambassadorial posts.

Finally, the sixth—and possibly the least important—category is that of college and graduate degrees of past and present ambassadors. Of a total number of thirty degrees earned, the vast majority (twenty-six) were undergraduate, and only five were granted in Senegal, the remainder having been earned in France and in such other countries as Tunisia. The fact that most degrees were earned outside Senegal is not surprising, given the late start of the University of Dakar, which was transformed from an institute of higher studies in 1950 to a full-fledged university in 1957. Six ambassadors are graduates of the William Ponty School in Senegal, and one is president of the William Ponty Graduate Association. The few graduates of the diplomatic section of the University's Ecole Nationale d'Administration do not yet have the experience to aspire to become ambassadors. An incipient trend toward more ambassadors with Senegalese degrees is nonetheless apparent in that the ratio of those with Senegalese degrees to those with foreign degrees was 1:11 between 1960 and 1962 and increased to 4:10 during the following four years.

On the basis of these characteristics and trends, a composite profile of a "typical" Senegalese ambassador appointed in the late 1960s is likely to have the following attributes. He would be in his thirties; there would be a 76 per cent or greater chance of his being Muslim, a 60 per cent or greater chance of his being Wolof, a 77 per cent chance of his having served in Senegal's civil service, a 93 per cent chance of his having had prior diplomatic experience—most likely in the Foreign Ministry—and more than a 50 per cent chance of his having at least an undergraduate degree, quite possibly acquired in Senegal.

But countries like Senegal are a long way from appointing such "typical" ambassadors with great frequency. Perhaps the single major obstacle is domestic political instability, and the consequent awarding of top diplomatic posts to prominent political leaders retired from government positions. In this connection, it is instructive to compare the list of Senegal's ambassadors in 1967 with that of early 1969.[21] The comparison yields several significant points. First, only eleven of the twenty-three ambassadors on duty in 1969 had been ambassadors since 1967, a turnover of about 50 per cent in a two-year period. Of these eleven, five served in the same posts (in France, the Kinshasa-Congo, The Gambia, Brazil, and Saudi Arabia), whereas six had been transferred to other countries (to Ethiopia, Mali, Tunisia, Belgium, the United States, and the Soviet Union). It is difficult, however, to extract causal relationships from the above information. It is likely that the satisfaction of the host country with the resident Senegalese ambassador (in France, the Kinshasa-Congo, and The Gambia) and, at least in Brazil, the remoteness of the ambassador from much Senegalese domestic politics, help to explain why five retained their posts. It may be of interest to note also that these five ambassadors shared a total of forty years of diplomatic experience, thus averaging eight years of experience each by early 1969. Very much the same is true of all eleven diplomats still in ambassadorial posts; their total diplomatic experience amounted to ninety years, with an average of slightly over eight years each.

Second, an attempt to explain in detail the meaning of the appointment of twelve new Senegalese ambassadors in 1969 is a risky undertaking because of lack of appropriate data at this time. At least half of these, however, had previous diplomatic experience. The new ambassador to West Germany is one of the most prominent political leaders of French-speaking black Africa and a member of Senegal's social elite. He has held several previous diplomatic posts, including the ambassadorship to France, and was the first executive director of the United

21. For the list of Senegalese ambassadors in office in the spring of 1969, consult *Europe France-Outremer*, CDLXXIII (June, 1969), 215–18.

Nations Institute for Training and Research. No doubt he owes his new post to his experience and prominence and the wide circle of friends and acquaintances cultivated over several decades, and to some extent because it may have been harmful to Senegal's international prestige had he not been given an important ambassadorial post upon termination of his assignment with the United Nations.

Another of the new ambassadors is fairly typical in the sense suggested earlier. He is a young career diplomat with a Senegalese university degree, who served as embassy counselor abroad and in Senegal as protocol chief of the Foreign Ministry. He had previously been appointed ambassador to Liberia. Socially prominent in Senegal and in The Gambia, he was apparently a protégé of Senghor and served for several years as technical adviser to the president of the Republic following a personal disagreement with the foreign minister.

The twelve 1969 appointees include another young, ambitious, socially prominent career diplomat; the *directeur de cabinet* of former Foreign Minister Thiam; the former secretary-general of a French-speaking African international organization; a distinguished lawyer; two cabinet ministers; and a sociologist who served as special assistant to the president of the Republic responsible for relations with the legislature.

An attempt to extract some possible general attitudes from the preceding biographical information must take into account at least three different categories of ambassadors. The first includes socially prominent Senegalese who tend to be people of the highest caliber, accustomed to making national decisions as a result of long, intimate, and relatively active contact with politics in Senegal. They are also at home in France, where they have served in government positions and cultivated extensive personal ties of long standing that can be used for the benefit of Senegal. At the same time, however, their friends are likely to include a number of former French colonial officials, and the alacrity with which they tend to press for change desired by Senegal may be a function of their interpretation of the legitimacy of the Senegalese government's policy orientation.

The second category includes ambassadors recruited out of

necessity. They are likely to be civil servants or businessmen and, as such, relatively conservative in the sense that they are unlikely to take major initiatives since they do not belong to the ruling elite in Senegal.

The third, and potentially the most important, category of ambassadors comprises the younger career diplomats. Their education is more specifically oriented toward international relations, although overlaid with the legalism of the French tradition. When interpreting the Senegalese national interest, they are less likely than those in the other categories to be influenced by the colonial past. In this sense, they are likely to be more "objective" than others; at the same time, they tend to be somewhat more impressed by their diplomatic status. Moreover, to the extent that they were educated in Africa and were spared much of the painful acculturation to a foreign, European country, they may have assimilated fewer affective aspects of Western culture. Finally, they have a sharper African focus and find it congenial to be among Africans and to question the present organization of the international community, hence to initiate change viewed as beneficial to their country.

A number of conclusions emerge from the above information. First, both the structure and operation of the Foreign Ministry are highly centralized and lend themselves to the working hypothesis that policy is made essentially by the president of the Republic. Second, the ministry has become a more effective instrument for carrying out foreign policy than it was in the immediate postindependence years. Improvements in policy coordination with other government departments, in the delineation of foreign affairs authority, and in the effectiveness of the central services point in that direction. Third, structural aspects of foreign policy indicate the growing importance of inter-African relations other than those with OCAM states. Fourth, the ministry's personnel policy is handicapped by the early reliance on nonspecialists and by difficulties in attracting many younger career people into the internal services. Fifth, the prestige of Senegal ranks relatively high as a criterion for sending resident missions abroad, although this may be decreasing. And, finally, there is a noticeable trend—other things being equal—toward the use of younger top diplomats whose outlook is apt to be more Senegalese and African than that of older colleagues and who are armed with greater expertise in international affairs.

CHAPTER THREE

Economic Protectionism
and Diversification

THE PROTECTIVE FRAMEWORK

Senegal has inherited an economic protective framework from
the colonial period which conditions much of her postindependence economic foreign policy. This framework consists of
(1) monetary arrangements with the former colonial power,
(2) trade arrangements with France and, to a lesser extent, with
France's partners in the European Economic Community, and
(3) French ownership and control of much of the modern business sector of Senegal.

Before examining in some detail the major characteristics and
trends of Senegal's economic foreign relations, it is useful to
cast a more general glance at some fundamental aspects of her
economic needs and environment as well as of her postindependence attitudes and policies. Senegal perceives the environment of economic foreign relations as having two dimensions:
a vertical dimension which encompasses extra-African relations,

100

and a horizontal dimension concerned with inter-African relations.

The vertical dimension includes Senegal's relation with France and with the European Economic Community as well as other non-African areas. To the extent that Senegalo-French economic relations result from structures erected during the colonial period, such as the franc zone, the two dimensions overlap. The Senegalese attitude toward the continuation or severance of these historical ties is based on stark, economic necessity. It is grounded in the proposition that what Senegal needs is actual development and not empty slogans. Inasmuch as Senegal is dependent on the vertical ties for the bulk of her trade and aid, there is no viable alternative but to maintain them. Senegal is independent politically, and the continuation of these ties is a voluntary act in the sense that Senegal has the right to abrogate them or change them drastically. To the extent that the justification for national independence was regarded as a response to a psychological need, then the possibility of choosing to discontinue or to continue the relationship answers much of that need. The formal choice is now Senegal's, not France's.

The European Economic Community plays an important role within the vertical dimension of Senegal's economic foreign policy. From the point of view of France's EEC partners, that organization serves as a device to secure new markets for capital goods and manufactures and to invest private capital, hence to enter areas of Africa previously foreclosed by French control. Part of the price they are willing to pay for these benefits is capital aid to the African Associated States, which is administered by the EEC's European Development Fund (EDF). The Associated States, in turn, derive four major advantages from their association: (1) an opportunity to create and maintain or expand markets for exports; (2) help in creating processing industries through European private investments; (3) public capital transfers through the EDF; and (4) the services of technical assistance personnel in connection with preinvestment studies and actual investments.

Monetary arrangements

Senegal's policy has been to seek to maintain, and later to enlarge and diversify, the protective framework inherited from the colonial period. A brief discussion of the franc zone, the most salient factor in the vertical dimension of Senegal's foreign economic policy, will illustrate the usefulness of that protective device. This monetary zone, which derived its name from that of the dominant currency, the French franc, was created after World War II. Although it was modified several times subsequently, its major provisions remained largely unchanged after independence. Its financial significance to Senegal is twofold: it is essentially a mechanism for backing the currency used by Senegal with a hard currency, the French franc, and it has prevented at least the monetary balkanization of French black Africa.

As befits a sovereign state, Senegal has the right to issue her own currency. The experiences of the Republic of Mali and Guinea suggest, however, that the political benefits from a national Senegalese currency are more than offset by the untoward economic consequences which would flow from it. There were rumors, around 1964, that Senegal in fact considered creating her own currency, possibly to facilitate economic relations with Mali and Guinea, both of which had national currencies. But these rumors were subsequently denied by President Senghor. A national Senegalese currency would pose knotty problems associated with its actual—as opposed to its declared—value in international transactions. Senegal has no access to precious metals for backing such a national currency, and arrangements other than participation in the franc zone are not available. The prospects of improving economic relations with the Republics of Guinea and Mali by "aligning" Senegal's currency with theirs, attractive though they were, nonetheless could not have compensated Senegal for the losses she would have incurred by abandoning the French-backed CFA franc.

The currency which Senegal uses, the franc of the Communauté Financière Africaine (CFA), is issued by a joint West African bank, the Banque Centrale des Etats de l'Ouest Africain (BCEAO), on behalf of Senegal, Mauritania, the Ivory Coast,

Dahomey, Upper Volta, and Niger. The headquarters of the BCEAO is in Paris, but its board of directors is controlled by a two-thirds majority of Africans. The one-third minority of Frenchmen on the board serves mostly to warn and admonish the African majority.

French monetary guarantee is more psychological than real, but nonetheless effective. Through the BCEAO, Senegal has an account with the French Treasury in which she deposits all her non-CFA currencies; these may be withdrawn anytime, or exchanged for French or other foreign currencies. Should her account be depleted, Senegal may continue to withdraw Franch francs in a theoretically unlimited amount: hence the guarantee which, in order to be effective, must be unlimited at least in theory. Holders of CFA francs can always be confident of exchanging them for a hard currency should they so desire.

In practice, there are operational limits to free and unlimited convertibility of CFA francs into French francs. First, BCEAO members pay a progressive interest on overdrawn accounts: 1 per cent up to $1 million, 2 per cent from $1 million to $2 million, and 2–2.5 per cent for larger amounts. Hence, BCEAO members are expected to maintain their accounts in balance. Second, the BCEAO is expected to maintain a reserve of 20 per cent of the value of currency it has issued, failing which the French government can take drastic measures, including the revocation of the monetary guarantee.

These restrictions tend to discourage overissue of currency and to maintain the value of French, and therefore indirectly of Senegalese, currency. The CFA franc is clearly tied to the fortunes of the dominant French franc and hence is likely to suffer untoward consequences from French economic and financial problems. But a number of advantages has in the past more than offset the price—actual or potential—which Senegal has to pay. First, as indicated, the French government guarantees the CFA franc, its free convertibility into other currencies (at fixed parity), and its free transfer among BCEAO member states. Second, since France has no exchange control, this arrangement obviates costly, undesirable exchange controls on the part of Senegal. Third, it encourages monetary stability. And, finally, it permits access to foreign currencies subject only to the requirement that conversion be done centrally, in Paris. This last requirement was abolished in July, 1967, following a French decision to allow unlimited free convertibility of the French franc and, consequently, of the CFA franc. Along with the other members of the BCEAO, Senegal is now in a position, for the first time, to exchange her currency without any restriction and to establish the kinds of bureaucratic measures needed to measure foreign capital flows into and out of Senegal.

Trade arrangements

Another aspect of the franc zone as a protective framework concerns Senegal's external trade. The framework is expressed most clearly in the regulations governing the three concentric circles of customs duties for imports into Senegal.

The first circle consists of countries whose imports into Senegal are exempt from customs duties. This includes France and, theoretically, the rest of the franc zone except such former French African mandates as Togo, Cameroun, Morocco, and Tunisia. The countries of the former AOF—minus Guinea—decided to create a customs union in 1959, the Union Douanière Ouest Africaine (UDAO), to continue the mutual free trade relations which had been imposed on them by France. As a result of the economic nationalism which followed their independence, intended in part to protect nascent industries, the UDAO became an empty shell as one country after another began to impose customs duties on other UDAO member states. The same countries formed another customs union in 1966, with the intention that future trade may be freed from the post-independence burden of excessive economic nationalism.

The second circle of the protective trade framework is made up of countries which must pay "minimum" customs duties. These apply to most of the countries with which Senegal has signed a trade agreement, and thus to which she has accorded a "most favored nation" status on the basis of reciprocity. This circle includes all African countries not part of the former French Union, so that Liberia, for example, trades with Senegal on the same basis as do the United States and the Soviet Union.

Finally, the third circle is defined by a "general" customs duty, three times larger than the minimum duty. This is a remnant, unchanged, of the colonial era. It was created by France as a mechanism to protect her economic interests from the potentially harmful effects of competition with such countries as Japan and China, and it applied to all members of the former French Union. Senegal is not entirely free to transfer a given country from the general duty status since such a decision must be approved by her partners in both the UDAO and EEC who seek to protect their advantage against competitors. Senegal, however, has interpreted the minimum category flexibly to suit her needs and has reduced customs duties accordingly.

The operation of the framework described above is somewhat more flexible in practice than its description would suggest. Other things being equal, countries which produce goods at a lower initial cost than those of, say, EEC countries, can still import and compete in the Senegalese market. Thus Japan, although falling into the general duty category from the viewpoint of customs duties, sells electrical appliances in Senegal at the same price for which equivalent products imported from the EEC are sold.

A number of other factors and postindependence developments tend to affect Senegal's foreign economic relations. One concerns quantitative import restrictions. These are generally imposed in accordance with the objectives of the former colonial framework, enlarged through the increasing participation of the EEC. Such restrictions have yielded to the needs of Senegal and to the characteristics of competitiveness of foreign products. Some import quotas have been applied by the Senegalese government in cases where French imports would have tended to harm domestic manufacturing industry. Moreover, according to a number of informants in the Dakar business community, import quotas were restrictive in practice only until about 1965 and have since become sufficiently liberal so as not to constitute a barrier to imports into Senegal.

Another important development which affects Senegal's external trade relations is the liberalization of some aspects of French economic policy and of associate membership in the European Economic Community. The French government has, in the past few years, actively sought to support Africa's industrialization by seeking to convince French firms that investments in Africa do not necessarily compete with metropolitan industries dependent on franc-zone markets. At the same time, the importance to France of the franc zone is decreasing, largely as a result of the improved competitive strength of the French economy, and this development may eventually help the African states' economy by allowing a greater diversification of trade.

Without gainsaying the immediate and considerable advantages which countries like Senegal derive from the continuation of their ties with the franc zone, the colonial framework also circumscribes Senegal's freedom of choice. Manifestations of disadvantages include Senegal's deficit trade with the EEC, the fact that foreign capital assistance is a palliative to imbalanced trade relations, the reluctance of resident French businessmen to reorient trade channels, the vulnerability of the CFA franc to the vagaries of France's currency and general economic health, and the structural obstacles to the growth of trade with non-franc-zone areas, in Africa as elsewhere. Senegal, in other words, is very much a junior partner.

There is evidence to suggest that the very existence of the colonial protective framework tends to discourage African initiatives to break away from it. It provides important elements of a short-term security that lulls recipients into a false sense of confidence and prevents them from asking questions about the long-range development of economic relations and diversification. The resultant lack of initiative is evident, for instance, in the fact that much of the postindependence liberalization of the framework resulted from events and decisions originating in Europe. Recognizing these problems, a French blue-ribbon committee chided African states by pointing out:

> The first temptation of a poor country is to consider its economic development as an "accelerated overtaking" of the most advanced industrial countries. . . . The creation, by us, of ultramodern enclaves, not related to the general equilibrium of the country, would often be unfavorable to real development. And yet such enterprises are often requested for reasons where psychology and politics have more room than economic calculation.
> The second temptation consists in wanting political, ad-

ministrative, and cultural structures narrowly copied from those of France which, being [top-heavy], are not adapted [to local conditions]. Too often independence, newly conquered by young nations, appears to be used less to insure indigenous development than to perfect their assimilation to France, as though they were reproaching [France] for having proclaimed it without fully realizing it.[1]

The growing Senegalese business community

The influence of the resident French business community in Senegal, though it remains considerable, is nonetheless being weakened. Two developments help to account for this, one external to Senegal and the other domestic. The first is the declining importance of France in Senegal's foreign trade, and the increasing commercial interests of other countries belonging to the European Common Market. As an associate member of the EEC, Senegal has extended progressive reductions of import duties and quotas to these European countries, and it was expected that most goods originating in these countries would enter Senegal without a customs barrier by 1969. The Associated States may impose protective fiscal or customs duties if they do not discriminate among the European Six.

One of the major obstacles to the development of Senegalo-European (non-French) trade is not evident from the structural arrangements between the EEC and its associated partners. Private conversations with businessmen from EEC countries other than France indicate spirited resistance by Frenchmen to what they consider foreign business activities. Some of these businessmen claim that they can make progress only by carefully playing what they call the French game. To the extent that Senegalese officials may be aware of this problem, it must be assumed that they tend to ignore it in the short run in view of the overwhelming importance to the national economy of the role played by the resident French business community.

In fact, one of the most important factors influencing Sene-

1. *La Politique de coopération avec les pays en voie de développement* (Paris: Ministère d'Etat chargé de la Réforme Administrative, 1963), pp. 84–85.

gal's foreign trade policy seems to be that business community. The Dakar Chamber of Commerce, Industry, and Agriculture is a public body which was created in 1964 to represent public as well as private interests. Its formal authority enables it to make recommendations and give advice to government officials on such questions as customs duties, taxes, import and export licenses, and general trade regulations.[2]

Inasmuch as the French resident business community, represented on the Chamber of Commerce, controls the lion's share of Senegal's external trade, it is likely that the businessmen's influence exceeds by far the authority recognized by legislation. Moreover, for all their undeniable contributions to the development of the Senegalese economy, these businessmen represent French firms whose headquarters are in France and whose economic policy may be decided not so much on the basis of the needs of Senegal as on considerations of profit resting on extra-Senegalese criteria. Their commercial interests transcend the borders of Senegal, and it would be surprising if their interests were identical with those of the Senegalese economy. Some Chamber of Commerce officials, in fact, readily agree in private that the Chamber, as an institution, follows a policy of consolidation, rather than diversification, of commercial circuits. They buy from those who buy Senegalese products, that is, preferably from France. According to the Chamber's former French president, the organization "intervenes directly with the public powers" to defend the interests of the private sector of the Senegalese economy.[3] Senegalese officials have tended to evaluate this problem by suggesting that they are confident that, first, the Chamber is only an advisory body to the government, which makes all decisions, and, second, that members of the Chamber have been able to distinguish effectively between their roles as private businessmen and as advisers to the government on national policy. Nonetheless, it would seem to be in the interest of Senegal to give equal opportunity to other EEC countries and

2. See Senegal, Loi 64–26, February 19, 1964, Journal officiel de la République du Sénégal (hereafter cited as JORS) (March 19, 1964), p. 395; and Senegal, Décret 66–578, July 13, 1966, JORS (August 8, 1966).
3. Charles-Henri Gallenca, Dakar-Matin (August 2, 1967).

thus to break the subtle control by French business and increase the competition among foreign businesses.

The second development pointing to an eventual decline in the influence of the French business community is the resurgence of Senegalese private enterprise. There is evidence to suggest that the government of Senegal has been overly cautious—or neglectful—in its evaluation and support of a small but growing group of Senegalese businessmen. According to one careful study, the "orthodox" view of the Senegalese as having, historically, neither taste nor aptitude for business is a superficial one. The nineteenth century witnessed a rapid increase in the number of successful Senegalese merchants. Many of them were subsequently ruined through the combined pressures of French business interests, Lebanese retail merchants, and French *petits-blancs* storekeepers, all assisted by the French colonial administration. It was this political development, an aspect of the "colonial situation," which reoriented many young and ambitious Senegalese toward the civil service for more secure careers.

A new, emergent group of Senegalese businessmen, from traditional, rural areas, took the initiative shortly before independence and sought to both further and protect their interests. The group prospered, partly because of support from the government after it had extended its control over the marketing of peanuts and the distribution of consumer goods in rural areas, a measure designed to put an end to usury in the countryside and to extract some development capital from agriculture.[4]

By 1968, Senegalese businessmen began to consolidate their various organizations and to enlist government support for a number of demands. The Union des Groupements Economiques du Sénégal (UNIGES) was formed in 1967 and during its first annual meeting in mid-1968 asked for stronger protectionist measures, more africanization generally, and the democratization of the Dakar Chamber of Commerce, which represented principally the French business community. A few months later, a number of important dissident Senegalese businessmen left UNIGES, although in agreement with its demands, and formed

---

4. This brief discussion is based largely on Samir Amin, *Le Monde des affaires sénégalais* (Paris: Minuit, 1969).

a rival organization, the Conseil Fédéral des Groupements
Economiques du Sénégal (COFEGES), with government sponsorship. For the first time since 1954, new elections replaced the
personnel of the Chamber of Commerce with a majority of
Africans; an African, Amadou Sow, became its president.
It is clear that the new Senegalese business groups are not yet
in a position to replace foreign business interests. Their resources
are modest, they have no easy access to capital, and they depend
on foreign business for imports and on the state for support.
But they have made a start. If they are successful in obtaining
more government support, then their role is likely to grow in the
future. The fact that the government sponsors COFEGES instead of the earlier organization does not necessarily mean that
the Senegalese business community will be prevented from
achieving its objectives. This sponsorship is in keeping with the
Senegalese political tradition of fusion and pluralism and demonstrates that the government has responded to new demands.
Whatever the precise relation between these new groups and the
government, it marks the beginning of a trend toward the growth
of Senegalese business and the corresponding decrease of foreign,
especially French, commercial influence.

FOREIGN TRADE

For countries like Senegal, foreign trade is much more important
than it is for countries such as the United States. The external
commerce of the United States makes up only a small percentage
of the country's total trade, and, consequently, state income is
derived largely from domestic sources. In Senegal, by contrast,
the bulk of state income comes from import and export duties
(in addition to foreign aid). The breakdown of Senegal's budgetary receipts for the 1967/68 fiscal year, for example, was approximately 4,566,250,000 CFA francs (80 per cent) from customs duties, 827, 500,000 CFA francs (14 per cent) from direct
taxes, and 337,500,000 CFA francs (6 per cent) from miscellaneous registration fees.[5]

5. *Bulletin statistique et économique mensuel* (Dakar: Direction de la
Statistique [nos. 11, 12], 1969), p. 36.

Volume and value

A brief profile of Senegal's external trade will reveal the major characteristics and trends of her foreign commerce. Table 1 recapitulates foreign trade figures for imports and exports broken down by volume and value. It should be borne in mind that the statistics, as well as the percentages derived therefrom, are those officially recorded by the government of Senegal. This is particularly important concerning inter-African trade, much of which still escapes official registration, if not notice, and thus may be of greater importance than the figures recorded in Dakar. For example, government statistics record Senegalese exports to the Ivory Coast for 1965 as amounting to 232 million CFA francs, whereas the Chamber of Commerce estimated actual Senegal exports at 921 million CFA francs for that period. Traditional trade links are allowed to persist even if officially frowned on: their disappearance would tend to lower the standard of living. Smuggling across political frontiers of such "modern" consumer goods as transistor radios and alcoholic beverages from The Gambia takes place so frequently that these "imports" can be readily found for sale in Dakar. Consequently, the statistical material used here should be considered only an approximation of actual trade currents between Senegal and other African states.

A number of important trends are apparent in these figures. First, the long-term (1961–68) trend for both volume and value of Senegal's exports and imports was upward. During the post-independence period of 1960–68 (trade statistics to 1960 indicate totals only for Mauritania, Soudan, and Senegal as one economic unit), the volume of exports rose sharply and steadily (interrupted only in 1967) by 48 per cent. The overall increase in the value of exports during this period amounted to 22 per cent, or less than one-half of the percentage increase in tonnage. Another dimension of this increase in export tonnage is the percentage growth between 1958—for three countries—and 1968 —for Senegal alone; in 1968, Senegal alone exported 27 per cent more tonnage than did the three countries in 1958, and the corresponding increase in value was 30 per cent.

Second, imports into Senegal between 1961 and 1968 increased only slightly in value but considerably in volume. The increase

TABLE 1
SENEGALESE FOREIGN TRADE, 1958–1968

	1958	1961	1962	1963	1964	1965	1966	1967	1968
Volume (in thousands of tons)									
Imports	788	740	772	793	944	1042	780	625	1000
Exports	766	1110	1143	1007	1363	1499	1577	1460	1650
Value (in billions of CFA francs)									
Imports	43.7	38.3	38.2	38.5	42.4	40.5	39.8	38.9	44.5
Exports	28.8	30.6	30.6	27.2	30.2	31.7	36.7	33.9	37.4
Deficit	14.9	7.7	7.6	11.3	12.2	8.8	3.1	5.0	7.1

SOURCES: *Commerce extérieur du Sénégal, 1957–1965* (Dakar: Service de la Statistique, January, 1957); *L'Economie du Sénégal* (Dakar: Chambre de Commerce, d'Agriculture et d'Industrie, July, 1965), pp. 192–205; *Bulletin statistique et économique mensuel* (Dakar: Service de la Statistique [nos. 3, 4], 1967), pp. 19–30; and *Bulletin . . . mensuel* (Dakar: Direction de la Statistique [nos. 11, 12], 1969), pp. 19–30.

NOTE: Figures for 1958 include Senegal, Mauritania, and the former Soudan.

in volume was relatively slow, but steady, from 1961 to 1965. It was followed by a sharp decline for the following two years and then almost reached the 1965 peak in 1968. The total percentage increase in volume during the postindependence period was 35 per cent. By comparison, the percentage increase in the value of Senegal's imports was 16 per cent. Total prices paid for imports rose slowly between 1961 and 1963, then more rapidly in 1964, declined until 1967, and rose again sharply in 1968.

Third, by 1966 Senegal's trade deficit was reduced to less than half of what it had been in 1961: from 7.7 per cent to 3.1 per cent after reaching a peak in 1964. Another way of expressing this relationship is the percentage of the cost of imports covered by exports. That "coverage" increased from 79.9 per cent in 1961 to 92.2 per cent in 1966, a considerable improvement in the balance of trade. An illustration of the dangers inherent in monoculture, however, is the fact that by 1968 the trade deficit returned to approximately the level of the immediate postindependence years. Largely because of a prolonged draught and its inevitable effect on the peanut crop, the 1968 coverage of imports by exports dropped to 84 per cent.

Senegal's most important exports may be divided into three major categories. The first includes peanuts and peanut products. Peanuts, introduced from France, were first grown commercially around 1840 by French merchants; some 77 tons were exported to France in 1841.[6]

As a cash crop, peanuts remained relatively unimportant until the French government decided, near the turn of the century, to implement a policy of financial autonomy for its colonies. This policy meant that the colonies, rather than the French taxpayer, were to bear the financial burdens of colonial administration, and the cultivation of peanuts as a cash crop was therefore emphasized in Senegal. By 1900, Senegal exported 100,000 tons; only nine years later the volume had increased to 224,000 tons; and by 1957 total production reached 677,000 tons.[7]

The second category consists of minerals, chiefly rich calcium

6. Félix Brigaud, Le Sénégal économique (Saint-Louis: Centre de Recherche et de Documentation, 1967), pp. 40–48.
7. Ibid., p. 41.

and some aluminum phosphates. Calcium phosphate deposits were discovered shortly before independence and estimated at forty million tons. Open air extraction was begun in 1960 by the Compagnie Sénégalaise des Phosphates de Taiba, which is now Senegal's most important private business company.

Finally, the third category is canned fish. In addition to traditional river and maritime fishing with pirogues and a number of small trawlers, whose catch is largely consumed locally, Senegal exports tuna, which is found conveniently off her coast. Tuna fishing on a commercial scale began in 1955, with French ships. Soon after, a Senegalese company was formed. It grew rapidly, especially after independence, and is now, with foreign financial assistance, building a complex that includes refrigeration and canning plants. The Senegalese tuna fleet now has five ships built in France and is approaching the objective of fifteen with the help of a Russian loan granted in 1967.

Table 2 recapitulates the trends in Senegal's most important exports, broken down into the major categories, and shows the percentage that each figure represents of total export volume or value for a particular year (compare table 1).

The major trend apparent in the figures in table 2 is an incipient but steady increase in the volume of exported minerals and canned fish. For the eight years covered, the per cent increase in the value and volume of minerals exported was 82 and 93, respectively, and the increase in canned fish was 67 per cent for value and 75 per cent for volume. This was accompanied by a decrease in the importance of peanuts and peanut products; peanut exports decreased from 52 per cent to 42 per cent in volume, and from 83 per cent to 72 per cent in value, of total exports. The trend is incipient in that the increases in export volume and value of minerals and canned fish still represent only small percentages of the yearly totals, except that by volume, minerals have replaced peanuts and peanut products as the most important item. It is expected that the absolute and relative amount and value of the minerals will increase in the future. Although not much real progress was achieved with respect to the export of canned fish—the slight increase in value resulted from high unit price—the Senegalese tuna industry is expected

TABLE 2
MAJOR SENEGALESE EXPORTS, 1961, 1966, AND 1968

	1961	1966	1968
Volume (in thousands of tons)			
Peanuts and products	578	611	690
Minerals	420	820	810
Canned fish	4	6	7
Value (in billions of CFA francs)			
Peanuts and products	25.46	28.59	27.00
Minerals	1.42	2.58	2.58
Canned fish	.96	1.30	1.60
Total	27.84	32.47	31.18

SOURCES: Extracted from *L'Economie du Sénégal* (Dakar: Chambre de Commerce, d'Agriculture et d'Industrie, July, 1965), pp. 203–4; and *Bulletin statistique et économique mensuel* (Dakar: Direction de la Statistique [nos. 11, 12], 1969), pp. 19–30.

to grow in importance once the necessary infrastructure is installed.

It should be pointed out that the basic structure of Senegal's exports has not changed appreciably. The three large categories of goods sold abroad, taken together, represent only a slight change in the percentage of the total value of exports (90.9 per cent in 1961 compared with 83.1 per cent in 1968), so that the country remains heavily dependent on three products for the bulk of her export earnings.

As already noted, the total value of imports increased slightly and the volume considerably after independence. The changes in the major categories of goods imported are evident from table 3.

These statistics indicate that there was no startling change in the overall distribution of the volume and value of imports. In terms of their relative share of volume, the different categories

TABLE 3
MAJOR SENEGALESE IMPORTS, 1961, 1966, AND 1968

	1961	1966	1968
Volume			
(in thousands of tons)			
Food, beverages, and tobacco	340	405	510
Cereals	201	260	265
Petroleum products	230	175	263
Manufactures	142	150	163
Raw materials	26	50	64
Value			
(in billions of CFA francs)			
Food, beverages, and tobacco	12.23	14.20	16.25
Cereals	4.53	6.50	8.80
Petroleum products	1.87	1.00	1.40
Manufactures	23.43	21.00	14.65
Raw materials	.82	2.10	2.25

SOURCES: *L'Economie du Sénégal* (Dakar: Chambre de Commerce, d'Agriculture et d'Industrie, July, 1965), pp. 199–200; *Bulletin statistique et économique mensuel* (Dakar: Direction de la Statistique [nos. 11, 12], 1969), pp. 19–30.

have undergone slight fluctuations or remained the same between 1961 and 1968. Food, beverages, and tobacco increased from 46 per cent to 51 per cent; petroleum products declined slightly from 31 per cent to 26 per cent; and manufactures declined from 19 per cent to 16 per cent. With two exceptions, the value of imports shows only slight fluctuations. One exception concerns manufactures, which decreased from 61 per cent to 23 per cent; the other concerns cereals, whose share increased from 12 per cent to 20 per cent. This increase in the per cent value of cereals imported into Senegal reflects the needs and habits of the large consumer sector of the modern economy, and illustrates the importance for Senegal of diversifying her agricultural production. In 1968, for example, Senegal's cereal imports included 185,000 tons of rice, 62,000 tons of wheat, some

3,000 tons of millet and sorghum, and an additional 15,000 tons of other cereals, requiring an expenditure of about 20 per cent of the cost of total imports.

It may be noted that changes in many categories of imported goods appear more significant when looked at from the point of view of per cent increase or decrease between 1961 and 1968. Thus, the volume of raw materials increased by 146 per cent; that of food, beverages, and tobacco by 50 per cent; and that of cereals by 32 per cent. The corresponding figures for increases in value are 174, 33, and 92 per cent. In terms of value, petroleum products decreased by 22 per cent, and manufactured goods by 37 per cent during the same period.

Geographic distribution

Table 4 recapitulates the geographic distribution of the value of Senegal's foreign trade from 1961 to 1968 inclusive. A number of important characteristics and trends emerge from the data. First, there is the preponderance of the franc zone, which includes France as well as her former African territories (except Guinea). During the period 1961–68, the zone accounted for between 92 and 77 per cent of Senegal's total exports, and for between 83 and 61 per cent of her total imports. Within the franc zone, France remains paramount as Senegal's trading partner, accounting for between 82 and 66 per cent of Senegal's exports and 65 and 44 per cent of her imports within the period mentioned.

Second, for all its dominant position, the franc zone has become less important to Senegal. The share of that zone in Senegal's foreign commerce has decreased for both imports and exports, although Senegal continues to be dependent on the area for nearly 80 per cent of her exports. Another aspect of the slow decline in the importance of the franc zone for Senegal emerges from a comparison, for the years 1961 and 1966, of her ten most important trading partners. In 1961, ten countries accounted for nearly 94 per cent of the value of Senegal's imports; by 1966 that percentage had declined to 85. The same is true for exports, for which the corresponding figures are 98 and 90 per cent. Within this concentration, the part of the franc zone has

TABLE 4
Senegalese Foreign Trade by Areas, in Percentages of Total Value, 1961–1968

	Exports from Senegal								Imports to Senegal							
	1961	1962	1963	1964	1965	1966	1967	1968	1961	1962	1963	1964	1965	1966	1967	1968
Franc zone total	86	92	92	79	85	81	84	78	83	73	72	69	70	67	65	62
France	72	80	82	75	81	75	80	66	65	62	62	57	54	53	48	44
Africa	14	11	10	4	4	6	2	3	14	9	6	6	10	9	5	6
Other	—	—	—	—	—	—	—	—	4	1	4	6	6	4	12	11
EEC total	78	83	85	80	86	81	83	74	75	71	73	68	66	67	62	59
less France	5	2	3	4	5	5	4	8	8	9	11	11	12	14	14	15
Africa total non-franc zone	14	11	10	5	6	8	2	3	15	10	8	7	11	10	5	6
Non-EEC western Europe	—	—	—	1	1	2	—	—	1	1	2	1	2	—	—	—
Asia	5	5	3	6	5	7	7	9	2	3	3	3	3	3	3	3
Americas	—	—	1	3	2	2	3	2	3	6	2	7	6	9	9	6
Eastern Europe	—	—	—	2	—	—	—	—	1	—	—	—	—	—	—	—
Middle East	—	—	—	—	—	—	—	—	—	—	—	—	—	—	—	—

Sources: Adapted from the general *Bulletin statistique et économique mensuel*; and the very detailed annual compilations, *Etat des importations: Pays* and *Etat des exportations: Pays*, both published by the Service de Statistique in Dakar, for relevant periods.

Note: Decimal fractions are rounded off to the nearest percentage point, and figures amounting to less than 1 per cent of total trade are not shown. Figures for the United Arab Republic re included under "Africa." Moreover, "other" franc-zone trade refers to Senegalese imports from Cambodia and Vietnam, which are excluded from "Asia."

declined. In 1961, the zone was responsible for 89 per cent of the sales from these top ten, but only for 69 per cent five years later; among the top ten buyers of Senegalese goods, the zone absorbed over 90 per cent in 1961, a percentage which fell to 85 in 1966. Probably the major reason for this development is that the franc zone is becoming less important to France. As French goods have themselves become increasingly competitive in world markets, the need for a highly protected economic space has receded. As a consequence, the share of the franc zone in France's own total foreign trade decreased steadily from 20 per cent in 1961 to 13 per cent in 1965.[8]

Third, with the exception of the total franc zone as discussed above and until 1966, Africa was Senegal's most important trading partner of any geographic region. In spite of the postindependence decline of Senegalese exports to Africa, she received more from exports to Africa than she did from the European Economic Community—minus France—in every year from 1961 to 1966. She also spent more for imports from Africa than from the EEC, minus France, in 1961 and 1962, but the margin between the amounts spent on imports for the two groups narrowed again after 1965. Data for 1967 and 1968 are only incomplete, rough approximations and consequently do not reflect the totality of Senegal's inter-African trade.

This African preponderance was largely the result, however, of the existence of the franc zone, which accounts for nearly all of Senegal's inter-African trade. Government efforts to stimulate trade with English-speaking African countries have had little success so far. This failure may be attributed to differences in monetary zones, fiscal legislation, and political outlook, as well as to sensitivities about different colonial administrative, cultural, and linguistic legacies. Further, as noted earlier, the French resident business community, which controls most of Senegal's foreign trade, cannot be said to have been overly enthusiastic in seeking new trade channels outside the franc zone. But Senegal's major problem in inter-African trade was its de-

8. Le Moniteur africain du commerce et de l'industrie (January 25, 1967).

cline following independence or, more precisely, following the breakup of the federal administrative structures previously imposed by France, the breakup of the Mali Federation, and the emergence of economic nationalism among the African states. Within the short period of two years, Senegal lost her position as entrepôt for French West Africa and, to some extent, for French Equatorial Africa; she also lost many of her markets for the manufacturing industries implanted by the French to service the French West African economic hinterland.

After national independence, Senegal's inter-African trade was characterized by two major developments. One was a drastic reduction in its total value: it declined by about 40 per cent in the five years following 1961. Senegal's exports to Africa decreased in value from 1.2 billion CFA francs to 992.5 million CFA francs between 1961 and 1966. Her trade deficit with these countries, although reduced by 17.2 per cent during that period, still remained at over one-third of the value of her exports.

The other major development in Senegal's inter-African trade relations was a shift away from the former Federation of French West Africa. Precise figures concerning preindependence commercial exchanges between Senegal and the AOF are not available, since the former was considered part of an economic unit which included Mauritania and the former Soudan. Nonetheless, an attempt was made to measure trade flows among the eight AOF territories in 1956. In that year, assuming that it was representative of the preindependence period, most of Senegal's inter-African trade took place within the AOF framework.[9] By 1966, Senegal's exports to AOF states had dwindled to 33.2 per cent of the African total, and her imports from AOF to 49 per cent of her inter-African trade.[10] The former importance of Senegal as an entrepôt of AOF commerce emerges from the fact that, in 1956, the value of her exports to AOF amounted to

9. *Comptes économiques de l'Afrique Occidentale Française, 1956, Rapport no. 6, échanges interterritoriaux* (Dakar: Haut Commissariat-Général, 1959).

10. This discussion of postindependence trade is based on figures published in *Etat des importations: Pays* and *Etat des exportations: Pays* (Dakar: Service de la Statistique, relevant years).

slightly over one-half that of total exports leaving Senegal; in 1966, the value of Senegal's exports to all Africa, by contrast, amounted to only 8 per cent of the total.

Another dimension of the shift away from her former AOF associates is the increasing importance of the larger Organisation Commune Africaine et Malgache. In 1966, the value of Senegal's exports to OCAM states represented 60.2 per cent, and that of her imports 72.8 per cent, of her total inter-African trade.

The importance of OCAM suggested by these figures, however, is somewhat misleading. This becomes apparent by looking at Senegal's inter-African trade from the point of view of another criterion, namely, that of African countries that accounted for at least 10 per cent of the value of her inter-African exports and imports. This "10 per cent" criterion reveals that significant African imports to Senegal originate in four countries: the Ivory Coast, 44.8 per cent; Madagascar, 18.2 per cent; Algeria, 14.8 per cent; and Morocco, 11.3 per cent. (Three of these countries also fall into the 10 per cent category from the point of view of volume: Algeria, 41.3 per cent; Madagascar, 19.1 per cent; the Ivory Coast, 16 per cent; and Gabon, 15.8 per cent.) Senegal's African exports go mostly to four countries: Madagascar, 19.6 per cent; South Africa, 14 per cent; the Ivory Coast, 11.6 per cent; and Mauritania, 11.5 per cent. (From the point of view of volume, three African countries bought more than 10 per cent of Senegal's total inter-African sales: Madagascar, 23.3 per cent; South Africa, 21.2 per cent; and Rhodesia, 15.2 per cent.) The total concentration of Senegal's "10 per cent" exports is only slightly smaller than her OCAM exports (56.7 per cent compared to 60.2 per cent), but her "10 per cent" imports exceed those from OCAM (89.1 per cent compared to 72.8 per cent). Both the "10 per cent" and the OCAM categories are much more important than trade relations with AOF, in spite of a resurgence of trade with the Ivory Coast.

Despite the concentration just described, Senegal has succeeded in diversifying some of her inter-African trade relations. One way to measure that diversification is to compare the number of countries with which products worth 1 million CFA francs or more were exchanged in 1961 and 1966. From this point of view, Senegal imported fourteen different products from nine

African countries in 1961, whereas the corresponding figures for 1966 were twenty-five and nineteen. In 1961, Senegal exported six different products to seven African countries, and twenty products to twenty-five African countries in 1966. Moreover, whereas only one of the African countries buying Senegalese goods on such a scale was outside the franc zone in 1961 (Guinea), in 1966 there were eleven such countries in Africa. Similarly, Senegalese imports in 1961 originated in five non-franc-zone countries (including Guinea), and in eight such countries in 1966. The number of African countries with which Senegal maintained significant trade relations, as defined by the figure of 1 million CFA francs, and counting imports and exports separately, thus increased from sixteen in 1961 to forty-four in 1966.

The third major geographic area with which Senegal maintains trade relations is the European Economic Community. Despite Senegal's status as an associate member, that area minus France does not loom very large in Senegal's total trade relations. Only since 1963 has the EEC less France sold Senegal more than 10 per cent of her imports. Until 1966, her trade with Africa was generally greater than with the EEC less France. This was true for the value of Senegal's exports for each year after 1961, and for the value of her imports for 1961 and 1962.

The remaining geographic areas with which Senegal maintains commercial relations (non-EEC western Europe, eastern Europe, the Americas, Asia, and the Middle East) are of relatively marginal importance to Senegal. None of these areas has accounted for 10 per cent of the value of total trade. With the sole exceptions of the Americas and of non-EEC western Europe in 1964, with regard to exports, the value of Senegalese trade with any of these areas was below that with African countries.

A variety of factors underlies the pattern and trends discussed above. The resilience of the franc zone, a structure inherited from the colonial era, is the result mainly of its relative homogeneity from the point of view of fiscal and customs patterns, of buying and selling habits, and of its difficult harmonization with other colonial systems obtaining in Africa. The common currency maintained after independence not only prevented the complete financial balkanization of former French Africa but also encouraged trade to remain within the zone. Thus, countries in North Africa and in OCAM have tended to replace former AOF states as sources of supply for Senegal.

Senegal's dependence on France can be attributed to a large extent to monoculture. The difficulties of finding alternative markets for Senegalese peanut products are compounded by different consumer tastes in other potential markets and by comparatively high production costs. (American-grown peanuts are less expensive in Dakar, for example, than locally produced competitors. Industrialists in Senegal have tried, without success, to sell peanut butter; attempts are now being made to improve the process by adding chocolate to the mixture and thus to capitalize on Africans' fondness for sweets.)

Industrialization has nonetheless tended to reduce Senegal's dependence on France. It is true that France still purchases the bulk of two of the three major export commodities from which Senegal derives most of its foreign exchange earnings: peanut products and canned fish. (It should be noted that France buys nearly all the crude and refined peanut oil Senegal sells, but only half of the oil cakes—the remainder is sold to Europe, Africa, and such occasional customers as the Canary Islands and Réunion.) France's share of the third commodity, minerals, is under 5 per cent; the rest is sold to other western European countries, to Asia, and to Africa. Senegal's ability to sell minerals is a function of demand, so that an important share of her phosphates have been purchased by the Republic of South Africa. The volume of Senegal's mineral exports to that country stood at 10,000 tons in 1962 and increased to 120,000 tons by 1965 (it declined to 14,000 tons the following year), which made South Africa the largest single African importer, by volume (68 per cent), of Senegalese goods. This increase is reflected also in the value of Senegal's exports to South Africa, which rose from 33 million CFA francs in 1962 to 388 million CFA francs in 1966, and during the latter year placed South Africa seventh among Senegal's African trade partners.

To summarize, the major trends apparent in the geographic distribution of Senegal's postindependence foreign trade are (1) the decreasing importance of the franc zone and of France, (2) the continuation of the importance of western Europe, (3)

the increase in Senegal's imports from France's five EEC partners (whereas exports to that area have remained relatively
stable), and (4) the overall decrease of Africa as a trading partner, with a pattern, however, that shows both concentration and
diversification.

On the whole, the geographic concentration of Senegal's external commerce remains enormous, although it was somewhat
more diversified in 1966 than immediately after independence.
Between 80 and 90 per cent of her total official foreign trade
takes place within a complex including the franc zone and the
European Common Market. Senegal's dependence on this complex was reduced, during this period, from 91 to 86 per cent for
her exports, and from 85 to 81 percent for her imports. Government statistics indicate several incipient, although weak, trends
which may lead to greater trade relations in the future at the
expense, in terms of total percentages, of the franc-zone/EEC
complex. From the point of view of exports, non-EEC western
Europe gained 2 to 3 per cent, and Asia gained 1 per cent; from
the point of view of imports, the Americas gained over 2 per
cent, and Asia increased by about 6 per cent of Senegal's total
foreign trade. Given the continuation of the direction of Senegal's foreign trade relations, it could be expected that greater
diversification of customers and sources of supply will take
place, at least in the long run.

FOREIGN ASSISTANCE

Bilateral foreign assistance

Bilateral public foreign assistance to Senegal is to a large extent
a continuation of the French post-World War II policy to inject
public capital into her African colonial territories. That policy
was based on the recognition that the economic and social development of colonial peoples is a prerequisite for their administrative and political development. It took expression in the Fonds
d'Investissement pour le Développement Economique et Social

(FIDES) and the Fonds d'Equipement Rural et de Développement Economique et Social (FERDES), both of which were concerned with long-range planning for economic development. Between 1960 and 1966, the major donor countries' public assistance appropriations to Senegal amounted to $267,730,670. During this period, Senegal thus received approximately $38 million per annum in bilateral foreign aid, or nearly 40 per cent of her annual national budget. France dominated the donors by a wide margin, being responsible for $226,197,400, or about 85 per cent of the total. Other major donor countries included the United States ($21,333,270), West Germany ($7,500,000), the Soviet Union ($6,600,000), and Canada ($6,100,000).

French aid has a number of important characteristics which makes it advantageous for such African recipients as Senegal. First, it has been a relatively constant and therefore reliable source. Most postindependence French aid was channeled through the Secretariat of State for Foreign Affairs in Charge of Cooperation (now located in the Foreign Ministry); the secretariat administers capital aid through the Fonds d'Aide et de Coopération (FAC) and loans through the FAC disbursing agent, the Caisse Centrale de Coopération Economique (CCCE). In addition, a number of other government depart ments appropriate and administer assistance for activities for which they have exclusive responsibility. These include (1) military aid; (2) price supports—until 1968; (3) treasury advances; (4) such other activities as air transportation and security, deemed by France to be in the "common interest"; (5) pensions to veterans of the French armed forces and former colonial administrators; and (6) contributions to multilateral funds such as the European Development Fund of the EEC, and the United Nations and its agencies. Some of this additional aid is administered by functional ministries and consequently is not counted officially as aid by French sources. (Thus, the French Ministry of National Education provides aid for Dakar University from its own budget.) Taking the cooperation budget of the Secretariat of State as a rough indicator of the general trend in French aid appropriations, that budget amounted to $230 million in 1960 and to $236 million in 1968; the intervening years fluctuated from a low of $224 million to a high of $263 million.[11]

France's bilateral aid to Senegal from independence to 1966, exclusive of military assistance and of the value of *surprix*—subsidies for Senegalese agricultural exports at prices higher than those of the world market—granted, is summarized in table 5. The percentage of loans has decreased considerably from 30.1 in 1960 to 7.4 in 1966, the average per year for the postindependence period being 14.2 per cent. Amounts for technical assistance were generally greater than for capital during the period (the reverse was true only in 1960 and 1964). The miscellaneous category is made up mostly of pensions paid by the French government to Senegalese citizens, veterans of either the armed forces or the administrative services; but the category also includes limited amounts for the administration of aerial security and such other financially limited activities as scientific research.

A second characteristic of French aid has been its flexibility. Prior to the African states' independence, French aid was designated not so much for the self-sufficiency of the territories as for the harmonious development of federal entities. If in the process such coastal areas as Senegal benefited from a much larger share of French aid than did their landlocked counterparts, this was the result of geographic location, which made them agents for the federal ensemble, rather than of their intrinsic importance. Senegal was singled out as a privileged recipient of French aid among the eight territories of French West Africa and consequently had a considerable head start over them upon acceding to independence. In other words, the early economic development of Senegal was to a large extent the for-

11. See *La Coopération économique entre la France, l'Afrique d'expression française et Madagascar* (Paris: Documentation Française [Note et étude documentaire no. 3330], October 25, 1966); "Aide financière accordée par la France au Sénégal sous l'égide du département ministériel de la coopération," typescript, Paris [1968]; "Aide financière accordée par la France au Sénégal sous l'égide d'autres départements ministériels," typescript, Paris [1968]; *Mémento de l'économie africaine, 1967* (Paris: Ediafric, 1967), pp. 308–10; and *Le Moniteur africain du commerce et de l'industrie* (September 13, 1967).

TABLE 5
French Bilateral Assistance to Senegal, 1960–1966
(in millions of U.S. dollars)

	1960	1961	1962	1963	1964	1965	1966	Totals
FAC	8,601,6	8,225,4	7,141,6	8,324,0	14,086,8	4,058,0	8,296,6	58,734,0
Technical assistance	6,020,0	9,360,0	11,240,0	9,680,0	9,580,0	11,040,0	10,982,0	67,902,0
CCCE	6,784,0	2,864,0	4,498,8	7,606,0	6,750,4	897,6	2,825,0	32,225,8
Dakar Univ.	1,082,0	1,382,6	1,694,0	2,083,4	2,513,0	2,070,0	2,083,6	12,908,6
Misc.	0	1,484,0	7,624,0	12,696,5	9,836,0	8,715,6	14,071,0	54,427,1
Total	22,487,6	23,316,0	32,198,4	40,389,9	42,766,2	26,781,2	38,258,2	226,197,5

Source: "Aide financière accordée par la France au Sénégal sous l'égide du département ministériel de la coopération," typescript (Paris, n.d. [1968]).

Note: FAC = Fonds d'Aide et de Coopération; CCCE = Caisse Centrale de Coopération Economique.

tuitous result of a French policy concerned with developing the federation.

After independence, Senegal benefited from France's flexibility in that the notion of economic development was adjusted to accumulated knowledge about the process itself. Before independence, the first priority appeared to be the immediate need for erecting a nonproductive economic and social infrastructure to lay the groundwork for future growth. In the postindependence period, partly because of a shift in priorities toward productive activities, the earlier emphasis changed. Both the leadership and personnel of the Secretariat of State for Cooperation have earned a reputation for innovation and are no doubt in part responsible for France's willingness to alter her earlier views regarding the nature and purpose of foreign aid. Some of the results of the French government's adaptation to the changing needs of Senegal may be illustrated by the drastic changes in the relative priorities given to economic infrastructure and to production in the allocation of public capital grants. A comparison between the period 1953–57, the year 1960, and the year 1964 shows that the share of capital allotted for economic infrastructure dropped from 49.9 per cent to 16.4 per cent to 6.5 per cent, respectively, whereas the share of capital allotted for production increased from 44.9 per cent to 82.5 per cent of the total allocation (it was 29.8 per cent for 1960).

There are other factors which may help account for the French government's adaptability. Senegalese leaders have continued to have easy access to top French leadership since independence. Because the French government centralized much of the administration of foreign aid in 1960, a trip or telephone call to one agency could bring about results which before independence would have required lengthy coordination among half a dozen government agencies. President Senghor's personal relations with General de Gaulle and Georges Pompidou are well known. Jacques Foccart, a former high colonial official who is responsible for African policy in the Presidency of the French Republic, and as such the most important of France's advisers on African affairs, has remained on good terms with Senegalese leaders. Senghor and other Senegalese leaders also have cultivated good relations with a string of former colonial officials placed at strategic spots within the French government structure. Most prominent among these is no doubt Yvon Bourges, a former French high commissioner in AOF, appointed secretary of state for foreign affairs in charge of cooperation in January, 1966. There can be little doubt that these contacts have had a generally beneficial influence from the point of view of Senegal.

The French government's receptivity to the changing needs and priorities of Senegal are evident also, in part, in France's policy concerning the distribution of technical assistance personnel. This is particularly striking with regard to the two categories of education and administration: French technical assistants for education nearly doubled (from 35.8 per cent to 70.8 per cent of the total) between 1960 and 1969, whereas they were reduced by more than half (from 33.9 per cent to 15.5 per cent of the total) in the same period for the more politically sensitive category of administration. It should be noted also that, whereas the overall postindependence trend in the total number of French technical assistance personnel serving in Senegal has been downward (from 1,656 in 1960 to 1,310 in 1969), Senegal nevertheless remains an important employer of such personnel, with 13.3 per cent of the total for the former African states in 1969.

Another advantage Senegal derives from French technical assistance personnel is financial. France is motivated in part by self-interest in placing abroad many former colonial officials lest they become a burden to the French economy. The consequence for Senegal is that it is less expensive for her to make use of expatriate Frenchmen than to employ her own nationals. Senegal is required to pay only part of the salaries of expatriate Frenchmen: a flat rate of $2,640 per annum per person ($1,560 until 1962) regardless of position, rank, or seniority. This financial obligation, however, does not apply to experts sent on short-term missions, or to the increasing number of French servicemen volunteering for "cooperation" rather than military duties—there were 65 of them in Senegal in 1964 and 169 in 1967. If it is assumed, conservatively, that the average Senegalese public official earns around $3,000 annually, then the saving to Senegal may be on the order of $540,000 per year.

Senegal's policy concerning the role of private foreign capital has encouraged the development of industry somewhat at the expense of commerce. The reasons for this choice antedate national independence and are rooted in the past role of small commerce in Senegal. In the eyes of Senegalese leaders, the commercial sector was tainted with the opprobrium of excessive exploitation. It served as an outlet for French manufacturers of relatively poorly made consumer goods in exchange for the cash crops exported to the metropole. Lebanese and French middlemen who came to monopolize small trade in the rural areas compounded this situation by charging exorbitant fees for their services and practicing usuary without effective legal restraints, thus helping to pauperize the peasant through perpetual indebtedness.

The industrial sector, by contrast, was looked upon with favor because it contributed to the modernization of the economy and brought capital, expertise, and employment to Senegal. A policy favoring investment in industry over commercial private investment was continued after independence. In order to keep attracting foreign capital, Senegal wrote a fairly liberal investment code offering advantageous concessions to potential investors.

The Senegalese government believes that, if it wants to continue to attract foreign capital, it must avoid giving the impression of being hostile to private enterprise. Moreover, national independence has actually increased Senegal's dependence on foreign private capital. Before independence, the private sector —which was mostly French—was secure in the knowledge that its interests were being looked after by a French colonial administration. Since independence, the private sector has depended legally on a politically sovereign Senegal and on the continued goodwill of its leaders. This helps explain why Senghor could afford to be critical of private enterprise before independence, whereas after 1960 criticism was transformed into public encouragement. As President Senghor explained in 1961:

> To nationalize, one must have national private capital and an adequate supply of national technicians. This is not the case with us. Since the goal is socialization, we shall reach it most surely by engaging in a dialogue with foreign

capitalists. It is a question of associating them with us under well-defined conditions. To be precise, it is a question, while retaining the direction of affairs, of guaranteeing them a fair share of the profits in return for their services. The essential condition is that the agreement enable the nation to develop its production and therefore its wealth.[12]

Senegal's policy has been successful in attracting considerable private investment in industry and manufacturing. Nearly three hundred new firms were established in Senegal between 1961 and 1966. Total foreign investments in industry and manufacturing increased from $12.6 million in 1962, to $22.9 million in 1963, $24.6 million in 1964, and $25.9 million in 1965. During this period, the percentage of private funds increased from 85 to 93.[13] Government sources indicate that the volume of industrial production in Senegal rose nearly 60 per cent between 1959 and 1966—the volume index rising from 100 to 159 in spite of a stagnation in construction and public transportation.[14] By the middle of 1967, over $30 million was committed for plants under construction, and an additional $17.5 million was committed for imminent expansion of existing plants and con-

12. *Théorie et pratique du socialisme sénégalais* (Dakar: Grande Imprimerie Africaine, 1966), p. 60. The discussion of French capital grants is based on data fom *A.O.F. 1957* (Dakar: Haut Commissariat de la République en Afrique Occidentale Française, 1958), p. 353; "Investissements de fonds publics français au Sénégal de 1947 à 1960," mimeographed (Dakar: Haute Représentation de France, February, 1961), annex 4; and France, National Assembly, *Journal officiel de la république française: Compte rendu intégral* (October 2, 1964), p. 3770. [Note: Figures for 1964 are as of September, 1964.] The following sources were used for the discussion of French technical assistance personnel: "Investissements de fonds publics français au Sénégal de 1947 à 1960," annex 3; *Rapport d'activité 1961/1966* (Paris: Ministère de la Coopération, 1964), p. 16; "Situation des personnels de coopération culturelle et technique au 1er mai 1967," mimeographed (Paris: Secrétariat d'Etat aux Affaires Etrangères chargé de la Coopération, 1967); and *Europe France-Outremer*, CDLXXIII (June, 1969), 213.
13. Figures adapted from *Mémento de l'économie africaine*, 1967, p. 297.
14. For details, see *Le Moniteur africain du commerce et de l'industrie* (March 29, 1967), and *Bulletin statistique et économique mensuel*, nos. 4, 5, 1967, p. 6.

struction of new enterprises. Of this grand total of almost $50 million, all but $7.5 million ($7.2 million from Russia and $360,000 from the EDF) came from private, mostly French sources.[15]

In order of descending importance, the major investments went into the development of the fertilizer industry, the construction of a sugar refinery, and the development of the tuna industry and the cotton processing industry. Prospects for cotton growing were particularly encouraging, after experiments in 1966 yielded the best results in former French Africa; the area for growing cotton was expected to increase tenfold, and total production of cotton grain to reach one million tons by 1970. Within a few years, Senegal anticipates that she will be one of the largest producers of fertilizer in black Africa. In addition to those mentioned, the products of processing and manufacturing plants under construction include seafood and by-products, vegetables, fruit juice, plywood, aluminum, cheese, and plastics; products for plants on which construction had been decided in 1967 include enamel, plastics, meat, margarine, and tomato concentrate. Prospects appeared favorable for continued growth following a sluggish period in the early 1960s.[16] Much of this activity is designed for import substitution in the short run; but some of it, chiefly canning plants such as those for tuna, fruit juices, and vegetables, are expected soon to yield export revenue.

In some important respects, the implantation of processing industries in Senegal has had the effect of increasing her dependence on a single outlet for exports. This is true notably of peanut oil. France's share in Senegal's exports of crude peanut oil increased from 88.5 per cent in 1957 to nearly 100 per cent by 1965; the respective figures which apply to refined peanut oil are 76.4 and 95.2 per cent. But the important question is not so much the desirability of diversification for its own sake as that of the advantages Senegal derives from this arrangement. Aside from the obvious ones resulting from the very establishment of these industries, Senegal needs—and gets—the protec-

15. For details, see Le Moniteur africain du commerce et de l'industrie (August 16, 1967).
16. Ibid. (March 29, 1967).

tion of a guaranteed market, for which there is no ready substitute available.

Multilateral foreign assistance

EEC multilateral capital transfers to Africa—the recipient of most such aid—have taken on special significance for Senegal. One reason is France's cautious but clear policy of shifting some of the burdens of her special trade and aid relationship with Africa toward the EEC. Another reason, a consequence of the first, concerns the French decision to discontinue the *surprix* for Senegal's peanuts. These *surprix* were special subsidies which made possible the maintenance of producer prices despite fluctuations in world market prices. The subsidies fell from an average of 22 French francs per kilo of unshelled peanuts for the period 1955–57 (followed by the devaluation of the French franc in 1958) to 1.05 francs for the period 1962–64, then to 0.99 franc for the 1964/65 harvest. Although the discontinuation of the French subsidy was postponed twice because of Senegal's internal economic difficulties, it took effect in 1968. (This has not measurably altered the guaranteed French quota for the quantity of peanuts and peanut products which she purchases.) At the same time, the European Development Fund has taken over part of the burden of subsidizing the price of Senegal's peanuts above world market prices during a transition period; the EDF subsidy began with the 1964/65 harvest, with 0.06 French franc per kilo; it was progressively reduced and terminated with the 1968/69 harvest.[17]

In terms of size alone, EDF capital transfers play a significant role in Senegal's economy. By March, 1967, the EDF had committed a total of $73,272,000 to Senegal, of which $45,049,000 was actually expended. EDF commitments were thus about three times those made bilaterally by the United States, and almost twice the amount of bilateral aid committed by the United States, West Germany, the Soviet Union, and Canada

17. For details, see *Mémento de l'économie africaine, 1967*, pp. 285–87; and *La Commercialisation de l'arachide sénégalaise en 1968–1969* (Paris: Banque Centrale des Etats de l'Afrique de l'Ouest, May, 1970), p. 11.

combined. As with French aid, Senegal benefits from a privileged position with respect to EDF appropriations: she ranked third among Associated States in the commitments made by the first EDF and fourth in commitments by the second EDF. As one of eighteen associates, Senegal received slightly over 10 per cent of the total appropriations to Africa by the second EDF ($58,728,000 of $553,715,000). Moreover, EDF commitments for Senegal reflect the same basic change in priorities as does French aid policy. Thus 89 per cent of the first EDF's appropriations to Senegal were allocated for social and economic infrastructure; the second EDF earmarked only 21.6 per cent of its commitment to Senegal for infrastructure, and 78 per cent for production, diversification of agriculture, and technical assistance, including the subsidy for peanuts and peanut products.[18]

Other multilateral assistance to Senegal, chiefly from the United Nations, has been estimated at $13,320,000 in commitments from 1960 to 1965. This amount includes the cost of national and regional studies, prospecting for minerals, educational support, and agricultural research. In addition, the International Development Association made its first loan to Senegal in 1966, in the amount of $9 million for railroad modernization.[19]

On the surface, it may seem that the continuation of French public assistance to Senegal is not highly dependent on membership in the franc zone. French motives underlying the aid effort have shifted considerably since the end of World War II. In 1945, French aid was justified mainly on humanitarian and economic grounds. First, France was indebted to her African territories and wanted to demonstrate her gratitude for Africans'

18. Adapted from figures in European Economic Community, *Dixième rapport général sur l'activité de la Communauté: 1 er avril 1966–31 mars 1967* (Brussels, June, 1967), pp. 304, 306–7; P. N. C. Okigbo, *Africa and the Common Market* (Evanston: Northwestern University Press, 1967), pp. 41–42; European Economic Community, *Troisième rapport général sur l'activité des Communautés: 1969* (Brussels, February, 1970), pp. 373–93; and *Fonds européen de développement: Situation trimestrielle des projets du 2ème FED en exécution* (Brussels, 1970).

19. *Mémento de l'économie africaine, 1967*, p. 310.

sacrifices in helping her win the war against the Nazis; Generals Charles de Gaulle and Jacques Philippe Leclerc both launched their anti-Vichy military campaigns from Africa. Second, the French economy had suffered severe blows, and she had neither ample foreign currencies nor easy access to raw materials. She therefore depended on her colonial holdings, which could, with the injection of public capital, help provide markets for noncompetitive exports and thus contribute to France's own economic recovery.

Since that recovery has taken place, other motives for French foreign assistance have moved into the foreground. First, from a general humanitarian view, France does not wish to see an economic collapse in Africa, which would also be a blow to French prestige throughout the world. Second, the new African states provide employment for the majority of still-active former French colonial civil servants.

But most important among today's motives for maintaining significant aid programs in black Africa is a combination of vanity and insurance. Economic motives have receded into the background and made room for more intensely felt considerations of national prestige. The French have not yet become accustomed to the end of their empire, an attitude expressed by the Cooperation Ministry as follows:

> [Foreign aid], to Frenchmen, is not only a sequel of the colonial heritage. It corresponds to a more profound need: it is a "destiny insurance." Frenchmen, consciously or not, fear that their country may become a diminished country, a "little France," which would not be on the scale of a world too powerful for her. They fear that France, by renouncing her traditional mission, this universalist and civilizing mission, this "imperialism of liberty," of which Giraudoux spoke, would renounce that which has made her real grandeur.
>
> [Foreign aid] is . . . the only means to assure for France, today and in the future, a real place in the world, to avoid a degradation of French prestige and influence, to permit France to remain a great power.[20]

20. "Dossier sur la politique française d'aide au tiers-monde," mimeographed (Paris: Ministère de la Coopération, 1966), p. 2.

From a practical viewpoint, concentrating French aid in former African territories has the advantage of maximum impact and of bolstering France's image. Such habitués of the French political scene as President Senghor are intimately aware of this attitude and seek to exploit it in part by appealing to French vanity. This is the meaning of such statements by Senghor as, if aid is continued, then "France will no longer be fenced in by the limits of the hexagon."[21]

But if we look below the surface, it becomes apparent that membership in the franc zone is, for Senegal and other African countries, a guarantee for public capital. From the point of view of strictly Senegalo-French relations, there is the danger that severing the zone relationship would activate domestic French pressures of long standing that would militate against the continuation of aid, at least on the privileged scale of the past. Cartiérisme, a kind of French isolationist theory according to which French resources ought to remain at home, is usually dormant; but its potency cannot be underestimated. Further, official French policy may be moving toward greater diversification and toward ceilings for foreign assistance. Senegal has not been greatly affected by this new turn of policy, but it is likely that her leaving the franc zone would have untoward consequences.

If Senegal were to be alone in leaving the franc zone, then the French government would be placed in a dilemma similar to that experienced at the time of Guinea's independence: either to seem to reward Senegal for having left the family of nations or to take measures designed to discourage others from following suit. If, on the other hand, a large number of—or even all—French-language states were to leave the franc zone, then this action would reinforce the tendency to diversify the recipients of French aid and, in the long run, probably deprive African states of at least some of the aid which they obtain as a result of their membership in the franc zone.

The quality—and no doubt the durability—of Senegalo-French economic relations appears to be largely a function of France's continued willingness to help Senegal. On a number

21. *L'Unité africaine* (October 27, 1966).

of occasions when it appeared that the French government was reducing its commitment to Senegal, President Senghor responded with sharp criticism of French internal forces advocating French retrenchment. In 1969, for instance, he spoke out publicly against French right-wing and left-wing extremists and expressed concern about their possible impact on French investments in Senegal. It is thus not unreasonable to suggest that if France were to abandon or drastically reduce her economic commitments to black Africa, and to Senegal in particular, that country would follow the dictates of economic national interests at the expense of cultural and linguistic attachments to France.

But given the present motivations underlying continued French assistance, such drastic changes are not likely to occur in the immediate future. It would seem to make good sense for France, which cannot afford a global foreign aid role, to continue her policy of concentration in Africa, and to take hesitant steps to include carefully chosen French-speaking countries, as well as some English-speaking countries, among the recipients of her assistance. Hence, the close economic relations between Senegal and France are likely to continue for some time.

INTER-AFRICAN RELATIONS

The horizontal dimension of Senegal's economic policy centers on the development of inter-African relations. As noted earlier, in spite of a relatively sophisticated economic infrastructure, Senegal remains a small, poor country. She needs an economic space larger than that provided by her national territory to return existing manufacturing plants to their optimum viability, to expand and diversify both agriculture and industrialization, and to find markets for her exports as well as suppliers of agricultural and finished goods produced by other African countries.

Senegal has pursued these objectives in her inter-African economic policy since 1960, although political problems tend to prevent their realization, and obstacles still remain. Her African policy of economic relations may be divided into two discrete parts. One concerns relations with the larger group of former

French states: this was expressed in the promotion of the Brazzaville group, which over time underwent a series of alterations to culminate in the Organisation Commune Africaine et Malgache created in 1965. The other part of Senegal's inter-African economic policy concerns her immediate neighbors and former partners in the Federation of French West Africa (Mauritania, Mali, and Guinea) as well as North Africa. That policy was set in motion once the early political disturbances resulting from sharply defined and ideologically expressed conflicts in West Africa had receded.

The Senegal River valley

Senegal's relations with her immediate neighbors resulted in early 1968 in the creation of the Organisation des Etats Riverains du Fleuve Sénégal. Before this step could be taken, however, a number of political frictions had to be overcome, and, until 1968, the immediate objectives of Senegalese policy were directed toward overcoming these frictions. The objectives concerned essentially a rapprochement between Senegal and Mali as well as Guinea, which involved, on the part of Senegalese leaders, patience, numerous negotiations, and influence on and through the French government and, on the part of Guinea, a realization that diplomatic isolation was essentially dysfunctional for her goals.

Senegal's inter-African economic policy was defined by President Senghor at Addis Ababa during the creation of the Organization of African Unity in the following terms:

> In a first stage, we must recognize . . . complementary diversities. We will even help to organize them into regional unions. I see three of them: North Africa, West Africa, and East Africa—while waiting for the liberation of Southern Africa. Each of these unions could, in its turn, be divided into smaller unions.

Once the Mali recriminations against Senegal, following the breakup of the Mali Federation, were quiescent, Senegalese leaders took advantage of the advent of their Second Republic, at the end of 1962, to make overtures to Bamako. Some contacts had been initiated by Senegal early in 1962, but these were interrupted abruptly after the discovery of an anti-Senegalese plot by rebels allegedly based in a training camp in the Mali Republic.[22] Negotiations were subsequently initiated by Foreign Minister Doudou Thiam and followed through by special emissaries who paved the way for a symbolic reconciliation meeting of the two heads of state. Both Modibo Keita and Senghor were reconciled publicly at Addis Ababa during the creation of the Organization of African Unity in 1963. Personal communications followed and culminated in reciprocal state visits, President Senghor spending one week in Mali in December, 1965, and President Keita returning the gesture with a visit to Senegal about one year later.

More important than the fanfare which accompanied and followed these presidential visits was Keita's declaration that "if in 1958 African leaders had followed the leaders of Senegal, and specifically President Senghor, then Africa would have been spared a rather painful experience." [23] At the same time, Senegalese pressures in France helped bring about a shift in French policy toward Mali which tended to remove the most important economic obstacle to a resumption of meaningful Senegalo-Malien economic relations. That problem was the Mali franc, which, although theoretically still within the franc zone, was an exclusively domestic currency whose value in inter-African exchange was between one-half to one-third its official parity with the CFA franc. Several agreements had been signed between Mali and Senegal concerning payments of Mali debts to Senegal, but the essential inconvertibility of the Mali currency remained

22. According to Senegalese government sources, the training camp for subversion was located near Koulikoro, an outskirt of Bamako. Among those later condemned by Senegal were Doudou Guèye, a Senegalese serving as President Keita's press adviser; Ibrahima Diaw; Moustapha Seck; and five others. The Senegalese information minister, Obeye Diop, declared that he had documentary evidence showing that Senegalese dissidents were trained in Mali in commando and infiltration tactics. See West Africa, no. 2334 (February 24, 1962), p. 207; no. 2336 (March 10, 1962), p. 263; and no. 2342 (April 21, 1962), p. 431.
23. Le Monde (December 10, 1966).

the chief obstacle. By the end of 1965, the Mali leaders had agreed to cooperate closely with Senegal in such regional ventures as the development of the Senegal River valley, and seemed to have abandoned their flirtation with the thesis that the sovereignty and territorial integrity of other African states could be violated in the name of political unity or the neocolonialist struggle.

Within Senegal's policy of furthering economic cooperation with immediate neighbors, it must be regarded as one of her major foreign policy achievements to have helped persuade the French government to change its attitude of coolness toward the Mali Republic. President Senghor has repeatedly and persistently suggested to the French that it would be in their long-range interest to move toward a rapprochement with Mali since this would reinforce the economic viability of West Africa as a region, of the Senegal River Development Project, and of the former French states in West Africa as a subregion.[24] Paris finally agreed, in 1967, to increase its assistance to the Mali Republic and to facilitate the reintegration of that country into the French-language ensemble. It should be added, however, that the prospects of Mali cooperation with Senegal and with France depend also on the success of Mali government leaders to secure the long-range support of some domestic factions which regard such association with less than complete satisfaction.

In attempting to secure the full cooperation of Guinea, Senegal's policy consisted of a mixture of patience and diplomatic pressures. Patience was grounded in the belief that time was on the side of the Senegal River, and diplomacy was used chiefly to help bring about a Guinean-French rapprochement.

Despite repeated official Guinean agreements to cooperate with Senegal within the OERS framework, the postindependence period was nonetheless marred by a strong undercurrent of Guinean hostility toward Senegal. The problem is partly structural since the success of OERS depends to a large extent on the member states' relations with France. The lack of common,

24. See, for example, Philippe Herreman's report in *ibid.* (April 28, 1966).

convertible currencies and the general restrictions on the movement of goods and persons are obstacles which could be surmounted in the short run only by common attitudes toward France.

Guinea's past hostility toward Senegal is rooted in a number of causes, reflecting preindependence and postindependence domestic, inter-African, and international problems. First, Guinean leaders believed that Senegal should have rejected the 1958 French constitution because that document did not permit the African states to become independent officially. Second, Guinea taxed Senegal with being a valet of imperialism because she preferred negotiations to other means of ending such conflicts as the Algerian liberation war.

Third, Guinea believed that the former Belgian Congo needed the support of other African states even if this meant opposing the legally constituted government of that country. Fourth, Guinea broke diplomatic relations with Britain over what she considered the dastardly failure of the British to settle the illegal Rhodesian rebellion by force, and she reproached the Senegalese leaders for not having followed suit. Fifth, Guinea and Senegal have for some years backed different segments of the nationalists in Portuguese Guinea. And, finally, President Touré became extremely sensitive to the possibility of internal subversion and regarded Senegal as a likely breeding ground and base of operations for anti-Touré forces.

On the surface, Guinean leaders had agreed to support Senghor's proposal concerning a concerted development of the Senegal River, whose source is in Guinea. President Touré had a number of meetings with President Senghor in which they declared their willingness to cooperate; joint Senegalo-Guinean bilateral talks took place regularly four times a year. But irritants remained and dominated the two countries' relations. Some of these irritants were removed in the course of events: the Algerians gained independence, the Congo settled down to less turbulent times, and Senegal shifted support to the nationalist group in Portuguese Guinea, which was also supported in Conakry.

Guinea's animosity toward Senegal reached a high point in June, 1966, when Conakry accused Senegal of harboring, training, and sending into Guinea large numbers of dissident Guineans specially trained by French instructors at a secret base to overthrow Sékou Touré. For the first time, Guinean government sources attacked President Senghor personally and publicly and demanded that Senegal apologize. The Guineans were disturbed by the series of military coups d'état in Africa, particularly by the overthrow of Nkrumah. They contended that some thirty truckloads of rebels, trained by French specialists at a secret camp near Saint-Louis, were loaded onto railroad cars fully armed and left Thiaroye in the direction of Tambacounda and Linguère near the Guinean frontier. This was flatly denied by the Senegalese government, which pointed out that it had prohibited an older undercover organization, Solidarité Guinéenne, and the newly created Regroupement des Guinéens au Sénégal from operating on Senegalese territory. It is understandable that the Guinean government was concerned, since there are some three hundred thousand Guinean residents in Senegal, and since one of the leaders of the Regroupement is David Soumah, a Guinean trade union leader who claims that Touré tried to have him assassinated.

Following Guinea's abrupt refusal to attend the First World Festival of Negro Arts and Literature, held in Dakar in April, 1966, these accusations were not tolerated by Senegal. Senghor announced the suspension of bilateral cooperation with Guinea —thus not affecting the Senegal River scheme—and closed the Senegalese embassy in Conakry, ostensibly for financial reasons.[25] Probably the most potent reason for Guinea's volte-face in her relations with Senegal was the increasing isolation of Sékou Touré in Africa. During the 1968 annual congress of the ruling party, the Guineans decided to change their policy and henceforth to cooperate with neighboring countries and to seek a rapprochement with France as well.

The Organisation des Etats Riverains du Fleuve Sénégal i

25. According to sources close to President Senghor, there are two things for which he will never forgive Touré. One is the boycott of the Festival, which Radio Guinea reportedly described as the "Festival des Sales Nègres," and the other is that the Guinean ambassador in Dakar was allegedly the only one who did not congratulate him for having escaped an assassination attempt in March, 1967.

a framework for the future development of the river valley. Its realization depends mostly on foreign assistance. The studies made so far envisage three major objectives for the project. One is year-round river transportation from its mouth at Saint-Louis to the Mali city of Kayes; another is expansion of agricultural production through irrigation and regulation of the river's flow; and the third is inexpensive electric power which could be used not only for domestic consumption but also for industrializing the river valley.[26] For Senegal's own economic development, the realization of the river valley project is of enormous potential importance. It will revitalize, and hence tend to integrate nationally from the points of view of economics and politics, the populations along the river's right bank. It will end the country's long dependence on imports for staple foods and release critical foreign exchange for development purposes, and it will increase export revenue by sales of surplus agricultural commodities and whatever manufacturing enterprises can be located in the valley.

The conclusion of the four-nation agreement to create the OERS was accompanied by a certain euphoria. Thus, Sékou Touré said that "all that is contrary to the interests of the four states must in the future be averted by each state." President Senghor declared that "little by little we shall build in this part of the continent a model organization, a model confederation, and why not tomorrow a model federation?" [27] In spite of this exaggerated optimism, the foundation was nonetheless laid for a future regional cooperation scheme based on the material interests of all participants. Although the OERS is not a supra-

---

26. The United Nations Special Fund, after preliminary studies begun in 1962, granted a subsidy of $5.8 million for studies of the technical aspects of the regional project. Plans envisage the construction of four dams: the most important at Gouina in Mali, and others at Saint-Louis and Saldé in Senegal, and at Tougé in Guinea. Other aspects of the project include the modernization of the port facilities at Gouina and at Saint-Louis, the latter having access to neither the sea, because of sandbars, nor the Dakar–Saint-Louis railroad; Saint-Louis, in fact, has been an economic backwater ever since the development of the city of Dakar, and lost its last claim to distinction when Dakar replaced it as Senegal's capital city shortly before independence.

27. L'Unité africaine (March 28, 1968).

national organization, its charter mirrors a concern with aspects of economic development transcending its immediate purpose. The charter provides at least a framework within which such problems as joint planning and development of the four national economies and educational, social, and cultural problems can be tackled in addition to the development of the river basin per se.[28] The eventual success of the OERS nonetheless depends on the quality of political relations among the member states and on the ability of Guinea's partners to convince that country of the value of future benefits. Guinea's official statements about the OERS have used political language, reflecting in part that country's limited material stake in developing the Senegal River valley. After 1968, President Senghor began lobbying the French government to help bring about a Guinean-French rapprochement since that would facilitate Guinea's cooperation within the OERS. One of the most crucial questions involved is whether Guinea would agree to rejoin the franc zone, a step from which she has shied away in the past, partly because it might be construed as a blow to her prestige as a "revolutionary," path-breaking African nation. That the Guineans and the Senegalese were still far apart in 1968 was evident when Sékou Touré, as the first president of the OERS, declared that the organization "must become a unitary state as soon as possible," whereas Senghor would not go beyond the suggestion that it may eventually become a federation.[29]

The Gambia

Relations between The Gambia and Senegal are a testament to the European balkanization of Africa. Other things being equal,

28. The OERS, a "confederation" of sovereign states, is headed by the Conference of Heads of State and Government, which defines joint policy and makes decisions unanimously. It is assisted by the Council of Ministers as an organ of execution responsible to the conference; and the administrative executive secretary supervises the activities of three General Secretariats: (1) on the River Basin, (2) on Planning and Development, and (3) on Educational, Social, and Cultural Affairs; finally, there is a Joint Parliamentary Commission with a mandate to inform state legislatures on joint developments. See ibid. (April 4, 1968).
29. Afrique nouvelle (March 28–April 3, 1968).

there should be no major obstacle to closer cooperation, and eventual integration, between the two countries. The preponderance of peanut production and the parent ethnic groups inhabiting the region suggest the possibility of a kind of Wolof League. But for the immediate future the two countries are intent on pursuing their separate development. This is largely —though not exclusively—the result of Gambian fears of losing their identity, now distinct from surrounding Senegal, which has twenty times the area and ten times the population of the small Gambian enclave.

The major obstacles to closer mutual relations have been summarized, in the words of one astute observer, as resulting from the colonial era, which "gave Gambia and Senegal different identities, and the resultant distinctions [which] made the rapid achievement of closer association almost impossible." [30] The Senegalese attitude is perhaps best expressed by a widely used current phrase, that Senegal and The Gambia are "condemned to live together." Both countries have so far preferred to maintain their separate educational, administrative, judicial, fiscal, and economic systems inherited from their respective mother countries. Their relations have consequently been more casual, characterized by few official overtures, and all encounters have been marked by "frankness and cordiality" but relatively little substance.

Cultural and political considerations rank high among the obstacles to closer cooperation. Whereas Senegal's elites retain a considerable attachment to elements of French civilization, those of The Gambia have remained comparatively isolated from other African areas. Gambia's capital city has been described as a "cloistered community, satisfied with its own fashion of life and resistance to change threatening . . . a possible loss of British identity." [31] Their mutual relations at times exhibit an almost palpable "my colonial power is better than your colonial power" attitude and display not merely vigilance but distrust of

30. Claude E. Welch, Jr., *Dream of Unity: Pan-Africanism and Political Unification in West Africa* (Ithaca: Cornell University Press, 1966), p. 260. Also see Harry E. Gailey, *A History of The Gambia* (New York: Praeger, 1965).
31. Welch, *Dream of Unity*, p. 269.

the other side's real intentions. Perhaps the major obstacle is a concern for retaining autonomy within present political borders, especially potent on the part of Gambian leaders who fear being swallowed up by their more powerful neighbor. That concern was reinforced after Gambian independence in February, 1965, and nourished by the occasionally cavalier attitude of some Senegalese officials.

Moreover, security considerations exert a centrifugal pull. Both countries are still cautious as a result of the experience of the Mali Federation, which they consider a dangerous example of external interference in domestic affairs. Senegal is fearful lest a weak, hostile Gambian government be used as a base for subversion, and has been particularly sensitive to the alleged activities of Portuguese agents in The Gambia. Since Gambians are not likely to accept any option to become a simple province of Senegal, Senegal is also apprehensive of the possible repercussions on Casamance of an arrangement allowing The Gambia more autonomy than parts of Senegal were the two states to agree on some type of political integration.

Economic cooperation with The Gambia has proved more difficult to achieve than a glance at the map would indicate. The general economic reasons favoring closer cooperation include, for The Gambia, slim prospects for viability as a lone entity as well as the similarity between her economic structure and Senegal's, in the sense that her chief export is also the peanut; and, for Senegal, her present inability to make use of the Gambia River to transport her peanuts at lower cost, and the possibilities of joint development of the river valley for irrigation and, possibly, hydroelectric purposes.

There are, however, other economic factors which tend to be centrifugal. Chief among these are, for The Gambia, her liberal trade policy, considerable income from smuggling consumer goods into Senegal, the reluctance of the EEC to absorb her peanuts, and the likely opposition of EEC African Associated States to The Gambia's inclusion among the beneficiaries of the European Development Fund; and, for Senegal, the knotty problems of harmonizing her restrictive trade policies to bring material advantages to The Gambia. Moreover, the combination of the difficulties involved detract from the chances of securing investments needed to develop the Gambia River valley. Since it appears questionable whether mutual benefits can result from a free trade area, both countries have agreed to restrict cooperation to "first steps" based on treaty arrangements which can lead to gradually increasing and mutually satisfactory results.

Senegal's policy toward The Gambia has been cautious in spite of the great potential economic importance of close cooperation. The Gambia, perhaps more than any other African state, is an incoherent anomaly whose only raison d'être is past colonial Franco-British rivalry. The Gambia River is the only one in West Africa deep enough for the inland navigation (some 250 miles) of vessels drawing up to twenty feet. Its importance for Senegal derives from its course in an area of Senegal which can be developed economically only if it can be traveled without the political obstacles of national sovereignty. It is an important outlet for agricultural goods and could serve for the transportation of cotton and sisal. Senegalese officials regard the use of the Gambia River as a cornerstone for the economic development of the Casamance region, and for marble and iron deposits that could be exploited with inexpensive water transportation assured.

North Africa

In view of the political obstacles to beneficial economic relations with her immediate neighbors (Mauritania excepted) in the years following independence, Senegal concentrated on closer ties with two North African countries, Tunisia and Morocco. With Tunisia, Senegal signed a trade agreement in 1961 and eight more cooperation agreements between then and 1966; Senegal also signed trade agreements with Morocco, one in 1961 and another in 1963, as well as a cultural agreement in 1963. Morocco was the only independent African state—except Rhodesia and South Africa—against which Senegal enforced economic sanctions; but this measure was only temporary and was removed after Senegalo-Moroccan differences were settled.[32] In fact, Tunisia and Morocco are the only countries with which Senegal has signed "friendship" treaties to underline her close relations with them, the result partly of personal ties between Presidents Senghor and Bourguiba and King Hassan II, and partly of mutually advantageous commerce. To judge from the published trade figures between Senegal and the three North African countries (including Algeria), trade has declined since Senegalese independence, both absolutely and relatively. Of Senegal's total inter-African trade, the share of her exports to North Africa decreased from 18 per cent in 1962 to 5 per cent in 1966, and the share of her imports was 28 per cent for both years after a peak of 51 per cent in 1964. Nonetheless, this exchange has remained third in importance in Africa, generally after the Ivory Coast and Madagascar.

OCAM

Another facet of Senegal's inter-African economic policy is mirrored in her initiatives, and subsequent active participation, regarding an association of French-speaking African states to coordinate common economic, technical, and cultural interests. Such an organization resulted from a preliminary meeting of twelve states in Abidjan in October, 1960, and had grown to fourteen members by 1968. President Senghor took the initiative in mid-September, 1960, less than a month after the collapse of the Mali Federation, by sending Prime Minister

32. After the 1963 discovery of anti-Senegal subversion attempts by a small group allegedly trained in Mali and implicating Morocco, Senegal applied "general" rather than the normal "minimum" customs duties to Moroccan goods as a reprisal. These restrictions have since been lifted. The Senegalese government has issued bans on all trade with Rhodesia and on imports from South Africa. Senegal still exports some phosphates to South Africa since she has to sell to whoever buys her exports. See Senegal, "Décret 63-524 du 17 juillet 1963 portant interdiction d'importation des produits originaires de l'Union Sud-Africaine ou en provenance du Portugal et de l'Union Sud-Africaine," JORS (August 3, 1963), p. 1051; and "Décret 67-463 du 28 avril 1967 portant interdiction de tout commerce avec la Rhodésie," ibid. (May 20, 1967), p. 713.

Mamadou Dia to confer with President Houphouet-Boigny of the Ivory Coast and to propose the creation of an "entente-like association" to promote cooperation in financial, economic, cultural, and technical matters.[33] This overture represented an abrupt shift in Senegal's inter-African policy. As noted earlier, Senghor championed political federalism between the end of 1956 and August, 1960. When it became clear that political unification in Africa would not work, he changed his orientation to one of functional cooperation among sovereign states, suggesting that Houphouet-Boigny take the leadership because Senghor was in no position to do so after the Mali failure.

Since political means of inter-African cooperation proved to be divisive, it was agreed to emphasize nonpolitical mutual interests. Before agreeing to a charter for the Union Africaine et Malgache (UAM) at Tananarive in September, 1961, the Brazzaville twelve created the most important of its specialized agencies, the Organisation Africaine et Malgache de Coopération Economique (OAMCE), in March, 1961, at a Yaoundé meeting; at the same time, they approved plans to create a common airline, Air Afrique, and named a Senegalese, Cheikh Fall, as its director.

The UAM was transformed under the impact of political events, but Senegal generally retained her emphasis on nonpolitical questions. The association was retained after the creation of the Organization of African Unity in 1963, transformed into the Union Africaine et Malgache de Coopération Economique (UAMCE) in March, 1964, at Dakar, then into the Organisation Commune Africaine et Malgache (OCAM) in February, 1965, at Nouakchott, Mauritania.

In spite of numerous organizational changes and political problems, the association has demonstrated its usefulness for its partners.[34] OCAM has retained two specialized organiza-

33. See *Afrique nouvelle* (September 28, October 5, 14, 1960). The political objectives of the organization—and its successors—will be discussed in the following chapter.

34. OCAM members are Cameroun, the Central African Republic, both Congos (Kinshasa-Congo joined in May, 1965), the Ivory Coast, Dahomey, Gabon, Upper Volta, Madagascar, Niger, Rwanda, Senegal, Chad, and Togo.

tions concerned with economic and technical problems (in addition to Air Afrique), the Union Africaine et Malgache des Postes et Télécommunications (UAMPT), with headquarters in Brazzaville, and the OAMCE, with headquarters in Yaoundé. The UAMPT serves chiefly to improve, create, and maintain communication links, and the OAMCE to coordinate economic activities.

Within Africa, OCAM members have so far agreed to improve inter-African trade: they have approved plans for a livestock and meat market and have instituted a common sugar market. The sugar agreement is a temporary measure designed to help OCAM's two major sugar exporters, Madagascar and the Brazzaville-Congo, overcome the transition period which follows the end of French subsidies for their sugar exports. It is therefore primarily a symbolic manifestation of OCAM solidarity. Senegal makes an annual financial contribution to the sugar market budget and has agreed to purchase an annual sugar quota from the inter-OCAM market. In a few years it is expected that Senegal's domestic needs will be covered by its own refineries, but it has been suggested that OCAM sugar be refined in Africa instead of in France to decrease costs and make OCAM states self-sufficient.

OCAM's primary concern in 1968 was the trade relations of the fourteen member states with Europe. OCAM president Hamani Diori was given a mandate to be the members' chief negotiator in Brussels for the renewal of the EEC Association; each state prepared position papers and sent them to Diori in an attempt to bring about a common bargaining position toward the EEC. Moreover, at their summit meeting in January, 1968, at Niamey, OCAM heads of state also agreed to press their common interests at the second of the United Nations Conferences on Trade and Development (UNCTAD). While deciding to act as a pressure group to represent their common economic interests, OCAM leaders made it clear no one should expect miracles from this type of coordination. But the extent of the coordination itself may be expected to bring about more

---

Mauritania withdrew from OCAM in July, 1965, but retained membership in the specialized organizations.

positive results than could separate démarches by fourteen individual states.[35]

The Poor and the Rich

Senegal and the Third World

In the past few years, the Senegalese government has become increasingly sensitive to stresses between the vertical and horizontal dimensions of the country's economic foreign policy. The stresses concern, first, the deterioration of the terms of trade of the developing nations, an issue which places these states in a position of relative unity against the developed, or wealthier, states; and, second, the common interests of the African states associated with the EEC, which seek to improve the terms of their association at the expiration of the Yaoundé Convention signed in 1963.

As have other developing states, Senegal has repeatedly emphasized the importance which she attaches to trade as contrasted to the transfer of capital and expertise. It goes without saying that foreign assistance will continue to be necessary for Senegal for some years to come, and Senegal recognizes the paramount role of technical assistance in the modernization process. Nonetheless, foreign trade has commanded an increasing amount of attention. From the point of view of its share of total income from foreign sources alone, trade appears to be crucial for the Senegalese economy. The total value of Senegal's postindependence exports, from 1961 to 1966 inclusive, amounts to 186.9 billion CFA francs; her income from public bilateral and multilateral assistance, by contrast, approximates 87.5 billion CFA francs, or less than half the previous figure.

Of greater import than this comparison, however, are the problems arising from the decline of her purchasing power.

---

35. In the words of Houphouet-Boigny, "We shall be taken seriously only to the extent that we are serious"; "We have interests to be served— the interests of our peoples. If it is true that 'man does not live by bread alone,' it is equally true that he cannot live on words." *Africa Report*, XIII, no. 2 (February, 1968), 55.

This phenomenon Senegal ascribes to the "deterioration of the terms of trade," which has become a major concern of the developing nations and which found expression in the United Nations Conferences on Trade and Development. Prior to the first UNCTAD meeting in the summer of 1964, President Senghor defined his views as follows:

> We think that, in the twentieth century, the essential problem, the essential cleavage, is that between underdeveloped and developed countries.
> The fact is that aid from developed countries, be they from the East or West, is inferior to the losses we sustain each year from the prices for raw materials: This is the essential truth and, so long as the world has not resolved this difficulty, we shall not go very far.[36]

Senegalese leaders argue that the revenue they derive from the export of primary goods has declined, whereas the price paid for imports has increased. As indicated earlier, the quantity of Senegal's exports between 1961 and 1966 increased by 42 per cent, whereas its value increased by less than 20 per cent. By comparison, the increase of imports during that period amounted to 5.4 per cent in quantity and to 3.6 per cent in value. In 1967, the Senegalese government published a study of how the deterioration of the terms of trade had affected the country. By comparing price indices for imports and exports, the study found that, taking 1957 as a base (100), the price index for imports had risen to 112.3, whereas that for exports had only risen to 102.7 by 1965. The study points out that Senegal's purchasing power declined by 8.5 per cent in eight years. Had it not been for external price supports, that decline would have amounted to 25.6 per cent for the same period.[37]

Moreover, artificial barriers to trade have prevented or made more difficult the sale of primary products as well as inhibited the production, by developing nations, of manufactures for export. The losses resulting from the gap, moreover, offset capital

36. L'Unité africaine (January 8, 1964).
37. "Commerce extérieur du Sénégal," mimeographed (Dakar: Service de la Statistique, 1967), pp. 34–35.

transfers from the rich to the poor nations. Consequently, along with that of other poor nations, the economy of Senegal remains "dominated" by, and is at the mercy of, the rich nations. As President Senghor put it, the fundamental reason for this disparity is the "egoism of the rich nations, which profit from injustice and deliberately prolong it." [38]

The problems of the poor nations do not stem from trade alone. At a time when trade is becoming more difficult and less remunerative for the poor nations, the rich nations appear to be saying, "Less trade and less aid." There are dangers that the so-called development decade will be followed, for want of having accomplished its aims, by one of despair. Mindful of rich nations' apparently increasing reluctance to continue their aid programs at a pace clearly recommended to them by the United Nations, President Senghor told his people in January, 1966:

> The Revolution of 1960, consecrating the principle of self-determination, which has liberated, massively, the former colonies, is not yet six years old and the rich nations already proclaim that they are tired of helping the poor nations. And thus they harmonize, for once, their actions and their words by effectively diminishing their aid. To take a significant example, on the morrow of World War II, during the time of the Marshall Plan, the U.S.A. with a national product of one fourth of today, earmarked $5 million for foreign aid. Now the American Congress voted, for the present fiscal year, only $3.36 million for economic and military aid.[39]

Senegalese leaders have suggested two solutions to trade problems, in addition to redoubling domestic efforts toward modernization and development. One solution—the long-term aspect—involves the world's rich nations and aims eventually at restructuring the world economy. Far from being the result of "free" economic forces beyond the control of men, the problem is sim-

38. "Ouverture de la première session du conseil économique et social de 1967," mimeographed (Dakar, March 15, 1967), p. 25.

39. "Exécution du 2ème plan quadriennal de développement économique et social," mimeographed (Dakar, 1966), p. 122.

ply the consequence of the rich nations' monopoly on world trade. Senegal is particularly sensitive to suggestions about a "free world market," which, like "free world prices," exists only in the mind of those nations which manipulate the world economic system for their own benefit.

Consequently, what is needed is the extension of the notion of human solidarity to the entire world, meaning chiefly to the rich nations. Senghor recognizes that there is nothing unusual about disparities between rich and poor and points out that human solidarity operates to redress the injustice within the boundaries of national societies. What is needed, therefore, is for the spirit of solidarity to cross these narrow, artificial national frontiers and to become operative for the benefit of mankind. As former Foreign Minister Doudou Thiam explained it,

> A world proletariat on the order of 75% of the population of the globe, disposing for their livelihood of only 15% of the world's revenue—85% of that revenue benefiting only one quarter of the world's population—this is the aberration.[40]

The strategy adopted to further these objectives reveals both realism and idealism. Realism is reflected in the assessment of the chances for the poor nations to influence the rich. The poor, by definition, have no power which they can bring to bear on others. An attitude suggesting that to count on the Third World countries to "bring the rich nations to their knees to make the desired concessions is utopian." [41] Senegal's strategy was defined as follows by President Senghor:

> Faced with this situation, how must we react, we of the Third World, we the proletarian nations? We must admit that, until now, we have not reacted: we were content to vituperate singly, "imperialism, colonialism, and neocolonialism." As if words, even words of vengeance, could kill this three-headed hydra. As for me, I see only one strategy which is efficient in resolving the problem: let the entire

40. *L'Unité africaine* (October 12, 1967).
41. Senghor, in *ibid.* (December 1, 1966).

Third World, all proletarian nations, unite. Not to insult, but to talk; at first among themselves and then, united in a common front, with the rich nations. To enter a dialogue, of course, but also to act in concert.[42]

Nothing suggests that Senegal has any illusions that the unity of the Third World countries, with their widely divergent interests and attitudes, will come about merely by dint of exhortation. Senghor alluded to this in a speech before the Senegalese Economic and Social Council: "But you know how much this enterprise, which would be only justice, appears illusory in the near future." [43]

It was this concern for injustice which explains the prominent role Senegal went on to play in connection with the trade issue. Senegal acted as cosponsor—with India—of the second UNCTAD conference in New Delhi early in 1968. Emissaries traveled to foreign countries in an effort to coordinate at least a basic outlook on the Third World's response. And Senegal advocated, then sponsored, the poor nations' conference to prepare for the confrontation in New Delhi; President Senghor, with his usual political finesse, suggested that it be held in Algiers, the capital of a "revolutionary" country. The meeting, which took place in December, 1967, bore the imprint of Senegal: it spread the term *economic Bandung*, which originated in Dakar; it was permeated with a new militancy resulting from the common objective articulated by Senghor; and it secured for Senegal increasing international prestige throughout the developing areas.

If the poor nations of the world have no power, and if the prospects of galvanizing them into common action are not good, then we may well ask in what the strategy consists. In full recognition of the existing handicaps, it is aimed at the moral fiber of the rich. One of the uses of dialogue in international affairs, in the absence of more concrete levers, is to manipulate ideas. Verbal assaults run the risk of alienating the recipients. Hence, the Senegalese strategy places the accent on attempts to convince others of the merits of her case. If they are reminded, time after time, of the plight of their fellow men, of the shame of exploita-

42. "Exécution du 2ème plan quadriennal," p. 123.
43. "Ouverture de la première session du conseil," p. 25.

tion, and of the economic advantages of more well-to-do partners that buy more, the perceptions which control their actions will, hopefully, change and so will their actions. For good measure, Senegal occasionally raised the specter of violent conflict should the rich remain unresponsive—although this addendum was probably intended more to mobilize sluggish Third World countries and to placate and attract domestic pressures than to frighten Washington or Moscow.[44] "If the rich nations," in the words of Senghor, "believe in the dangers associated with such a division of the world, then their conscience will be awakened and they will respond." [45] For all the uncertainties beclouding Senegal's policy, a strategy of moral pressure is preferable to no strategy; what common attitudes and actions may thus be generated are preferable to no common attitude and action; and what results this policy may reap will be, one hopes, preferable to no result.

To be sure, the results obtained thus far by the United Nations Conferences on Trade and Development are something less than spectacular. If nothing else, however, the activities of Senegal have contributed to the articulation and consciousness of a major international problem and to the institutionalization of the world community's economic revisionists. Progress is being made; development takes place. But the problem is a relative one: it concerns the rapidity and scope of progress and the increasing gap between the eighty-eight poor and thirty-three rich countries.

The total value of developing states' exports has decreased and continues to decrease relative to the world's total exports. From 31 per cent in 1948, it dropped to less than 20 per cent in 1966.

44. Thus Senghor told a domestic audience that there is "a last argument: the Third World includes 2 billion men of a total of 3.3 billion. Not to help them, to continue to impoverish them while the rich nations become richer, is to push them toward despair, toward any adventure, including that of the Third World War, which would mean the end of our humanity." "Exécution du 2ème plan quadriennal," pp. 124–25. Cf. Senghor's statement on the eve of the New Delhi UNCTAD conference: "It is certain that, should the Third World be backed against hunger and despair, then it could turn only toward China and take with it the road of misery and revolt." *Jeune afrique*, no. 370 (February 2–11, 1968), p. 17.

45. *L'Unité africaine* (March 2, 1967).

The share of developing countries' exports in primary products—foodstuffs and beverages, not minerals—was nearly 45 per cent in 1953, but 5 per cent less twelve years later. Moreover, as is well known, developing countries stand to benefit only indirectly—if at all—from the reduction of external tariffs for industrial goods which followed the Kennedy round of negotiations; presumably, exchanges among advanced nations will increase their growth rate and their demand for primary products.

The Algiers Charter of the developing countries, which Senegal supported, was the planning stage for the organized protest of UNCTAD in New Delhi in February, 1968. The demands formulated by the eighty-eight fall into three categories: (1) negotiation of a new international agreement on primary products; (2) preferential tariffs for manufactured goods exported by developing to developed countries; and (3) increased financial assistance to reflect the previously set objective of reaching 1 per cent of the developed countries' Gross National Product. What these amount to is a fundamental revision of the present reluctance of the rich to help the poor. What they are saying is that present international cooperation is insufficient and that it must be improved through a global approach (including increased participation by the socialist countries).

At the same time, the Third World framework served to reinforce the conviction of such countries as Senegal that the international system must provide benefits at least equal to those which they receive through association with the European Common Market before they could consider realistically abandoning that association. For all the theoretical appeal of a global approach to solve these economic problems, the present realities of the Eurafrican Association spell protection and benefits not otherwise available. Consequently, Senegal continues to advocate that present protection and benefits not be given up without a viable alternative.

Senegal and the EEC

The second solution—the short-run aspect—to economic imbalance suggested by Senghor concerns the EEC. While the impact of ideas designed to coax more justice out of the world economic system runs its course, Senegal's economic foreign policy has maintained the more concrete relationship with the EEC, more susceptible of bringing immediate results. The initial association of Senegal and thirteen other African states with the European Common Market took place without their consent shortly after the signature of the Rome Treaty in 1957 and was thus the result of colonial history. The association was renegotiated at Yaoundé, Cameroun, in 1963, and thus placed on a contractual basis among partners legally expressing their free choice as independent states. It was renegotiated in 1969 after the expiration of the 1963 agreement, and the period preceding 1969 therefore presented an opportunity for the African Associated States (now numbering eighteen) to pressure for desired changes. For Senegal, as for the other associates, the question was not whether to continue the association—other African states were admitted or are knocking at the door. The question was, rather, under what conditions to continue it, that is, what concessions could be obtained in 1969 which would most benefit the Associated States.

The importance of EEC association to Senegal is largely rooted in the nature of her economy. Barring acceptable alternatives, Senegal is dependent on the EEC countries for the bulk of her export earnings and of foreign public and private investment. This dependence had been understood by Senegal's leaders long before national independence. Senghor's interest in Eurafrican ties dates back to the time when he became conscious of his country's economic needs. In 1949, for instance, he complained that the French delegation to the Council of Europe did not include an African representative. He therefore reminded the French legislature of the existence of the French Union and of the economic needs and interests of the African territories:

> We wish that, among the French delegates, there also be representatives of the Overseas Territories, in order to remind not only other European delegates, but also the metropolitan delegates, of their duties toward the French Union. . . .
> Let the Council of Europe not forget. Let it, also, have

among its major preoccupations that of liberating Africa from misery, illness, and ignorance.[46]

At least two methods of changing the nature of the association after independence were considered, and rejected, because of their questionable chances for success. One was transformation into a really free trade association. Such a free association would be discriminatory in practice against the interests of some African states: it would favor the relatively wealthy at the expense of those which need the association most. Further, it would also draw strong objections from other Third World countries for very much the same reasons. Another change, considered in the light of the new association agreement signed between the EEC and Nigeria, was for the EEC countries to dissociate public capital assistance from trade relations. But this would have meant their abandoning the European Development Fund as a wedge to obtain trade concessions in Africa among the eighteen Associated States.

The only option open to the Senegalese, then, was to seek to influence the EEC, in combination with other OCAM states, to modify at least some aspects of their policies. In cooperation with OCAM, Senegal therefore walked the thin line of persuasion in which one of her chief arguments was the Europeans' concern lest they be openly labeled neocolonialist by the Associated States. In short, Senegal's policy toward EEC association was to maintain the general structure for want of a viable alternative, but to try to improve the terms.

The major grievances of the associates concern price stabilization and minimum quotas for their exports into the EEC. As with world markets, Senegal and other associates argued for continued, and increased, protection of their goods in the markets of Europe. Their demands were presented through the common front of the Organisation Commune Africaine et Malgache, which gave its president, Niger's Hamani Diori, the mandate to represent its interests vis-à-vis the EEC. In addition

46. "Recueil des interventions faites à l'assemblée nationale française par le Président Léopold Sédar Senghor de 1946 à 1958 en sa qualité de Député du Sénégal," mimeographed (Dakar, n.d. [1967?]), p. 25.

to this concerted pressure on Brussels, OCAM states are active in the association's Parliamentary Conference, a body made up of legislators from EEC and associated countries.

Associate members' complaints regarding trade with the EEC have been directed to the fact that their exports to EEC countries, between 1958 and 1966, rose at a rate of only 3 per cent, whereas EEC imports from Asia rose over 5 per cent and those from Latin America increased over 8 per cent during the same period. The value of Senegalese imports from EEC countries other than France has steadily increased since independence: from 3.7 billion CFA francs in 1961 to 6.6 billion CFA francs in 1968. By contrast, the value of Senegal's exports to that area decreased after 1961, until, as a result of a sudden fourfold increase in sales of unrefined vegetable products, the level increased in 1966. It is obviously in Senegal's interests to be able to sell more of her products to the European countries with which she is associated. But Senegal maintained a deficit trade balance with EEC countries other than France after independence; this deficit varied from 1.7 billion CFA francs in 1961 to 3.5 billion CFA francs in 1968, and averaged approximately 3.2 billion CFA francs per annum. By 1968, her total trade deficit with these countries amounted to over 24 billion CFA francs, which exceeded the capital committed to her by the European Development Fund during the period, a fund to which France, incidentally, contributes one-third.

Unfortunately, Senegal's difficult problem of doing without the French *surprix* for her agricultural exports comes at a time when there is an increasing interest in Europe for other vegetable oils. European countries have accented production and use of oils from sunflowers, rapeseeds, and soy beans; these have been imported into EEC countries from eastern Europe, and France herself reportedly has built two new refinery plants to handle the new imports. The entry into—and acceptance by— European Common Market countries of peanut oil is therefore handicapped in two ways. First, only the French consumer has so far developed a taste for peanut oil; and, second, what chances the Senegalese product has of gaining the favor of other Europeans are made more precarious because of competition from other oils which modern technology makes virtually tasteless and, presumably, unobjectionable.

Other grievances presented by Senegal and the associates to the EEC include the reduction of domestic EEC tariffs on primary products (some years ago the Ivory Coast caused a ripple in Afro-European relations by pointing out that West Germany earned more from domestic taxes on imported Ivoirien coffee than she spent on foreign aid to the Ivory Coast), assistance in opening markets for African manufactures, and a more equitable distribution of the capital disbursed by the EDF. In the words of a Senegalese official, Senegal looks forward to "better justice which would end the pillage of our national economies, operated for the benefit of international trusts without giving even the European consumer a meaningful advantage." [47]

Finally, the Associated States are subject to inter-European quarrels which have unfavorable repercussions in Africa. Some EEC states, for instance, used their trade relations with the Associated States as a means of pressure on France in connection with President de Gaulle's veto of British entry; and West Germany's dissatisfaction with her parsimonious share of EDF-supported contracts in Africa has been a bone of contention affecting a project vital to Senegal's development, Dakar's water supply from the Guiers Lake.

To sum up, it is instructive to look briefly at the difficulties Senegal is experiencing in her foreign economic relations in the light of available remedies. These difficulties may be classified into four overlapping categories. The first is dependence on the external environment, the result of monoculture. The second is decreasing amounts of aid from the wealthy countries. The third is the deterioration of the terms of trade, a problem directly connected with the nature and structure of the world

47. Daniel Cabou in *L'Unité africaine* (December 21, 1967). On the 1969 negotiations to renew the association, see I. William Zartman, "The EEC's New Deal with Africa," *Africa Report*, Vol. XV, no. 2 (February, 1970). The discussion of Senegal's trade with the EEC less France is based on *Mémento de l'économie africaine*, 1967, p. 305; and *Bulletin statistique et économique mensuel*, nos. 4, 5, 1967, pp. 21, 30, nos. 11, 12, 1969, pp. 19–30.

economy. And the final difficulty is the economic nationalism of the new African states which followed political independence.

In the case of the first two factors, dependence and less foreign assistance, the remedy is diversification of Senegal's internal economy and of foreign and trade sources. For the terms-of-trade problem, the remedy is a fundamental change in the world economy. And in the case of inter-African trade relations, the remedy is regionalism as a steppingstone to subsequent wider African unity.

Remedies to all four sets of problems are being sought and pursued simultaneously by the Senegalese government. That she has been able to make comparatively little progress reflects, partly, a certain lack of initiative on her part, but also, and probably in much greater measure, her dependence on the international economic system. All four sets of problems have pulled Senegal, in the short run, toward a reinforcement of the protective framework inherited from the colonial past. Diversification, both internal and external, occurred chiefly through the framework, namely, the EEC. Likewise, the structure of worldwide trade relations and the African states' economic nationalism have also pulled Senegal toward the protective framework: the EEC offers both substantial trade and aid, and OCAM states are becoming susceptible to more regional cooperation. By contrast, the international economic system (including the socialist states) has not demonstrated much willingness to exert great efforts to offer a satisfactory alternative for the benefits which Senegal presently derives from the protective framework.

To be sure, there is some evidence that, in the long run, Senegal will be able to accomplish her foreign economic objectives. But in the short run, Senegal could give up the protection which she enjoys only at some risk to the welfare and standard of living of her people. The few examples of African states which have taken the plunge into immediate diversification of all economic foreign currents, whether willingly or not, are not sufficiently convincing to invite emulation. Until the external environment is willing to adjust itself, to respond to the needs of such developing states as Senegal, there appears to be no viable alternative but to follow the broad course set by that country's foreign economic policy: to work for improvements by stages while maintaining whatever ties are needed in the short run.

Senegal's economic foreign policy since independence has a number of achievements to its credit. As indicated earlier in this chapter, Senegal's economy is being diversified from the point of view of both foreign assistance and trade, despite the overall dearth of domestic resources. To be sure, some of the diversification must be ascribed to purely external factors over which Senegal has little or no influence and to which she merely adjusted herself. These external factors include the increasing competitiveness of the French economy and the decreasing importance of the franc zone, as well as the willingness of EEC countries to take over some of France's aid and trade interests in Africa.

At the same time, some postindependence improvement was the result of Senegalese policy. Perhaps the most important result was achieved by using the vertical dimension to influence the horizontal. External sources were tapped successfully in laying the foundations for strengthening inter-African economic relations. The OERS owes its existence in large part to the interest which Senegal, in collaboration with her three African partners, could generate at the United Nations, in the EEC, and in France. Senegal's policy of encouraging foreign investments is helping to diversify her exports with the assistance of French, American, and Soviet capital. Senegal, then, has been able to influence the external setting with a measure of success in improving her economic condition. Moreover, she has played an important role in articulating the common interests of Third World countries to present one of the greatest challenges addressed to the conscience of the fortunate, rich nations.

It is obvious that political independence does not allow such African countries as Senegal to play an important role in the international economy. Independence has allowed Senegal to take stock of her problems, to begin to become conscious of what she must do in order to become part of the world economy. In the decade after independence, Senegal has set a course designed to enlarge the circumscribed space of her national territory. In part as a result of her own initiatives, her economic horizon was broadened to include contiguous areas, the wider group of French-language states and—at least potentially—the rest of Africa, as well as the vertical dimension of extra-African ties.

CHAPTER FOUR

Practical Nonalignment

POLICY GUIDELINES

Perceptions

It goes without saying that Senegalese leaders did not make their appearance on the world scene armed with a well-defined set of theoretical notions concerning the nature and workings of the international environment. As late as 1968, President Senghor said, "We are becoming increasingly aware that external events somehow influence our very existence and that we must, consequently, pay particular attention to them." [1] But neither did they step into their roles as statesmen from a theoretical vacuum. This section attempts to define the perceptions, major objectives, and guiding principles of Senegal's decision-makers in international affairs.

1. *L'Unité africaine* (January 11, 1968).

Foremost among their perceptions was that of the continuing dependence of Senegal on external assistance. As indicated in chapter one, Senegal's leaders had no illusions about the magic of national independence; they regarded it as nothing much more than the signature of an agreement which altered very little of substance to the continued need for outside help. In fact, political independence seems to have confirmed their prognostications, and Africans have on occasion termed it a "poisoned gift" since it brought in its wake a whole range of problems with regard to the continuation of economic assistance from external sources. In a discussion of Senegal's foreign priorities, Doudou Thiam said, "There is first the necessity to assure rapid development for our country. Consequently we entertain political relations with countries capable of helping us and willing to do so." [2]

The thrust of the decolonization process, from the viewpoint of Senegal, was toward continued cooperation rather than a break with the former metropole. Senghor's commitment had been, and remained, to the progressive decentralization of the political setting of the French Union, and this progression culminated in political independence for the African territories. He had envisaged the Community as a loose confederation, and this was replaced by contractual ties between France and the African states. The legal framework, however, did not fundamentally alter the expectations for future collaboration with France, if only because such collaboration was considered to be as essential after independence as it had been before. As Senghor put it, "Our desire for independence can accommodate a strong association with France, a country which we need." [3] The French government had, on its part, clearly declared its intention of continuing to bear the burdens associated with widespread, long-term assistance to the newly independent states.

A second important perception of Senegal was the need for

2. Taped interview, August 4, 1967.
3. France, Travaux préparatoires de la constitution: Avis et débats du comité consultatif constitutionnel (Paris: La Documentation Française, 1960), p. 157.

continued inter-African links. Not only were Senegalese leaders accustomed to frequent, close contact with other African leaders within the framework of the French Union, but their fears of isolation in Africa were reinforced after the breakup of the Mali Federation. Thus, there were economic as well as psychological considerations which led Senegal toward cooperation at least with the former French African states.

In inter-African affairs, Senegal considers herself to be left of center, although it would be more accurate to describe her as a moderate, slightly-right-of-center African country. Probably no country in Africa is at a "center" of inter-African political behavior, if only because foreign policy orientation tends to vary with specific issues. Nonetheless, Senegal has a larger incipient middle class than most African states, and relatively close postcolonial ties with France; moreover, she is comfortable with a general pro-Western orientation, and inclined to a brand of realism that accents principles which, in the African context, may be said to prefer evolutionary to revolutionary change.

A third major element of Senegal's perceptions concerns the larger international setting, which appears to be dominated chiefly by the two superpowers and their maneuvers for alliances and friends. The cold war, or the clash of national interests, between the United States and the Soviet Union and their respective friends may seem remote when seen from Dakar. But the struggle between the two giants nevertheless presents dangers to the new African states: when two elephants fight, says a well-known African proverb, the grass gets trampled. Notwithstanding the presumed commitment to peaceful coexistence at the global level of international relations, both America and the Soviet Union continue to pursue their respective and often conflicting interests. In the words of Thiam:

> Peaceful coexistence never stopped the race for bases, the frenetic search for allies and for strategic raw materials, the fabrication and accumulation of instruments of mass destruction under the pretext of deterrence, local wars conducted by proxy, indirect participation in civil wars, injection of arms and sometimes of camouflaged units under the

guise of volunteers, if not under the name of mercenaries, the instruction and equipment of foreign soldiers.[4]

Objectives

Senegal's foreign policy is designed to achieve three major objectives. The first, as suggested in chapter three, is economic growth and development. Since independence, this goal has changed from a relatively passive acceptance of the international economic order to the pursuit of, ideally, radical change in that environment. According to Foreign Minister Thiam,

> What is the problem? The problem is to lay the foundations of a new world society, to make a new revolution, to destroy all practices, all institutions, all rules . . . to the extent that [they] consecrate injustice and exploitation and establish an unjustified domination of the minority over the majority of humanity.
> The problem is to build a new system based not only on the theoretical affirmation of the sacred rights of peoples and nations, but on the effective enjoyment of these rights. The freedom of self-determination, the sovereign equality of peoples, international solidarity, will all be vain . . . as long as the relations among nations are not examined in the light of economic and social facts.[5]

The second major objective derives from Senegal's notion of justice, in this case the end of the colonial era. It should not be surprising—or overlooked—that a country whose political colonial status ended in 1960 should remain sensitive and committed to the need for ending that dependence elsewhere in Africa and throughout the world. As Thiam put it, "The African states agree unanimously to the need for rapid decolonization in Africa and, more generally, in the world." [6]

4. *L'Unité africaine* (October 12, 1967).
5. "Intervention de Monsieur Doudou Thiam, Ministre d'Etat chargé des affaires étrangères de la République du Sénégal, à la XXIème session de l'assemblée générale de l'O.N.U.," mimeographed (Dakar: Ministère des Affaires Etrangères, 1966), p. 19.
6. Doudou Thiam, *La Politique étrangère des états africains* (Paris: Presses Universitaires de France, 1963), p. 113.

Third, the desire to maintain national independence takes the form of a commitment to keep intact the political boundaries inherited from the colonial powers. Modifications of these boundaries should take place only with the agreement of the states and populations concerned. But the notion of self-determination, invoked by some dissident regionally or ethnically based African leaders, is essentially defined by, and stops at, the international frontiers of the colonial era. Senegal's position on a number of such issues, from Moroccan claims over Mauritania prior to and after 1960 to Biafra in 1968, indicates that recognition and maintenance of the territorial integrity of the new states is one of her main objectives. Although she has not been directly threatened by a neighboring country, the location of The Gambia serves as a constant reminder of the significance of territorial integrity; it may harbor potential dangers to Senegal and thus emphasizes daily the importance of respect for political sovereignty as a condition for inter-African cooperation.

Principles

The operating principles designed to serve as guidelines for Senegal's foreign policy are pragmatic: they reflect the country's objectives as well as the concrete problems which confronted the new state after 1960. Leaving aside the more theoretical—and philosophical—commitments of President Senghor, which are discussed below, there are two guidelines which underlie Senegal's foreign relations: a twin commitment to peace and nonalignment.

Peaceful methods. Dedication to world peace is one of the more readily identifiable and ubiquitous commitments of foreign policy makers. The speeches of Senegalese leaders make frequent references to international peace and often single it out as their number one objective in their relations with other states. In practice, however, peace tends to be an ideal and a method rather than a goal per se or a concrete policy. For Senegal, peace is an object of profound theoretical and rhetorical reverence as well as a general principle for achieving national objectives. As President Senghor recognizes, "Peace is not an end in itself. It is not even a solution, but the means to search for solutions, which must still be found." [7] The search for peace, however, has not blinded Senegal to the manifold difficulties involved in attaining or maintaining it; her spokesmen have recognized that in practice the search for peace is like the search for a means of squaring the circle.

This a priori preference for peace is accompanied by a belief that violence may help to define problems but does not solve them. Peace as an objective in the conduct of international relations has its roots partly in the weakness of Senegal and partly in a desire for order. The weakness of such countries as Senegal and the lack of viable alternative policies to peaceful intercourse are self-evident and need no elaboration. For Senegal to adopt nonpeaceful methods to secure, say, economic benefits would be useless at best, and dysfunctional or dangerous at worst. Senegal has more to gain from applying moral pressure than from adopting a militant stance in foreign affairs, especially in her relations with the larger powers on which she is dependent.

But a peace policy functions also to maintain a modicum of international order within which the new states can develop. Without favoring the status quo, Senegal nevertheless insists that it is essential, especially in inter-African relations, to articulate and honor in practice a number of elementary principles as guides for action if the continent is to avoid anarchy. If, for example, the principle of noninterference in the internal affairs of other independent states is constantly violated, then "independence is no longer possible, peace is no longer possible, coexistence is no longer possible among African states." [8]

In fact, Senegal has consistently adhered to the belief that such principles are essential. This is not always the case elsewhere in Africa, and Senegalese leaders have attempted to convince others that it would be to their common advantage were they to base their foreign policy on principles rather than to operate with ad hoc responses to individual problems as they arise. To some African states, for instance, the only valid principle seems to be that of "revolution," interpreted as vast and

---

7. Liberté I: Négritude et humanisme (Paris: Editions du Seuil, 1964), p. 308.
8. Taped interview with Doudou Thiam, August 4, 1967.

rapid changes affecting the present structure of international—
and in some cases domestic—politics. From the point of view of
inter-African relations, the problem is that anything can be justified in the name of revolution: attacks on other countries, the
violation of their sovereignty, the very notion of the legitimacy
of constitutionally elected governments if these governments
happen not to share the revolutionaries' views, and the subversion of other countries' governments. In short, a commitment to
revolution can justify any action intended to change violently
the domestic and external policies of other countries.

The importance of emphasizing peaceful methods in the relations among states derives also from a longtime preference
for conciliation on the part of Senegal's leaders. Independence
was achieved without violence and bloodshed, after a series of
efforts to decentralize the decision-making authority vested in
French or French Union executive and legislative bodies. When
former Prime Minister Dia addressed himself to this aspect of
Senegalese policy, he explained:

> Our policy has attempted to avoid useless crises, and
> violent tests when these were not indispensable. We have,
> on the contrary, faithfully made use of dialogue, . . . while
> safeguarding the most precious of human riches . . . , I
> mean friendship—which in its African form we feel essen-
> tially as fraternity. Thus we were able to cross the threshold
> of decolonization without bloodshed or hatred.[9]

Senegal's preference for conciliation also reflects her desire
for moral equality with other states and for the respect that accompanies equality. Conciliation is thus viewed as a specific contribution which Africa can make in international affairs. Hence
Senghor suggests that the African tradition of palaver be placed
at the disposal of the international community and be used to
compromise and adjust differences. As he declared to the General Assembly of the United Nations, "International 'dialogue,'

9. Senegal, *Déclaration prononcée par Monsieur Mamadou Dia, président du conseil des ministres de la République du Sénégal devant l'assemblée
nationale et les délégations invitées aux fêtes de l'indépendance du Sénégal*
(Dakar: Imprimerie Nationale du Sénégal, 1961), p. 4.

the instrument of peace and international cooperation, is the major contribution which . . . Africa wishes to make." [10]

It should be noted that Senghor's concept of dialogue as it applies to international relations is not the same as traditional mediation or conciliation. The function of these two activities is to help create the atmosphere needed for subsequent dialogue among antagonists. Senghor assumes that a viable solution, or adjustment, of differences can result only from a direct confrontation between opponents. Without international dialogue, Senghor explains, "the thought and reality of the antagonist . . . is presented as caricature," [11] and as a result compromise and cooperation are not possible. To an audience in Latin America, Senghor pointed out that international dialogue was never more needed than "in the century of dichotomies and prejudices, of confusions and simplifications, of ideologies without spirit and aesthetics without imagination." [12]

One implication of the desire for equality concerns the proper method to search for Truth. Equality requires that all be heard and suggests that no nation has a monopoly on truth. In the eyes of leaders of developing states, this applies especially to former colonial powers and to the world's superpowers. But if no people or nation has a monopoly on truth, this raises the question of where truth is located and how it can be discovered. Senghor's answer is not much different from that of other African leaders. He suggests that

> from the equality of nations there flows a consequence, that the truth belongs to no people, to no nation. . . . It follows that each people, each nation, each race holds a part of the truth. It is the purpose of dialogue to unite

10. United Nations, General Assembly, *Allocution de M. Léopold Sédar Senghor, Président de la République du Sénégal* (A/PV. 1045), October 31, 1961, p. 32.

11. *Ibid.*, p. 12.

12. Senegal, *Voyage officiel aux Etats-Unis du Brésil de S. Exc. M. Léopold Sédar Senghor, Président de la République du Sénégal, 19 septembre– 25 septembre 1964* (Dakar: Grande Imprimerie Africaine, 1964), pp. 22–23.

these partial truths in order to make a human truth which must be recognized [*doit s'imposer*] by all peoples.[13]

This version of truth serves the purpose for which it is intended, namely, to justify listening to the voices of new states. It cannot, however, serve as a guide to policy since it is impractical—unless, that is, the world were run by superpragmatists. In theory, Senghor's suggestion amounts to a kind of "truth by pieces," to a global jigsaw puzzle which need only be assembled by willing partners. The a priori assumption that truth is a function of geography merely begs a number of important questions. Which part of truth is located where? What is the proper mix for the ultimate combination?

The process of assembling pieces of truth in order to get a universal composite truth is similar in result to the analogy of the bright, shiny star which becomes self-evident to anyone merely willing to lift his head skyward. It assumes that there is an absolute on which everyone can agree and, more important, will act on when sighting it. Regardless of this kind of criticism, however, it should be kept in mind that the purpose of this formulation of the nature of truth is less an exercise in logic than a justification for acceptance by others on a basis of full equality, much like the legal fiction of the sovereign equality of nations. Senghor reinforces the need for equality by calling on African states in general, and Senegal in particular, to offer their utopias to the rest of the world. He says,

> A people which does not believe itself to be the bearer of a unique message is finished: let it be stored in a museum. The Negro-African is not finished before having begun to speak. Let him speak, and above all let him act. Let him bring, like a leaven, his message to the world.[14]

Since peaceful methods are intended only as a general guide for policy, they have obvious limitations in practical affairs.

13. *L'Unité africaine* (June 17, 1965).
14. *Nation et voie africaine du socialisme* (Paris: Présence Africaine, 1961), p. 89.

These limits are hypothetical in the sense that the country has not been involved in armed conflict, except for her assistance to the United Nations operation in the Léopoldville-Congo. Her pronouncements and behavior nevertheless suggest that force is legitimate in three types of situations. The first type concerns helping to reestablish domestic order provided that the legal government calls for outside help and that the international community at large, or at least a significant segment thereof, mounts a collective operation which can be justified before world public opinion.

⏚The second legitimate use of force concerns the right of states to defend themselves against external aggression; this includes clearly identifiable subversion by outside forces, although the problem of a response to subversion is more difficult to cope with in practice than in theory.⏚And, third, force is recognized as legitimate if directed against decolonization where the colonial power has remained unmoved by the winds of change. This viewpoint was clarified, for example, in the unilateral declaration of independence by Rhodesia's white minority. In this case, Senegal called on Great Britain to use force against what she considers the illegal regime of Premier Ian Smith; but she refused to accede to some Africans' pressure to break diplomatic relations with Britain, on the grounds that this would accomplish nothing and would, moreover, erase whatever influence Senegal might have on the British government in helping to solve the Rhodesian problem. By contrast, Senegal approves the use of force by the nationalists of Portuguese Guinea because the government of Portugal has steadfastly refused to consider starting the decolonization process for her African territories and has thus placed herself outside acceptable limits of moral behavior on that issue.

Another guideline which influences Senegal's foreign relations is a belief that ideological affinity is not by itself a sound basis for alignment in world affairs. This conviction rests on pre-independence experiences which demonstrated the superficial nature of such ties. To attribute the end of colonialism to, or to expect the end of neocolonialism from, the international solidarity of like-minded people is not merely an error but a gross misreading of the historical record. For all their rhetoric about oppression and exploitation in foreign lands, the French Communists, for example, nonetheless helped send French troops to battle with Ho Chi Minh. One of the ironies of the history of decolonization is that it was right-of-center or moderate European governments who granted national independence to most colonial territories. Moscow's espousal of the anti-imperialist cause was prompted less by a desire to liberate overseas colonies—she had none—than by a desire to embarrass cold war rivals. African nationalists have, moreover, experienced at home the paternalism of Communists who offered advice and services after World War II.

Nonalignment. Another major principle serving as a general guide for Senegalese foreign affairs is that of nonalignment. Much has been written about this post–World War II phenomenon, which, to judge from some of the comments made, may appear as either immoral, irresponsible, or at least confused and confusing. It may be useful, as a starting point in a brief conceptual exploration of nonalignment, to indicate what it is not. First, nonalignment is not neutrality. In the words of Doudou Thiam, "In politics, neutrality is an illusion. Politics means taking sides . . . [but] the essential point is not to take sides systematically." [15] And, second, nonalignment is not a careful balance of support among major contestants on the international scene as, for instance, among the antagonists in a bipolar cold war struggle for influence.

As a next step, it is useful to distinguish between theoretical nonalignment, on one hand, and practical nonalignment, on the other. Theoretical nonalignment may be defined as a psychological element in the foreign policy decision-making process. This involves the desire, on the part of Senegal's leaders, to make their own decisions. It grows out of the colonial period, when Senegal was not able to make such decisions because of external political control, and therefore is part of the decolonization process. Theoretical nonalignment thus involves self-respect and dignity, which demand that others not merely recognize but also respect the legitimacy of decisions reached independently from external powers; Senegal, like other African

15. Thiam, *La Politique étrangère*, p. 106.

states, no longer wishes to be taken for granted. It means that a policy decision, to qualify, must be preceded by an independent evaluation of the merits of each case. It is the interposition of one's national judgment between an international relations problem and a policy decision. Theoretical nonalignment, then, is a flexible guide for policy rather than an immutable policy. It is intended as a general direction to be followed rather than as a detailed road map with a specific itinerary. It is useful for understanding some of the limits on policy, such as an insistence on territorial integrity, or criticisms of undue foreign pressure, or such foreign policy motives as suggestions for African contributions in international relations.

Practical nonalignment may be defined as consisting of policy outputs designed either to prevent or to alter undesirable aspects of the international environment. By definition, practical nonalignment deals with concrete issues, such as decolonization, inter-African cooperation, and an equitable distribution of the world's riches.

The distinction between theoretical and practical nonalignment addresses itself to the conceptual puzzle of reconciling divergences between declarative and behavioral aspects of African foreign policy. Conceptual attempts to assess theoretical and practical nonalignment under one analytical roof are confusing because they make no allowance for gaps between statements and behavior. According to this "one roof" approach, nonalignment, first, is considered not to be a policy, but then it is evaluated in terms of policy decisions. The limitation of this approach is that it does not distinguish clearly between legitimate psychological components of the decision-making process and equally legitimate policy outcomes. Consequently, it tends to suggest that nonalignment is a screen concealing logical inconsistencies at best, and hypocrisies at worst.

Furthermore, the distinction leads to recognition that theoretical nonalignment is not necessarily incompatible with alignment in practice, since the latter encompasses the universe of policy outputs. Thus, countries which are in practice aligned from the point of view of ideology or economics may be said to be theoretically nonaligned, provided that their leaders are satisfied that a particular decision was taken by them rather than imposed by external powers. This conceptual dichotomy removes the logical difficulty of the "one roof" approach and facilitates assessment of practical foreign policy decisions without the encumbrance of apparent inconsistencies. Thus, practical economic alignment may be judged on the basis of economic dependence and be regarded as legitimate; it need not be considered an aberration or a deviation from principles articulated at another level.

Practical nonalignment can be subdivided, as suggested earlier, into negative and positive elements, depending on the objective sought by policy decisions. A policy designed to prevent the spread of the cold war or of other undesirable influences to Africa would be a negative example of practical nonalignment. By contrast, a policy designed to further majority rule in southern Africa, or to change the international economic environment for Africa, may be called positive practical nonalignment.

In short, theoretical nonalignment is chiefly a psychological factor, whereas practical nonalignment is closely related to the African states' perceptions of their concrete national interests. Practical nonalignment may thus encompass not only alignment policies but also conscious policy decisions which in effect abridge a state's sovereignty should this abridgement be seen to be in the national interest. International relations, according to Thiam, "often demand reciprocal concessions and limitations on sovereignty. The essential point is that these limitations of sovereignty take place in sovereignty." [16] Senegal's foreign policy makers have in fact limited their country's sovereignty in a number of important structural ways. Leaving aside Senegal's willingness to abridge her sovereignty in inter-African affairs before independence, these limitations include membership in the Union Africaine et Malgache de Défense (UAMD) (although this has existed only on paper), a defense and foreign policy agreement with The Gambia, and the foreign policy and defense agreements signed with France. The existence of the agreements mainly reflects a number of overlapping considerations, expressed in two types of relations. The first type of relation, inter-African ties, is concerned with possible subversion

16. *Ibid.*, p. 110.

from within, exemplified by the agreement with The Gambia, and with externally supported subversion, exemplified by the inter-African defense agreement. The second, ties with France, is designed in part to help deter internal disorders and external attack, to secure economic benefits, and to act as a concession for obtaining political independence—thus reflecting to some extent French strategic and other interests in Senegal.

The pursuit of political, defense, and economic objectives has led Senegal to sign an agreement on external defense and foreign policy with The Gambia, a territory completely enclosed by Senegal save for an outlet to the Atlantic Ocean. The defense agreement calls for mutual assistance against external and, presumably, internal threats and obligates Senegal to assist The Gambia in organizing and training military and paramilitary forces. Both countries have also agreed to set up a Joint Permanent Secretariat on External Security and Defense. The agreement further provides for the permanent exchange of information and for consultation on foreign affairs problems.

By far the most significant limitation on Senegal's sovereignty resulted from some of the cooperation agreements signed with France at the time of independence. One of these concerned foreign policy, another defense.[17] The first singled out the "persistence of ties of friendship" with France and provided for (1) mutual exchange of information and consultation on foreign policy matters, (2) French support for Senegal's candidacy for membership in the United Nations, and (3) preferential status for the two countries' resident diplomats.[18]

The Senegalo-French defense agreement was undoubtedly of greater import. It explicitly recognized that Senegal alone was

17. France, *Journal officiel de la république française—Communauté: Accords franco-maliens*, July, 1960 (Paris: Imprimerie des Journaux Officiels, 1960). In an exchange of letters with the French government, Senegal agreed to honor the Malien-French agreements after the breakup of the Mali Federation. Quotations in this section are taken from the above document.

18. Both countries' representatives would have the official title of High Representative in addition to that of Ambassador; moreover, the French ambassador was made the dean of the Senegalese diplomatic corps, whereas African ambassadors in Paris would enjoy a "privileged place" among the diplomats accredited to France.

responsible for her external and internal defense but permitted her to ask for the assistance of French armed forces for such defense; the decision whether to supply the forces was to be made by the French government. The principle of "mutual assistance for defense" was embodied in three specific subjects on which commitments were made. First, France agreed to help Senegal organize, equip, and train her national armed forces. Second, Senegal agreed to have French troops stationed on her territory.[19] And, third, both countries agreed to a joint policy on strategic materials.[20] That policy also requires exchange of information, obligates the partners to purchase from and sell to each other such raw materials, and, "when the defense interests so require," to limit or prohibit exports to third countries.

To what extent have these agreements affected Senegal's sovereignty, and what is their relation to nonalignment? The one regarding strategic raw materials has remained inoperative since none was discovered. Almost a decade of efforts to find oil and natural gas deposits on land and offshore have proved fruitless. Should such materials be found in quantities sufficient to make exploitation attractive, the French would no doubt retain a substantial interest. But Senegal's own interests would be subject to negotiation, and there is no reason to believe that she would not press for the best bargain possible. The diplomatic agreement, conferring special status on the French ambassador in Senegal, is but a small gesture which reflects the "special relationship" between the two countries. Moreover, a commitment for consultation in general matters of foreign policy is not, per se, an abrogation of sovereignty; it does not commit Senegal to common action.

The presence of some twenty-five hundred French soldiers in Senegal seems to be a function of French strategic considerations

19. French troops are under the jurisdiction of Senegalese law, except for violations committed inside a military base or while on duty. French military units also enjoy free use of Senegalese roads, port and railroad facilities, postal and telecommunications facilities, air space, and territorial waters—subject to prior notification of troop movements.

20. These were defined as including oil and natural gas, uranium, thorium, lithium, beryllium, helium, and their elements and mineral components.

and of Senegal's possible need for them for internal security.[21] Although they may be used to secure internal order, there is no evidence that this has happened in Senegal. The French refused to place their soldiers at the disposal of Modibo Keita in August, 1960, when he requested assistance to end Senegal's "secession" from the Mali Federation. It is true, of course, that Senegal's existence as an independent political entity—independent at least from the former Soudan and with the same top leadership group—hung in the balance and literally depended on what the French would or would not do. Had the French intervened, that intervention could have led to the emergence of a different leadership in Senegal, possibly with a somewhat different foreign policy outlook. The French refusal to take sides in 1960 probably reinforced the government's belief that it could rely on France as a dependable friend presenting no threat to the country's sovereignty and territorial integrity.

Moreover, the possibility that Senegalese leaders may, in the back of their mind, count on French military assistance to help prevent or contain internal disruption cannot be overlooked. In view of the many military takeovers in black Africa in recent years and the confusion and vacillation of Senegalese military officers in 1962 during the Senghor-Dia struggle, French troops garrisoned near Dakar may well be intended partly to serve as a deterrent to a coup d'état by Senegal's armed forces. President Senghor has apparently been successful in retaining the allegiance of his military leaders through a combination of constitutional arguments, isolation of prospective dissidents, and distribution of professional rewards—the country spends about 7 per cent of her national budget on defense, a percentage which ranks among the highest in independent black Africa. It is true that the circumstances in which French troops could intervene effectively to prevent a takeover by Senegalese troops are circumscribed by the speed with which such a coup d'état can be accomplished.

Nonetheless, there are examples of successful French armed

21. For details, consult Chester A. Crocker, "France's Changing Military Interests," *Africa Report*, Vol. XIII, no. 6 (June, 1968); and "External Military Assistance to Sub-Saharan Africa," *Africa Today*, Vol. XV, no. 2 (April–May, 1968).

intervention to protect an incumbent African regime. French forces were flown into Gabon in 1965 to protect former President Léon M'Ba from ouster by his own armed forces. More recently, over three thousand French troops were used in Chad to help the regime of François Tombalbaye cope with serious internal armed rebellion. (The use of French troops stationed in Dakar may well give rise to serious criticism that Senghor is indirectly responsible for helping to maintain other African regimes in power, and to demands for the withdrawal of French armed forces from Senegal.) The possibility of French military intervention in the future cannot be dismissed entirely. Senegal retains considerable strategic and prestige value in French official eyes, and no one can predict the effects of successive poor peanut crops or of political restlessness on Senghor's ability to retain the continued support of her own armed forces.

Similarly, French troops in Dakar are not there primarily to protect Senegal from an external attack—although such an eventuality cannot be ruled out as impossible under all circumstances. Such hostility as has been directed against Senegal in the past from neighboring states runs no risk of being translated into armed attack. The presence of French troops, however, plus the defense agreement, may act as an actual or perceived deterrent to larger and more frequent Portuguese incursions than have occurred.

It is difficult to estimate what influence, if any, the presence of French troops in Senegal has had on the internal security of the country. Between independence and 1965, an antigovernment plot was officially discovered about every two years, and it was believed that the plotters received help from external sources. In 1961, a secret arms cache was found in Casamance. In 1963, there was an alleged plot masterminded from Mali territory and, according to Senegalese sources, supported by Morocco. In 1965, the Senegalese government discovered another alleged plot; an apparently pro-Chinese or pro-Russian group, partly trained in Havana, had entered Senegal from Mali and fanned out to eastern Senegal and Casamance. This group was, however, reportedly rooted out with the official help of Mali authorities, which had resumed their cooperation with Senegal beginning in 1963.

The presence of the French, then, does not seem to have prevented these incursions; what challenge there was against Senegalese authorities was presented in the form of infiltration and preparation for subversion against which a French army response may not have been appropriate. French intelligence and communications agents normally collaborated with the Senegalese government in these activities, as they do in connection with the activities of the Portuguese. But whether such cooperation was essential to the government's success in preventing subversion is another question. Cooperation with neighboring African states is probably more useful to Senegal in preventing subversion than are the French forces in Dakar.

The fact nonetheless remains that Senegal allows foreign troops on her territory. In addition to possible reassurance that her borders will not be violated, Senegal derives—and appreciates—economic benefits in the form of French expenditures. President Senghor said that the withdrawal of French military units from Senegal in 1964 resulted in an estimated annual loss of some 8 billion CFA francs, nearly 10 per cent of the country's annual revenue.[22]

It may be germane to raise the question of nonalignment in connection with the Senegalo-French defense and foreign policy agreements. It is clear that they represent an example of practical alignment, from which Senegal's leaders believe that they derive valuable benefits. The defense agreement does tend to circumscribe Senegal's freedom of choice to the extent that she need not be fully consulted before French troops are used elsewhere in Africa, and to the extent that she invites external criticism for allowing the armed forces of a foreign country—a former colonial country, at that—to be stationed on her soil. At the same time, the foreign policy agreement does not necessarily have the same effect. Senegal has been able to influence French policy, particularly with respect to Mali and Guinea. But when their respective national interests diverge, their policies may also diverge, as they did in the Middle East crisis in June, 1967, over the question of diplomatic recognition of

22. *West Africa* (October 10, 1964), p. 1137.

the People's Republic of China, and over the general usefulness of the United Nations.

To the extent that Senegal may yield to French pressure concerning international issues, this is likely to be the result of careful calculation of the advantages and disadvantages of a particular issue against the value of overall relations with the former metropole. In this sense, it would be normal interstate behavior, which rests in part on a combination of external pressures. The same pressures are at work in inter-African relations, and Senegal has adjusted elements of her foreign policy with respect to the French-language states because she values continued cooperation with them more than opposing them on a given issue.

It is much more difficult to answer the question whether the agreements represent an example of theoretical nonalignment. It must be remembered that the agreements are a holdover from the preindependence period, in the sense that they were signed simultaneously with the one that transferred political sovereignty from France to Senegal and were thus part of a bargain whose objective was political independence. Following the signing of these agreements, Modibo Keita, head of the Mali Federation at the time, commented that "[this] alliance with the French Republic is particularly dear to the Mali Federation, whatever the circumstances, whatever the future." [23] This judgment, coming from one of Africa's "radicals," almost makes audible a sigh of relief at having overcome a major obstacle in the negotiations. To have convinced the French government to grant independence to the Mali Federation without the shadow of the consequences which befell Guinea in 1958 was an achievement. Given the circumstances, there was no point in jeopardizing it. In other words, the goal of independence for the Mali Federation seemed preferable to whatever restrictions on forthcoming sovereignty were embodied in the agreement.

It can be argued, then, that signature of the agreements did violate theoretical nonalignment because the Soudan and Sene-

23. Quoted in Maurice Ligot, Les Accords de coopération entre la France et les états africains et malgache d'expression française (Paris: La Documentation Française, 1964), p. 29.

gal were not free to make the decision. But it could also be pointed out that theoretical nonalignment was possible only after political independence. Since both events took place at the same time, they cannot be separated subsequently by the concept of theoretical nonalignment, which is a postindependence phenomenon. As suggested above, their continued existence after independence falls into the practical alignment category, which need bear no substantive relation to prior, theoretical nonalignment. But their signature was part of a bargain to secure political independence.

CULTURE AND INTERNATIONAL RELATIONS

Personal characteristics

Given the working hypothesis of this study, namely, that Senegal's foreign relations are to a large extent determined by President Senghor, it is useful to extract a number of salient personality characteristics and predispositions from his experiences before he became actively involved in his political career, which may be assumed to influence his country's external relations. Two personal characteristics stand out for their potency and constancy.

First, Léopold Senghor has a large capacity and willingness to work hard. Accustomed from his early childhood to daily physical exercise, he endured without complaint the spartan life under the guidance of the Fathers of the Holy Spirit in Senegal. His later life at the Sorbonne, during the early 1930s, was austere. In addition to performing the various duties as head of state, government, and party with the punctuality of clockwork, he corresponds and reads widely. Fellow students at the Lycée Louis-le-Grand encouraged him to read widely outside assigned materials, and he was awarded the coveted agrégation in French grammar in 1935 after having prepared for it while completing his military service in France. He has retained a penchant for scholarly research and meditation. In 1967, when asked how he would have lived his life over again, he answered, "It is probable that I would have earned my doctoral thesis . . . and become a professor at the Collège de France." [24]

A second important personal characteristic of Senghor's is an unusually strong will. As a child, he says, "I had a cholerous temperament," [25] which earned him a reputation for bad conduct and caused him to lose two years in primary school despite considerable scholarly achievement. His early restlessness led his mentors to dissuade him from becoming a priest. He ascribes his subsequent ability to overcome, or at least to keep beneath the surface, his "natural" temper to the rigorous discipline of his Roman Catholic teachers. His self-discipline and somewhat austere notion of duty are revealed in his definition of pleasure, not as frivolous pursuit, but as the by-product of hard work: "Pleasure is not happiness; happiness is mainly the feeling of duty, of work well done." [26] Among his collaborators and subordinates are many who believe that once he has made a decision, he will alter his efforts to realize his objective only after all other possibilities are exhausted. This trait may help explain, for example, why he clung to the Mali Federation long after advisers and observers were convinced of the experiment's failure. Along with his strong will must be ranked an extraordinary capacity for faithfulness to his ideals. The intensity of his commitments has made him search for, and contribute to, philosophic depth beyond the range of most statesmen. To a newly appointed foreign ambassador who presented his credentials and suggested that Senghor is both an optimist and a pragmatist, he replied, "I am an optimist and a dreamer. These two attitudes . . . are not opposed . . . , they are complementary." [27]

In addition to these characteristics, two personal predispositions must be singled out as bearing on the direction and style of his foreign policy. One is that Senghor was fortunate in that his most salient environmental experiences rested on relative prosperity and security. His father was a merchant whose trade

24. Jeune afrique, no. 303 (October 30, 1967), p. 46.
25. Jean Rous, Léopold Sédar Senghor: Un Président de l'Afrique nouvelle (Paris: Didier, 1967), p. 15.
26. Ibid., p. 46.
27. L'Unité africaine (December 28, 1967).

income enabled him to acquire substantial real estate and to raise a large family comfortably. Senghor's own memories single out his family's social position and his love for his mother and other relatives. He probably never experienced the full weight of the colonial heel—although he was, as a sensitive man, often profoundly resentful of snubs by ignorant or illiberal Frenchmen. When he came to Paris as a twenty-two-year-old student, he found easy acceptance by students and professors.

It is plausible to suggest that the security of his early life and of later personal friendships, plus the recognition earned from academic achievements (he taught French to French children in France), have helped make Senghor into an international man, at home in Africa as well as in Europe. Moreover, this security may also be at the root of his predisposition toward conciliation.

Another outcome of his Paris student days was the close ties of friendship with such fellow students as Georges Pompidou. Pompidou, in fact, greatly influenced Senghor. It was he who encouraged him to read, who shared his intellectual discoveries, who "converted" him to socialism after a flirtation with royalism —in short, who made him feel at home. During World War II, Pompidou saved the manuscript of *Hosties noires*, which Senghor had written while a prisoner of war of the Germans and had smuggled out with the help of an Austrian anti-Nazi professor.

It would be rash to assert that Senghor was influenced by Charles de Gaulle; it is nevertheless clear that he held the French general in enormous esteem, as did most other leaders of French-language Africa. De Gaulle stands out not merely as "the man" of Brazzaville who, in 1944, began the process of liberalization that culminated in political independence. But de Gaulle's later willingness (albeit grudging for a while) to accept and promote decolonization, his known sympathies for developing areas generally and African states in particular, and his continued special interest in Senegal—Senghor and his aides always had free access to the Elysée and to de Gaulle's chief advisers—no doubt helped shape Senghor's views of his country's ties with France. Senghor's admiration for de Gaulle was not always without some reservations. In May, 1958, when it appeared possible that French Air Force units stationed in Senegal would join French army rebels in Algeria, Senghor prepared for the worst and openly helped form an organization protesting an army takeover. After the danger had passed, and it became clear that de Gaulle favored a constitutional government ready to redefine the relations between Africa and France, Senghor again seems to have regarded the general as an ally who understood and approved at least some of Senghor's values. Senghor relates the story, for instance, of de Gaulle's answer to the governor of a French colony who complained that one of his officials wanted to marry an African. "You are a petit-bourgeois, Monsieur," said de Gaulle, "the future belongs to racial mixtures." [28]

Within the dualism of his African and French experiences, Senghor has woven strong affective ties with France. Much of his intellectual life revolves around things French, despite the humiliation instilled by the French colonial tabula rasa and "prelogical mind" concepts. To a certain extent, in fact, Senghor can be said to have an a priori prejudice, among things foreign, in favor of things French. This is reflected, for example, in his concern for internal French structural changes affecting Senegalo-French relations. When the French government decided, in 1966, to abolish the Secretariat of State for Cooperation as a separate entity and to place it under the jurisdiction of the French Foreign Ministry, Senghor deplored the move as one that would cause an estrangement of Senegal from France; "For us," he explained, "Frenchmen are not foreigners like the others." [29]

The unity of mankind

Much of Senegal's foreign relations is conditioned by President Senghor's views on the importance of culture. This concern has pervaded the thought of Senghor since his student days in

28. Quoted in Gisela Bonn, *Léopold Sédar Senghor: Wegbereiter der Culture universelle* (Düsseldorf: Econ, 1968), p. 131.
29. *Le Monde* (November 30, 1966). In this sense, it is also significant that the Senegalese government published a pamphlet justifying the handling of the 1962 Mamadou Dia affair that was really addressed to criticism by French intellectuals.

Paris. At the time he became associated with the periodical *L'Etudiant noir* in 1934, he made it clear that he considered man's cultural endeavors as his summum bonum and that such other activities as politics were consequently subsidiary. The primacy of culture is most evident in his concept of negritude, in his advocacy of a world-wide French-language community known as francophonie, in his major speech about arabité and africanité at Cairo University in February, 1967, as well as in the peace prize awarded him in April, 1968, by German book publishers. Senghor's cultural mask was carved out of three successive concerns—for the experiences of Africa and Europe, and for the future of mankind. His mask symbolizes two present cultures plus that of a presumed ultimate pan-human encounter.

The cultural dimension of Senegal's foreign policy is more important than are others, in the sense that it conditions much of Senghor's thinking about inter-African and wider, international affairs; provides a framework without which many of his ideas and actions are not fully comprehensible; asks questions about—and suggests answers to—problems transcending mundane, everyday worries of ordinary politicians; and lifts man's self-image to heights theoretically capable of inspiring men everywhere to conceptions of nobility frequently left behind in our technological age. More specifically, the cultural dimension may be said to perform a number of functions in international relations. It emphasizes the underlying unity of *Homo sapiens* as a basis for world-wide cooperation. It provides a basis for justice among peoples. It promotes the security of pride and identity among black Africans and, by extension, black people everywhere. It helps lay the foundations for future African unity. It seeks to promote the material welfare of Africans. And it offers a contribution by Africa to the world.

Senghor suggests that the world cannot be understood only in terms of the conventional divisions made by students of international affairs. A fuller perspective requires attention to a different breakdown: a number of civilizations which share an underlying unity increasingly evident in a vast movement of pan-human convergence. Each of the world's civilizations possesses all traits of mankind but has cultivated only some of the offerings of which mankind is capable. He buttresses this hypothesis with a number of arguments.

First, the differentiation of *Homo sapiens* into the present families—the negroid Grimaldi, the caucasoid Cro-Magnon, and the mongoloid Chancelade branches—was the result of interaction between men and differing environments and was thus preceded by unity. Senghor assumes that racial physical differentiation began in Africa some forty thousand years ago during the Upper Paleolithic era. Moreover, differentiation was not unilinear; it followed a pattern of *métissage* which tended to perpetuate underlying unity and to blur the validity of racial analytical categories.

Second, if differentiation is ascribed essentially to the interaction between man and environment as the basis of today's civilizations, then is there any evidence that this environment is changing? For Senghor, the answer is unambiguously positive: in fact, both environment and man's behavior are changing. This belief is reflected in, and supported by, his theory of history, an overall framework for perceiving the world, whose elements were plucked from such European thinkers as Marx and other utopian socialists and heavily influenced by Pierre Teilhard de Chardin, a French Jesuit and scientist.

To Senghor, the evolution of mankind is governed by a moral purpose: raising the social consciousness of the human species. He postulates an eventual peaceful world resulting from the gradual symbiosis of the world's civilizations into a civilization of the universal. Following an ever increasing global social consciousness, fashioned in large part by the necessity of facing problems common to mankind, the interpenetration of today's national segments of mankind by culture and technology will produce a world civilization whose members are closely attuned to, and willing to cooperate with, one another.

This civilization of the universal will be achieved in three successive stages. The first stage was that of "consciousness," during which man acquired both knowledge and the consciousness of knowledge. Consciousness brought about an awareness of the universality of mankind. The second stage, that of "socialization," began with the scientific discoveries of the Renaissance and resulted in the spreading—and conscious sharing—of human knowledge. In order to avoid conflict springing from increased tensions—including those inherent in such weapons of mass destruction as explosives and gases—and from the simultaneous increase in the earth's population, men everywhere must weave ever closer social relations with one another, pool techniques and knowledge, and thus essentially solve humanity's common problems.

Anxieties arising from the bomb, evidence that the world is growing smaller and more crowded, the decreasing usefulness of nationalism, and mutual cultural interpenetration must be interpreted in this light. The final stage of historical development is that of "communion," which will be characterized by an end to religious, ethnic, national, and social conflict among men. Thus Senghor's ideal concerning the civilization of the universal reflects—or parallels—the brotherhood of man long heralded by poets and composers, and the widely accepted notion that cultural evolution, or that of the world's civilizations in the Senghorian sense, tends toward convergence through continuous and increasing contacts resulting in cross-fertilization.

Third, Senghor reinforces his theory of history by suggesting that great civilizations are interdependent, mixed civilizations. "Cultures," he said, "are like living beings: they must assimilate foreign elements in order to grow and perpetuate themselves." [30] The history of mankind provides examples of such greatness, past and potential, on a scale intermediate between national compartments and the ultimate world civilization. Such were those of Greece, Egypt, India, Sumer, and China. Today, despite antagonistic ideologies and material interests, "there is an opportunity for the United States of America and the Union of Soviet Socialist Republics to be at the crossroads of races and civilizations." [31] The same reasoning applies to such smaller countries as France, whose greatness Senghor ascribes in large part to culture contacts with Greek, Roman, Spanish, Italian, and Anglo-Saxon influences:

30. "Un Humanisme de l'union française," *Esprit* (July, 1949), p. 1025.
31. *Liberté I*, p. 96.

It is often Europeans of foreign origin, like Stravinsky or Picasso, who have brought France exotic riches. If Paris was, since the end of the nineteenth century, the intellectual and artistic capital of the world, think of the large number of foreigners included in what could be called, for fifty years, the Paris school. Think of van Gogh, van Dongen, Chagall, Picasso, for painting; of Honegger, Stravinsky, Satie, whose mother was Scottish, for music. . . . All great critics have underlined the decisive contributions of the Far East or of black Africa in French contemporary art.[32]

Part of Senghor's attraction toward the final symbiosis of a world civilization is that it accommodates his commitment to justice: all present civilizations must contribute their offering on the basis of equality. None of the world's present civilizations—the African, the European and its offshoots, or the Asian—is superior to another. The civilization of the West, or that of technology, has fallen into the trap of assuming a linear progression from backwardness to modernization and of identifying itself as the only source and direction of future civilization. By focusing essentially on the technical aspects of man's quest for mastery over nature, it has tended to confuse the end with the means and to lose sight of the primacy of man. It is dangerous to concentrate on the achievements of material wants alone, to become fascinated with opulence and gadgetry. It is dangerous because men may be so intent on contemplating their technetronic navels that they callously overlook their fellows dying from want of food or fuel.

One of the major functions of Senghor's theory of history is to make room for Africa's contributions to a future world characterized by an end to religious, ethnic, national, and social strife. If none of the world's civilizations is superior to another, then all have something to contribute, and the contributions of all are needed to achieve the ultimate end. A universal civiliza-

32. "Recueil des interventions faites à l'assemblée nationale française par le Président Léopold Sédar Senghor de 1946 à 1958 en sa qualité de Député du Sénégal," mimeographed (Dakar, n.d. [1967?]), p. 15.

tion must be the result of "reciprocal assimilation of one civilization by another." [33] A civilization which refuses to accept the gifts of others would soon begin to stagnate. An illustration of the kind of contributions which Africans can make, of particular interest to Americans, is his poem "To New York." In it, Senghor deplores that city's "mental muscles" and the skyscrapers which "eclipse the sun," longs for "a tender word in the absence of lips," and admonishes the city to "let black blood flow into [its] blood, to remove the rust from [its] steel joints, like an oil of life." [34]

Senghor's view that Africans needed a focal point for self-expression was at the root of negritude and has remained a constant theme in his writings. The theme is expressed in the notion of the "production" of civilization; part of the process of recapturing lost pride is for Africans to be aware of the need for creating, in addition to receiving. Creativity is inherent in the continuity from rehabilitation as the preindependence goal, through participation via independence, to contribution in the postindependence period. "Our aim," said Senghor, "is to bring our stone to the building of universal civilization, the one of the year 2000." [35]

Like other Africans, Senghor has remained sensitive to instances of non-African behavior which implies the denial of African equality, particularly regarding the need for African contributions. Thus, when the Society of European Culture (which considers America its offspring) suggested that the future world civilization would be an amalgam of European and European-derived values, Senghor immediately protested; he pointed out that this was an inadmissible, arrogant cultural imperialism which completely overlooked the intrinsic values of Asia, Latin America, and Africa. Moreover, being at home

33. *Liberté I*, p. 150.
34. Gerald Moore and Ulli Beier, eds., *Modern Poetry from Africa* (Baltimore: Penguin, 1963), p. 53.
35. In Jean Toulat, *Français d'aujourd'hui en Afrique noire* (Paris: Perrin, 1966), p. 45. In another context, he wrote that "there is nothing worse for men than to be content to be, that is to consume, not only the material goods produced by others, but also to be simple consumers of the ideas, the thoughts, the culture of others." *L'Unité africaine* (January 5, 1967).

with ideas, Senghor derives an aesthetic pleasure from the conviction that he, as an African and a member of the Third World, participates in shaping the future. "What is exalting," he said, "is the satisfaction of one's ambition to participate in the quest for definitions, for shedding light . . . and [to be] present at the meeting of [common] accomplishment." [36]

To some extent, Senghor's suggestion of the need for an African contribution to the world has a psychological, instrumental function: it may be seen as a transfer of the need for participation from the individual to the state or continent. Whereas Senghor believed earlier that the road to salvation led through individuals' sharing in the common decision-making process, he later suggested that civilizations share in decision-making on a wider, world scale. Participation appears as a constant, the scope as a variable. Senghor rests his case for Africa's contributions to the world not so much on a full inventory of specifics as on the right and the need for these African contributions. An African state, and by extension, Africa, must acquire a sense of the vitality of its mission—lest it be relegated to an ethnological curiosity. A sense of mission is, to be sure, a common ingredient in a viable nationalism; but in this case it seems to spring also from a psychological need for dignity and self-respect writ large.

Senghor's negritude as a working hypothesis is concerned more with the recognition of its continued existence than with the specific content or the evolution of that content. He holds that Aimé Césaire, Léon Damas, and he did not create negritude but rather recognized it and asserted it. "My only merit, I am convinced, is to have been a conscious and constant militant of negritude for 35 years," Senghor recently pointed out. The point is that it be recognized as a civilization, on a par with Arab, French, or Anglo-Saxon civilization. This point has been missed by the "tigritude" critics, who concentrate their attention on some aspects of earlier negritude. They reproach negritude for its tendency toward the idealization of Africa's past and argue that there is no need for "a tiger to proclaim its tigritude." This criticism does not, however, take issue with

36. *Ibid.*

Senghor, who argues that although the tiger may not speak of its stripes, the stripes nonetheless exist and must be recognized, and who, moreover, admonishes Africans to avoid cultural narcissism. Senghor also takes issue with those who find negritude too abstract by pointing out that the concept is "an abstraction *from* reality." [37]

Senghor distinguishes between civilization, a descriptive term, and culture, a moral concept. Civilization is the man-made environment which reflects man's adaptation to and influence on his physical setting. As Senghor uses the term, it is a taxonomy of man's behavior, ideas, and artifacts; it includes the spectrum of technical and moral values as well as the ways in which these are used, such as dialogue in politics and syncopation in music. Culture, by contrast, is a dynamic concept which raises the all-important question of the nature and purpose of man. It is the guiding spirit of civilization, "the spirit . . . which gives original style to a civilization." [38] Culture in this sense is not the superficial ornament of art, literature, or music. It is revolutionary in that it seeks to change existing relations between man and nature and, more important, between man and man, in the light of standards of morality and justice. Man is essentially a creator of culture, a moral being dedicated to the pursuit of justice, and his other activities are, by definition, subordinate to that end.

A number of important theoretical consequences flow from or are connected with the foregoing general outlook. In contrast with such other African leaders as Nkrumah, Senghor believes in the primacy of cultural over other types of activities of man. Since man's moral purpose is the creation of culture, only that purpose can justify politics and material well-being. As Senghor put it,

> Culture is not an appendage of politics, which one may cut without damage. It is not even a simple means of politics.

37. "Remise du diplome de Docteur Honoris Causa à Howard University, allocution du récipiendaire," mimeographed (Dakar, n.d. [1966?]), p. 2; *L'Unité africaine* (December 14, 1967).

38. *Séminaire organisé à l'occasion du congrès de l'union nationale de la jeunesse du Mali* (Rufisque: Imprimerie Fédérale du Mali, 1960), p. 68.

Culture is the prerequisite and the end of all politics deserving that name.[39]

His commitment to the whole of mankind is obviously incompatible with a theoretical precedence of narrow nationalism, either in Africa or elsewhere, or with any separatism of race, religion, or civilization. On this level, the question is not one of choosing Senegal, Africa, or Europe, but one of choosing man. As he wrote in 1960,

> Our humanism . . . cannot, without peril, stop in West Africa, or even in Africa. An efficient humanism must be open: it excludes . . . nationalism, pan-Negrism. . . . The only "pan-ism" which fits the needs of the twentieth century, let us dare proclaim it, is pan-humanism.[40]

It should not be surprising that a man of Senghor's poetic vision should seek to manipulate images. To the pessimism of "realists" and other students of international affairs, Senghor opposes a utopian humanism which regards the end of the colonial era as a major turning point in the history of mankind, and calls for drastic changes in the relations among peoples: hence his expectations—and admonitions—that knowledge be transferred and wealth be equalized on a world-wide scale for the benefit of all. Senghor frequently refers to his conviction that men are moved in part by symbols; it is neither illogical nor unrealistic to assume, in consequence, that important facets of the behavior of men can be changed by changing the symbols which motivate it.

Negritude

Senghor's cultural thought, developed in addition to or simultaneously with the general theory discussed above, was channeled into a number of specific strands related to different sets

39. *Ibid.*
40. *Ibid.*, pp. 69–70.

of problems. The first was negritude, a black cultural nationalism originated by Senghor and two other black students in Paris during the nineteen-thirties. Negritude was at first a reaction against French cultural pretensions as well as a function of widespread intellectual criticism of the role of the Cartesian tradition; during this period Senghor reinterpreted negritude in the light of political and other priorities; he suggested that the emotive and humanist ingredients of black culture be preserved at the same time that Africans acquire the techniques for modernization, and that these qualities be offered to a dehumanized, technological world.

Early negritude was an instrument of liberation from a black identity crisis induced by some aspects of France's assimilation policy. That policy rested on the noble ideals of the French Revolution, according to which men are created equal everywhere. Men encountered in foreign, unfamiliar lands were therefore presumed to have the same innate capabilities as did Europeans and needed only to demonstrate these capabilities to be accepted as equals in fact. From the point of view of the recipients of that theory, the problem arose from the nature of the test used to elicit the demonstration. That test was the complete assimilation, by black people, of the standards and behavior of French civilization. And the corollary was that, before assimilation, the world of the blacks was an uncivilized void. In the eyes of Europeans, the world still centered on their subcontinent, and the "obvious" backwardness and inferiority of others was rationalized into such theories as the "prelogical mind" of unfortunate non-European natives.

It was only a matter of time before such sensitive Africans as Senghor would react against Frenchmen calling into question the very existence of the values of African civilization. After having briefly and innocently accepted the French tabula rasa thesis, Senghor set about to rediscover and rehabilitate his African cultural heritage and became a leading apostle of negritude. Arguing on the basis of cultural relativism, Senghor pointed out the logical and functional fallacies of a doctrine of white supremacy—or of anyone's supremacy, for that matter. "It is their human qualities which confer rights on men, not their

cation to equality, which is capable of serving the needs of others in another age. Bread, to Senghor, was less important than the psychological nourishment of equality. No doubt Senghor's personal experiences in France oriented his perceptions to some extent. He recognizes that the success of negritude was the result in part of at least two important trends in French contemporary ideas. One was the insecurity and anguish which followed World War I, leading to an undercurrent of irrationalism that questioned and ridiculed conventional European values and from which France emerged tarnished by absurdities. The other was the work of French scholars taking a fresh look at assumptions about the relative value of differing civilizations. They learned—and taught— that African civilizations, if only one made the effort to understand them within their own context, were far from the wastelands they had been portrayed to be. "The great lesson of my professors at the Sorbonne," Senghor wrote, "was to forget their lessons to discover my truth." [47]

The success of negritude in overcoming the cultural crisis is no doubt also related to Senghor's views on neocolonialism. Seen in a historical perspective of widespread culture contacts, that phenomenon does not appear to Senghor as the immovable manichaeistic monster it has become in the eyes of some. The colonialism of old, Senghor believes, has left the world stage never to return. For a political leader in an Africa still sensitive to newly recovered pride, Senghor has a remarkably detached view which is probably ahead of its political times. A glance backward into history indicates that past colonialism, in addition to leaving ruins in its path, has also contributed new ideas and techniques.[48] Perhaps more important, there is little to be gained from a morbid fascination with the seamy side of colonialism. The colonial era created "two blind spots in our eyes, the

47. L'Unité africaine (July 4, 1968). Elsewhere, Senghor notes that France "invited us to make, of its museums and of its university teaching, . . . cultural instruments, I mean instruments of liberation and progress." Liberté I, p. 314.
48. "Europe was not the loser as a result of the Roman conquest, and neither was India following the Aryan conquest, nor the Middle East and North Africa following the Arab conquest." Séminaire, p. 70.

ulcers of our inferiority complex and the resentment of the conquerors," [49] both of which must be healed before a more balanced judgment is possible. What is needed is the fresh outlook of responsible, free men:

> Let us cease vituperating against colonialism and Europe and making them responsible for all our ills. Aside from the fact that this would not be entirely just, it is a negative attitude, which reveals an inferiority complex, the very [complex] with which the colonizer inoculated us and of which we are, secretly, the accomplice. It is too facile an alibi for our laziness, for our egoism as intellectuals, for our failures. [50]

Senghor's one-time certainty that he had defined negritude for all time has receded into a working hypothesis. At first, because of the intensity of his quest for identity he allowed himself to assume that he had discovered the very essence of black African culture. He subsequently recognized that his judgment was somewhat hasty. As he expressed it in 1968,

> When I was younger I would gladly have represented myself as a spokesman for Africa, or at least for negritude. In the meantime experience has taught me the differences between Negroes and between other African peoples, and it would be presumptuous on my part to speak on behalf of either. [51]

Nonetheless, his basic notion of an African culture and civilization which must be recognized as equal to all others remains an anchor in his thought. Shortly before Senegal's independence, he addressed himself to that question; he suggested that it was difficult to give negritude specific content outside of references to African traditions and to the general observation that African culture tends to breed warm personal human relations. He also proposed an inventory of the content of negritude

49. *Deutschland-Berichte*, IV, no. 11 (October, 1968), 19.
50. *Séminaire*, p. 70.
51. *German Tribune* (October 5, 1968), p. 7.

and of the encounter of civilizations, from which could be derived an eventual understanding of the dynamics of the ultimate symbiosis. No doubt his other interests and responsibilities have prevented him from pursuing that line of inquiry more fully. But his commitment to understanding and promoting the values of African culture resulted in the first Festival of Negro and Negro-African Arts, held under his sponsorship in Dakar in April, 1966.

A black-white African bridge

For many years Senghor has sought to enlarge his concern with negritude by adding to it, from the viewpoint of a continental Africa, the predominantly white civilizations north of the Sahara. This line of investigation was reinforced after independence in 1960 and after the creation of the Organization of African Unity in 1963. In contrast to the political reasoning of some African leaders interested in furthering African unity, Senghor predictably followed his inclination to build on cultural grounds. In a speech during the opening ceremonies of the OAU, Senghor outlined one of the common grounds of an all-African civilization as follows:

> What binds us is beyond history—it is rooted in prehistory. It has to do with geography, with ethnic factors and, therefore, with culture. It is anterior to Christianity and Islam; it is anterior to colonization. It is this cultural community which I call africanité.

This outline contains an element characteristic of Senghor's thought, namely, a perspective higher than that of current and popular preoccupations with neocolonialism. He believes that any unity effort based solely, or even primarily, on colonialism and its "sequel" of underdevelopment is doomed to failure because it is too fragile, does not define Africa, and belongs largely to the past. Moreover, it would imply logically that African unity would crumble once colonialism and its undesirable consequences are removed completely.

The context of Senghor's successive statements on the need

for cooperation between black and white Africans suggests that he seeks to use cultural notions to influence political events. Several statements were made during the life of the Mali Federation, in 1959. These were designed to promote the integration, within the new African federation, of Senegalese and Soudanese by singling out common elements of culture. Sensitivity to political factors remains evident in Senghor's subsequent views. His disquisitions on the similarities of black and white African civilizations were accompanied by moves toward a rapprochement with North African countries, motivated partly by close personal affinities between him and President Bourguiba and King Hassan II, and partly by trade relations with North Africa. After 1963, following a temporary disagreement with Morocco over that country's alleged participation in a plot against the Senegalese government, close mutual relations resumed so that Morocco became one of three countries with which Senegal has signed a special friendship treaty. Moreover, the importance of North Africa for Senegal derives in part from past difficulties in setting up the four states bordering on the Senegal River as a subregional cooperation group; access to the north tends to diversify Senegal's foreign relations and to bypass Guinea and Mali should the need arise. Furthermore, the pro-Arab stand of Senegal during the 1967 Middle Eastern crisis was designed to help promote cooperation with North Africa, with Guinea, and with Mali.

Aside from such preoccupations, Senghor suggests that evidence from prehistory, physical and cultural anthropology, and linguistics indicates the existence of a common African background which should be exploited in laying the foundations of unity. "If we want to build a united Africa," he wrote, "we must do it solidly and, therefore, build it on our cultural convergences and not on our political divergences." [52] He regards arabité (or arabism, as the Arabs call it) as an element complementary to negritude in a dynamic relationship producing an African civilization.

52. "Les Fondements de l'africanité, ou négritude et arabité," mimeographed (Dakar, 1967), p. 106.

Senghor presents these African convergences as resting on three sets of factors. First, man was born in Africa. Rejecting the discredited thesis that Hamites or Asians are responsible for African civilization, Senghor believes that *Homo faber*, man the toolmaker, emerged in Africa during the Lower Paleolithic era and may well be the ancestor of *Homo sapiens*. Although American anthropologists are accepting an interpretation according to which the agricultural revolution occurred first in Kurdistan, on the flanks of the fertile crescent, Senghor maintains the older theory which places that revolution in the Nile valley and in Mesopotamia and holds that it was created by negroid peoples.

Second, and perhaps more in keeping with what anthropologists regard as valid today, Senghor postulates that such subspeciation as present differences between black and white Africa are the result of the interaction of environmental factors and genetic drift. Racial differentiation—through mutation of chromosomes—began some thirty to forty thousand years ago in Africa and continued elsewhere as peoples spread over the globe. Senghor holds that negroid people preceded such others as the caucasoid Cro-Magnon in the Mediterranean and in Europe.

The third, and perhaps most important, part of Senghor's theory concerns the underlying similarities and convergences among the peoples of Africa. The point is that if present differences among Africa's civilizations are the result of environmental factors, and if that environment cannot be expected to change *sui generis* in the foreseeable future, then Africans should recognize and proclaim the fundamental similarities which underlie their differences. What black Africans and Arabo-Berbers have in common can be stated briefly. First, they have racial or ethnic affinities, or both, testifying to the mélange which accompanied differentiation and migration. Second, they have common philosophic and religious beliefs: commitments to broad cultural and humanitarian values, to social justice, and to monotheism. Third, they share a belief in the importance of symbolism as expressed, for example, in abstract art or in the imagery which pervades their Weltanschauung. And, fourth,

Senghor suggests that there are similarities—and instances of convergence through mutual contact—in the structure of Arab and black African languages.

Francophonie

Another recent dimension of the cultural basis of Senegal's thinking about international affairs was the call, in mid-1966, for tightening the organization of francophonie, a loose community of French-language states and nations throughout the world. The proposal for such an ensemble originated with Presidents Senghor and Bourguiba, was defended and popularized by President Diori of Niger, and subsequently adopted as an official goal by the Organisation Commune Africaine et Malgache at its January, 1968, summit meeting.

The proposed French-Language Commonwealth (FLC) would encompass countries according to their location in three linguistic concentric circles. The first includes the former French territories in black Africa (Guinea and Mali presumably at a later date) and France; the second, Morocco, Tunisia, Algeria, and Lebanon in Africa, plus former Indochina; and the third circle would consist of countries where French is spoken by important minorities, specifically, Switzerland, Canada, Luxembourg, and Belgium. Haiti and the former Belgian colonies in black Africa could become members by virtue of their affinities with either the second or the third circle.

Senegal has suggested that organizing the FLC could proceed easily on the present foundation of international structures serving most of the states involved, especially those in the first concentric circle. These structures are of two kinds. One includes postindependence descendants of the French Union, such as the bilateral and multilateral cooperation agreements between African states and France or between African states. The FLC could serve to enlarge fields of mutual cooperation covered by regular meetings of African and French education and finance officials, and to create a joint advisory council on higher education, in which President Senghor has had a longtime interest. Further, the Parliamentary Union representing the legislatures of member states could, in a manner reminiscent of the Federal Council of the former French African federations, submit recommendations to national executives and thus exert popular pressures for strengthening existing ties.

The other kind of international structure has emerged since African independence. Among the most prominent examples are the Association des Universités Partiellement ou Entièrement de Langue Française, created in 1961 in Montreal and presided over by Jean-Marc Léger, a Canadian author and journalist; the United Nations Committee for the Defense of the French Language; and the International Council of the French Language, created in France in 1967 with the support of the Académie Française.

Cynics may well question the usefulness of such a project, which groups together peoples on four continents of whom many, from the point of view of conventional international relations, have very little in common. Can relatively superficial and unassimilated cultural similarities become a solid foundation for international cooperation? Is it reasonable to expect the Kerguelen Islands, Haiti, and the Islamic Republic of Mauritania to discover the resilience of their mutual ties simply because they—or their leaders—speak French? What is the significance for international affairs if the Canadian province of Quebec, Cambodia, and the Kinshasa-Congo respond as one to the poetry of Verlaine or the prose of Malraux? Or can one expect that, with their French cultural heritage reasserted by a few prophets, such divergent states as Guinea and Mali on the one hand, and Gabon and the Ivory Coast on the other, are bound to forget their differences and concentrate on what cultural affinities they may have been endowed with by French colonization?

What Senghor has in mind, however, can be understood only by considering the way he defines francophonie. "As for me," he wrote, "the notion of francophonie is a reality to the extent that it voices a feeling of solidarity at the level of a community of civilizations and of cultures which express themselves in French." [53] Keeping in mind Senghor's views about the pan-human convergence of differing civilizations, a reading of his

53. Senghor to author, November 20, 1968.

recent writings and speeches conveys the impression that francophonie is a new, Senghorian twist of the geography of world civilizations. These include overlapping categories: the civilizations of Africa, America, Asia, and Europe, the last in turn subdivided into the two which have made the greatest impact on the world, those of Britain and France. Francophonie, then, is an additional category of relations which qualifies as one of the world's great civilizations whose contributions are essential to achieve the ultimate goal.

Two kinds of motives account for President Senghor's initiative with respect to francophonie. One of these is primarily cultural and is an extension of his concern with the need for building cross-cultural bridges without regard to racial distinctions. Senghor believes that any effort to promote solidarity and cooperation in today's world must be global in scope so as to break down artificial barriers resulting from environmental influences:

> We cannot remain mutually isolated. In order to be ourselves fully, we must advance toward convergence with others. It is in this spirit that we conceive the necessary encounter of civilizations and of cultures, be they arabité, negritude, francophonie, or other forms of culture.[54]

In the same vein, negritude in the 1970s is no longer what it was twenty or thirty years before; it was adapted to the new environment of autonomy and independence. Whereas early negritude was an instrument of cultural liberation, the new negritude is an instrument of universalistic humanism. It is a negritude open to the fertilizing winds of other civilizations within the overall framework of mutually beneficial exchange through contact. At the same time, an enriched negritude can continue to make its rightful contributions to the emerging universal civilization, to become a respected producer—instead of remaining a passive consumer—of civilization.

According to Senghor, the civilization exemplified and spread by France qualifies as one of the world's greatest on several

54. *Ibid.*

counts. It qualifies, first, because of the relevance of its ideals of humanism and universalism, which ignore "racial" divisions, and, second, because of its real and permanent impact on former colonial areas. President Senghor believes that Africa has been marked by European colonizers much more than would-be African purists are willing to admit.[55] The profound differences between, say, English-language and French-language Africans have by now become classic. These differences do not result from language alone; they are manifest in different approaches to almost any given topic. One need not disregard tensions among French-speaking Africans to appreciate the existence of other extra-African influences. Anyone at home in both French and English culture—not merely languages—quickly detects undercurrents among young and old ranging from interested tolerance to veiled animosity. Partly in jest, they refer to each other as "francophonies" and "saxophones." Moreover, Senghor suggests that fears of francophonie dividing Africa are groundless at this level of generalization, which accents the overlapping and complementarity of different civilizations.

The third reason for which francophonie qualifies is the advantages which Africa can derive from that civilization. There is no question that Asian, American, or other European civilizations have much to offer to Africa. Other things being equal, German, British, or United States technological prowess is at least as valid as that originating in France and French-speaking modern countries. But for people speaking, reading, and thinking in French it is far easier, and at least in the short run more

55. One example of French influence on the elites of the former Soudan is as follows: "Among all our leaders, there is none who has not vibrated with Le Cid, who has not burst out laughing with Scapin, or whom Harpagon has not made both smile and quiver. We have admired, we do admire, and we shall always admire the pioneers of human dignity and freedom: Mirabeau and Danton, St. Just the precursor, Victor Hugo the voluntary exile, Gambetta and his commune, Jean Jaurès, his fire and attacks, France's millions of dead for the defense of liberties, but also Romain Rolland." L'Essor hebdomadaire (July 4, 1959). For a recent sample of an anglophone African who appears to have some difficulty understanding Senghor and negritude, partly because he limits himself to one secondary source, see Ayi Kwei Armah, "African Socialism: Utopian or Scientific?" Présence africaine (Fourth Quarter, 1967).

effective, to use French as a preferred medium of communication.

Moreover, Senghor rests his case for francophonie in part on linguistic and aesthetic characteristics of the French heritage. These include the qualities of a language which is a precise means of communication, which can impart complex technical knowledge to its adherents with comparative ease, and which is likely to remain a universal tongue. The aesthetic gratifications inherent in French-oriented civilization are useful building blocks in promoting cross-cultural understanding and cooperation—a feature to which members of more pragmatic civilizations are sometimes not sufficiently sensitized.

The other major motive of Senghor's francophone initiative is economic and reflects a clear understanding of the material interest of Senegal and other French-language African states.[56] The economic objectives of francophonie are an attempt to insure or at least facilitate the continuation of important elements of French assistance and at the same time to diversify the sources of such assistance by adding French culture areas. This attempt applies to three specific elements of foreign economic relations.

The first is the continued future availability of expatriate technical assistants. Such cadres are needed in Senegal for at least another ten years. Until now the African states have served as important markets in which to place former colonial officials, who make up about half the total French expatriates serving abroad. An increasing proportion of them, however, is due to retire soon; and they can be replaced neither by younger, inexperienced men fulfilling their military obligations nor by civil servants, for whom the need in France is increasing. One of the purposes of francophonie, then, is to attract to Africa expatriate cadres from such other modern nations as Switzerland and Canada.

56. As Senghor defined it, francophonie "must deal with cultural questions, on one hand, and with economic questions on the other." *L'Unité africaine* (June 30, 1966). Elsewhere, he said that "the chief result of my conversations with Canadian authorities, at the federal and provincial levels" was that Senegal is going to get more technical assistance. *Jeune afrique* (October 30, 1966), p. 41.

The second area is that of the deterioration of the terms of trade. Given the OCAM states' preference for artificial supports for their sales and purchases abroad, and the reluctance of rich nations to grant the desired concessions, French support for the Africans takes on greater importance. In fact, the French government is one of the very few rich nations which has consistently seconded the Africans' demands for protection in international markets. Hence, a francophonie whose kernel consists of OCAM states could be useful in pressuring France into continuing support, and international economic forces and organizations into accepting the protection sought.

Finally, the third aspect of the proposed FLC's economic objectives concerns French aid generally. For several years the French government has been thinking about greater diversification in aid recipients; since the total, absolute amount of French assistance is not likely to increase, this inevitably means a reduction of such aid to Africa. This trend was accentuated following the popular unrest in France in 1968 and its consequences for the French economy: hence the need to attract other aid sources, hopefully in part from French-speaking donors.

Important parts of Senghor's occasionally abstruse dissertations on cultural problems are conscious attempts to change environment from the point of view of specific cultural, political, and economic problems. No doubt the future will evaluate the degree of his successes. But the outline of such an evaluation may be sketched today. The success of early negritude is attested by generations of Africans who have used it, as Senghor suggested, as an instrument for cultural liberation. Other, post-independence strands of his thinking such as africanité, francophonie, and a world civilization are but taking their first steps. Their success, moreover, depends on vastly more complex and numerous factors than did the relatively simple African-French confrontation.

To conform with the "utility" tests we are wont to apply to theoretical constructs, we may raise the question of the effectiveness of Senghor's vision to change the world. The obvious answer that may commend itself is that it is not very useful in understanding the world as it is. Such problems as the lassitude of the rich to succor the poor, the violent conflicts occasionally flaring up all over the globe, or the ethnic, political, and material conflicts within Africa are too tenacious to yield to Senghor's faint and visionary stabs at men's consciences. People in Nigeria, Israel, or Arab countries march to entirely different drummers and have no taste for philosophical frivolities.

But this kind of answer overlooks Senghor's point. He is not describing the world as it is today; he is turning his eyes toward the future. Conventional wisdom appears less than adequate for a profound appreciation of the seemingly revolutionary forces which tug at the secure theoretical fortresses of the past. Such traditional notions as democracy, collective security, racial superiority, free world markets, and ideological jousts are being emptied of content and connotation.

Men like Senghor are not merely conscious of these changes; they are asking the obvious question, "Where do we go from here?" Senghor's ideal answer, couched in the terms of a panhuman convergence toward a peaceful world of men sharing their particular heritage and benefiting from that of others, is broad enough to allow for experimentation and attractive enough to warrant the undivided attention of mankind. Just as men are, to a large extent, responsible for the way they have shaped the past, so they will be responsible for the kind of world they create in the future. What Senghor suggests is that the two broad alternatives of continuing in accustomed molds, on one hand, or striking out for new creations, on the other, pit against each other habitual pessimism and novel optimism. As a manipulator of ideas, Senghor knows that men's behavior results in part from the images which project an increasingly complex reality, and that many traditional images are badly out of focus. His message is simple: An effort ought to be made to create a new image of peaceful, harmonious cooperation instead of conflict.

His message fulfills two requirements central to his cultural concerns: it comes from Africa and thus is a creative offering from that continent, and it focuses on a universalistic humanism of stimulating relevance to the world. Man ought to devote himself not merely to the pursuit of material welfare. His greatest rewards will be reaped from the cultivation of the separate condiments of distinct civilizations enriched by those of others. The eventual, universal banquet will make available the best that each civilization has to offer, and the spices will be accepted and savored widely and freely on their own merits.

THE AFRICAN FRENCH-LANGUAGE ASSOCIATION

Senegal's inter-African relations are concentrated chiefly within the French-language association of states of which she is a leading member—President Senghor is referred to as the association's vice-dean. This association rests on a number of common ties, including economic dependence on France, the influence of French language and culture, the defense of territorial integrity and national sovereignty, and a preference for functional inter-African cooperation and for moderation and reason in interstate relations. Member states also make frequent attempts to harmonize their views on particular foreign policy problems, but there is no expectation that this can—or should —be done successfully. Because of differing domestic problems, regional contexts, and geographical areas, member states agree that it is impossible to find agreement on all foreign policy problems. Moreover, the association has remained a fairly closed corporation. New members must be approved unanimously; the approval of two new members (both French-speaking states) reflects political concerns, chiefly the defense of territorial integrity. Further, ties with France, as well as the benefits from the European Development Fund, militate against the admission of English-language states even if these shared the association's defensive objectives.

Insurance against isolation

Senegal's inter-African policy after the breakup of the Mali Federation made what was on the surface an abrupt volte-face. From having been a champion of political inter-African ties, Senghor became an advocate of nonpolitical functionalism almost overnight. For Senegal, the failure of the Mali experiment meant the failure of long efforts to prevent economic isolation.

The Mali Republic—the new name for the former Soudan—
severed all economic and political relations with Senegal in a
last blow to Senghor's hopes. And since three-fourths of Senegal's total inter-African trade was with the Soudan, the blow
was a painful one; it lost the vast hinterland which it was designed to serve. Hence, Senegal, after the sudden Mali action,
needed other partners.

Moreover, French African leaders generally were uncomfortable at the prospect of the isolation from one another that
resulted from national independence. For one and one-half
decades, they had been accustomed to frequent and close mutual contacts in Paris, Dakar, and throughout the former federation. Hence, they experienced a psychological need for the
security of familiar company. The abstract notion of African
unity popularized by Senghor also acted as a stimulus for the
maintenance of past contacts. That notion had found favorable
echoes among the elites of the African states, and the incumbent
political leaders were conscious that the image must take a
more concrete shape. As Senghor described it, it has grown into
a "mystique of unity [which] undeniably exists today." [57]

Since the prospective smaller circle of states around Senegal
was broken and since the major obstacle to cooperation with
the Ivory Coast no longer existed, Senghor suggested the formation of a larger group which would encompass most of the
former territories of the two French African federations. The
Senegalese government openly admitted that its previous policy
was not only a failure but also a mistake. The prime minister
wrote:

> Our error was that under the pretext of fighting balkan-
> ization, we did not take into consideration . . . territorial-
> ism. We allowed ourselves to be seduced by the mirage of
> the construction most satisfying to our spirit and, taking
> our ideal for reality, we believed that it would be sufficient
> to condemn territorialism.
>
> We must therefore begin with these micro-nationalisms
> —which are the reality in this strange universe of Africa
> in the twentieth century—to create modestly, progres-

57. *Afrique nouvelle* (April 3, 1959).

sively, the base of . . . [a] large African nation. Future
cooperation will be restricted to a flexible coordination of
national policies.[58]

Fortunately for Senegal, circumstances favored a positive
reply by the Ivory Coast. Several factors accounted for the new
Ivoirien willingness to cooperate with Senegal in setting up a
French-language association of states. The first was economic:
the disappearance of the former Federation of French West
Africa and of its potential successor, the Mali Federation. As
indicated earlier, the Ivory Coast was in many ways the most
economically developed of the former territories in AOF. She
stood out for a consistent favorable balance of external trade
and had opposed political federalism in Africa on the grounds
that she was being used as a milk cow since her enforced subsidies to AOF exceeded the returns she received from it. With
the collapse of the Mali Federation, there was no longer any
handicap to economic and technical cooperation with other
independent African states.

The second set of reasons was political. As president of the
interterritorial RDA, Houphouet-Boigny had good reason to
believe that inter-African political ties were utopian. The RDA,
a movement rather than a party, was based on the autonomy
of its territorial components. What preindependence inter-
African cohesion it could muster depended largely on the relatively weak grip of territorial leaders on domestic politics. But
once that grip tightened in the period surrounding independence, cleavages among RDA leaders came into the open. As
Houphouet-Boigny reflected, "the political unity of the RDA
not being possible, we were led . . . to suggest . . . administrative and economic coordination." [59]

Moreover, the demise of the Mali Federation also removed
from inter-African competition a political pole of attraction
which the Ivory Coast regarded as inimical to her influence.
Houphouet-Boigny, in fact, had created the Conseil de l'Entente in April, 1959, as a counterweight to the Mali Federation,

58. Mamadou Dia, *Nations africaines et solidarité mondiale* (Paris:
Presses Universitaires de France, 1960), p. 140.
59. *Afrique nouvelle* (September 11, 1959).

with the Ivory Coast as its center and Houphouet-Boigny as its leader.[60] The purpose of the Entente, in contrast to that of the Mali Federation and the Ghana-Guinea union created in 1958, was ostensibly nonpolitical: to coordinate common interests, especially in matters economic and technical. But the unstated function was to assure inter-African influence for the Ivory Coast.

Union Africaine et Malgache

Senegal therefore took the initiative in September, 1960, one month after the Mali fiasco. Senghor asked Houphouet-Boigny to convene a round-table discussion of all former French African leaders, since Senegal was hardly in a position to take official leadership. Mamadou Dia traveled to Cotonou, capital city of Dahomey, to meet with Houphouet-Boigny and suggested the creation of an "Entente-like association" to facilitate cooperation in matters financial, economic, social, technical, and cultural.[61] The Senegalese initiative, with the support and official leadership of the Ivory Coast president, led to two meetings in the fall of 1960—one in Brazzaville and one in Abidjan—out of which emerged the twelve-nation agreement to create such an association.[62] The association was formalized at a meeting of experts in Dakar and took shape as the Union Africaine et Malgache in September, 1961.

The structure of the UAM, as well as the timing for the creation of its specialized agencies, proclaimed its limited objectives. The emphasis on technical and economic cooperation was highlighted by the fact that the most important of these

60. One of the four Entente leaders, President Hamani Diori of Niger, expressed the nature of the personal ties which underlay the Entente by saying that "the quasi-religious respect, the profound admiration which we harbor toward President Houphouet-Boigny . . . constitute the strongest guarantee of our Entente." *Afrique nouvelle* (November 26, 1962). The Entente included the Ivory Coast, Dahomey, Upper Volta, and Niger.

61. See *ibid.* (September 28, October 5, 14, 1960).

62. The twelve states included, in addition to Senegal and the Ivory Coast, four from AOF (Mauritania, Dahomey, Upper Volta, and Niger), the four states of former French Equatorial Africa (the Central African Republic, Gabon, Chad, and Brazzaville-Congo), Madagascar, and Cameroun.

agencies, the Organisation Africaine et Malgache de Coopération Economique, was formed even before the UAM charter
was signed; at the same time the UAM leaders agreed to establish a common airline, Air Afrique. Other agencies subsequently
created include the Union Africaine et Malgache des Postes et
Télécommunications with headquarters in Brazzaville, and the
Union Africaine et Malgache de Défense with headquarters in
Ouagadougou, capital city of Upper Volta. UAM policy was
defined by a semiannual conference of the member states' chief
executives. An administrative secretary-general, appointed by
the conference, assisted the UAM president to implement decisions and oversee the work of the deliberative and consultative
specialized agencies.[63]

Despite the intended emphasis on economic cooperation, the
twelve UAM states, or the Brazzaville group, as they were called
before September, 1961, found themselves involved in inter-
African political controversies. This was the result partly of
"internal" and partly of "external" factors. One of the psychological consequences of national independence was a perceived
need for having an immediately visible impact in international
relations, be it ever so humble. The French African states had
been active, as indicated earlier, in interstate relations as a result of the nature of the French framework. Their desire to
become visible after independence was thus also grounded in
previous experiences which had preconditioned them to play an
international role. As the UAM leaders stated, they agreed to
seek common attitudes on international political problems "in

63. Only the UAMD showed signs of incipient supranationality, although
it never performed such functions. The UAM charter foresaw the use of
collective armed force in self-defense after consultation with national governments; but the UAM leaders decided, at their 1962 Libreville summit
meeting, that the use of armed forces would be automatic upon the
request of a member state. Moreover, the leaders decided that the consent
of member states was not needed for the use of armed forces on their
territory if "the scope, violence, or the speed of aggression" was such as to
interrupt "the free play of its institutions or the exercise of its sovereignty."
The UAMD, however, has existed only on paper. See Afrique nouvelle
(August 31, 1962; September 6, 1961; October 8, 1962; and February
21, 1962); Fraternité (March 31, 1961); and Le Monde (September 7,
12, 1961).

order to impose ourselves on the attention of international opinion." [64]

One issue in which the Brazzaville group became involved as a result of such "internal" motivations was the Algerian liberation conflict. In view of its close ties with France and simultaneous sympathies for the Algerians' cause, the group believed that it was especially qualified to try to help settle the conflict. (Senegal's role and policy in that respect are discussed in greater detail below.) Meeting in Brazzaville at the end of 1960, the twelve states affirmed their commitment to Algeria's self-determination and called on France to end the war through negotiations. It was the emphasis on conciliation which generated vocal opposition on the part of some African leaders and provided one of the elements of inter-African discord. At their initial meeting in January, 1961, the Casablanca group called for unequivocal assistance for Algeria on the grounds that the liberation struggle should be carried to a victorious end rather than being compromised through talks with the French.

Between 1960 and 1962, a series of "external" issues confronted the UAM states with the need to respond, and helped define their position as one of the poles of an inter-African split. One such issue arose when Morocco claimed sovereignty over the newly independent Islamic Republic of Mauritania. Although relations between Mauritania and the other territories in AOF had never been particularly close because of that country's almost exclusively Arab heritage, the Brazzaville group supported the new state against Morocco's intentions. To the Brazzaville leaders, the real issue was not the historical and religious considerations underlying the Moroccan claim, but that of the protection of territorial integrity of new states. If one African country were allowed to incorporate another, then the precedent did not augur well for the future stability of the continent. Artificial though they were, national boundaries had to be respected to provide at least a minimum of security and could be adjusted only by mutual consent. The issue led directly to the institutionalization of the African cleavage through

64. *Afrique nouvelle* (December 13, 1961).

the creation of the Casablanca group, called together by the Moroccan government to seek support for its demands.

The other major external issue concerned the former Belgian Congo. The policy of Senegal and of the UAM on that issue followed earlier commitments. The problem arose when the new Congolese central government was unable to maintain internal order in the face of strong opposition groups. The two major contending forces in the Congo—one led by President Joseph Kasavubu, the other by Patrice Lumumba—solicited inter-African support, casting the issue in terms of ideological tenets that functioned as an invitation for an inter-African contest. UAM leaders defined legitimacy in the Congo in terms of the central constitutional government, whereas Casablanca states used the criterion of ideological affinity and hence recognized the Gizenga government in Stanleyville and subsequently supported Lumumba in his struggle against Kasavubu. The crucial issue was that of intervention in the domestic affairs of another African state: it drove another wedge between the two African groups, since one justified it on the basis of a judgment about the acceptability of Congolese domestic leaders whereas the other justified it on the basis of the principle in support of legal governments.

The dynamics of inter-African politics

The creation of the Organization of African Unity (OAU) in 1963 provoked a crisis within the UAM. Several African leaders, among whom President Sékou Touré figured prominently, asked that the UAM be disbanded in deference to the new all-African organization. A larger number of African leaders pressed the argument that, inasmuch as the Casablanca group was defunct, the UAM should likewise be dissolved. From the point of view of the UAM leaders, however, their organization should not and could not be equated with the Casablanca group. That group had in effect ceased to exist by late 1962, mostly because the issues which brought it to life had been settled, but also because some Casablanca leaders had second thoughts about their initial support of such ancillary issues as Egypt versus

Israel with which they were not directly concerned. By contrast, the UAM was a going concern, some of its activities having been honored by emulation on the part of the Casablanca nations and its principles copied by the OAU. UAM leaders were therefore reluctant to disband some of their specialized agencies.

In view of the underlying tensions among the UAM states and those of the former Casablanca group, UAM leaders were cautious lest their technical agencies be taken over and subjected to political pressures as a result of incorporation into the new OAU. They had worked for several years to create structures for inter-African cooperation; perhaps they also took a certain proprietary interest in these structures and wanted to avoid their destruction at the hands of an OAU whose leadership included the most outspoken critics of the UAM and its principles.

In spite of these misgivings, UAM leaders realized that the creation of the OAU had opened a new chapter in the history of inter-African relations and that some adjustment was indicated. Their answer was to transform—but not to abandon—the UAM. This was done in part to forestall strong criticism by African leaders arguing that its continued existence was a danger to the OAU. Inasmuch as the debate took place against the background of political animosity between two African organizations and of the failure of the one group, it was an issue which derived its importance in part from the psychologically negative consciousness of failure and resentment on the part of the former Casablanca group. Hence, it was decided to placate the critics by at least taking the political sting out of the French-language organization.

The UAM leaders, meeting between July, 1963, and March, 1964, renamed their organization Union Africaine et Malgache de Coopération Economique, to underscore the changed priorities from the political to the economic. Its stature grew through the recruitment of an additional member state, Togo, admitted at the July, 1963, summit meetings in Cotonou. As a further concession to the OAU, it was decided that the specialized agencies could, if circumstances should warrant it, be subsequently turned over to the OAU.

Beneath these general concerns, shared more or less among all UAM leaders, there remained divisions regarding the purpose of their organization. On the surface, this was evident in the long delays needed to bring about an agreement. The OAU was formed in May, 1963, and the charter of the transformed UAM was signed only in April, 1964. UAM leaders were divided into three schools suggesting three solutions to the crisis prompted by the creation of the OAU. Some wanted to abandon the political functions of the UAM and concentrate on economic and technical cooperation; others preferred to decide on the basis of effectiveness of functions; and a few favored merging the UAM into the OAU outright. They did agree to dissolve the UAM caucusing group at the United Nations and took pride in having solved a dispute between Niger and Dahomey.

But the crucial disagreement concerning the future political content of the organization was that between Presidents Senghor and Houphouet-Boigny. It has been widely suggested that their disagreement was the result of previous rivalry between Senegal and the Ivory Coast. This rivalry no doubt contributed to the two countries' disagreement regarding the UAM's functions. But the primary reason for the disagreement was rooted in the two leaders' views of their national interest as reflecting the situation of 1963–64 and not the period of the preindependence federation.

The Ivory Coast was making swift progress toward the modernization of her economy. She was intimately associated with the three other Entente countries, which provided a ready market for some of her exports. What progress she had made was the result of ties not so much with the larger French-language ensemble as with France and the Entente countries. Houphouet-Boigny's inter-African relations had become concentrated on the Entente and he was staying away from most larger inter-African meetings of heads of state. The economic usefulness of the UAM, to Houphouet-Boigny, was thus relatively marginal. Consequently, the Ivory Coast looked on the UAM from the point of view of its political usefulness. This priority became evident when Houphouet-Boigny made a number of overtures designed to enlarge his sphere of influence: he courted the leaders of Mali and Guinea by using his position as leader of the Entente as a steppingstone. Had these overtures been successful, the result would have further isolated Senegal.

Senegal, by contrast, was preoccupied primarily with the need to enlarge her economic frontiers. Consequently, Senghor emphasized the prospective economic functions of the UAM, in both its horizontal and vertical dimensions. Senegal was engaged in negotiations to improve economic relations with two groups of African states. The first group included Nigeria, Sierra Leone, and The Gambia, which led Senghor to suggest the formation of a West African grouping of states cutting across linguistic barriers. And, second, his efforts to create a regional subgroup encompassing the riverside states of the Senegal River had made some progress. Experts from the four states involved, meeting in Bamako in July, 1963, had recommended the internationalization of the river basin and creation of an Interstate Committee; this was followed by a summit meeting in Nouakchott, capital city of Mauritania, in December, 1963, when the heads of state agreed on a common policy for the exploitation of the river.

Another factor in the mind of the Senegalese was the possible influence of a purely economic and technical association on relations with Mali and Guinea. Relations with both countries had improved since the end of 1962, and Senghor hoped that the depoliticization of the UAM might well lead to a resumption of at least some of the preindependence economic interchange. Further, Senghor was concerned lest the politicization of the UAM endanger material assistance from France and Europe. As he expressed it, "The major problem is that of our economic independence which . . . can be resolved only through the reinforcement of our horizontal solidarities." [65] Although there was no imminent danger that European aid to Senegal would be reduced measurably, it seems likely that Senghor reasoned that a dramatization of the need for material assistance would be less likely to detract from the EEC's commitment than would an emphasis on inter-African political quarrels. By accentuating the importance of the economic and technical nature of the UAM, Senghor sought to propitiate the economic

65. *Afrique contemporaine*, III, no. 13 (May–June, 1963), 2.

framework on which the modernization of Senegal depended.

If it could be said that the creation of the UAMCE represented a "victory" for Senegal in its dispute with the Ivory Coast regarding the political content of the French-speaking association of states, this was to be short-lived. President Houphouet-Boigny continued to insist on the priority given to political problems. He underscored his opposition to the UAMCE by a number of moves designed to undercut, and to show the political uselessness of, the new organization. He sought to revive old RDA ties and called on the leaders of Upper Volta and Niger, as well as Mali and Guinea, to join him in widening and strengthening cooperation with the Ivory Coast.

Since it was obvious that the UAMCE merely papered over a serious malaise concerning its proper political functions and that the perpetuation of the disagreement could result only in weakening the organization, Senghor conceded Houphouet-Boigny's point. He therefore decided to mend his fences with the Ivoirien leader in a series of meetings with the presidents of the Ivory Coast and other Entente leaders. The reconciliation, facilitated through the good offices of André Guillabert, a prominent Senegalese legislator and diplomat who was also a close friend of Houphouet-Boigny, paved the way for a more frankly political stance in inter-African relations.

As interpreted by Houphouet-Boigny and his friends, inter-African political relations were dominated by a thorough disillusionment with the OAU. The cleavage between the African "moderates" and "radicals" persisted and, more important, threatened to render the OAU useless in its ability to engender cooperation among its member states. The vocal minority in the OAU, whose influence was out of proportion to its numbers, continued to insist that the all-African organization behave in a manner approved by only a few members. The minority insistence that no regional African organization be allowed to function was defeated officially as a result of strong representations on the part of those who believed that regional organizations had something to contribute to Africa.

This did not, however, deter the minority from continuing to inject into the OAU their notions of what was right even if this did violence to the sovereignty and territorial integrity of sister states. On the Kinshasa-Congo question, for instance, they refused to recognize the right of that state to send the legal prime minister to attend international conferences because of their distaste for the incumbent, Moise Tshombe. In fact, Algeria, Morocco, and Ghana declared that they would boycott such a meeting, thus sacrificing the right of a sovereign state to send a delegate of her own choosing. The issue involved was whether to support the legally constituted government of another African country regardless of the policies pursued by that government. The minority chose to support the domestic opposition in the Congo and therefore remained silent in the face of a Congolese government appeal to provide an inter-African military force to replace the foreign mercenaries it was using to put down armed rebellion.

From the viewpoint of the OCAM states, the basic problem of the OAU was not so much that it was relatively ineffective as an international instrument for solving problems; it would have been easy simply to ignore it and to concentrate instead on the common interests of the OCAM members. The danger was that, unchecked, the weakness of the OAU could be manipulated by the vocal minority and pose a threat to the territorial integrity and sovereignty of all independent African states. OCAM leaders were not willing to accept the minority proposition according to which the principle of noninterference in the internal affairs of sister states should be ignored if a leader or government does not behave in accordance with their expectations. On that issue, the position of the OCAM leaders had not changed: such interference is legitimate only if it serves to reinforce the legal government of a given country, regardless of one's estimate of what that government symbolizes.

The reaffirmation of the political tasks of the French-language association took expression in yet another organizational change. At a summit meeting in Nouakchott in February, 1965, the UAMCE was transformed into the Organisation Commune Africaine et Malgache. The OCAM charter specifically committed its members to "mutual consultations on foreign policy problems."

The two major substantive decisions made by OCAM leaders during the summit demonstrated their commitment to noninterference. One of these decisions concerned the Léopoldville-Congo. In order to prevent the Congo's isolation in Africa as a result of the "radicals'" interference, and to avoid inviting the cold war into Africa, the OCAM leaders responded favorably to a request by the Congolese government and admitted the country as a member.

To be sure, the personality of the Congo's prime minister, Tshombe, provoked an element of disagreement among OCAM leaders, just as it did at the level of the OAU. But the majority of OCAM leaders, in spite of the delicacy of the Tshombe issue, gave priority to the principle involved rather than sacrificing it to the subsidiary issue of the incumbent of a particular office. Their willingness to rapidly come to the aid of the legal government of the Congo was reflected in the ambiguity which surrounded that country's admission as a member state. The official admission took place in Abidjan in May, 1965. That meeting had been called by Houphouet-Boigny rather than by the OCAM's acting president, Moktar Ould Daddah of Mauritania. Moreover, the Congo was admitted by a majority of OCAM states, whereas the OCAM charter, elaborated and signed subsequently, required unanimity for admission of new members. The procedure used for admission, however, was never called into question, since by the time the OCAM charter was signed Tshombe was no longer his country's prime minister; his removal from that post disposed of a bone of contention among OCAM states.

In addition to accepting the Congo into their fold, the OCAM leaders also made a strong declaration in support of order in that war-torn country. Their communiqué committed them to "bring back peace in the Léopoldville-Congo by helping the legal government to national reconciliation in order and freedom." [66] The Senegalese position was spelled out further by

66. *L'Unité africaine* (May 26, 1965). Belgian officials apparently tried to convince OCAM to provide an inter-African force to be used in the Congo. A Belgian delegation to the OCAM summit included the Belgian ambassadors in Switzerland and Mauritania, who talked with Senghor, Houphouet-Boigny, and Presidents Tsiranana of Madagascar and Tombalbaye of Chad. President Senghor, however, vetoed the suggestion unless it be taken over by the OAU. See *L'Unité africaine* (February 1, 8, 1965).

Doudou Thiam: unequivocal support for the legal government, OAU supervision of forthcoming national elections, an inter-African police force under the control of the OAU, and a general amnesty in the Congo. The point was that this type of intervention was legitimate since its purpose was domestic order at the behest and under the control of the legal government. Senegal opened an embassy in Léopoldville to underscore her support.

The other major OCAM decision taken at the 1965 summit meeting in February was rooted in the same concern for non-interference. It addressed itself to alleged conscious efforts on the part of the government of Ghana to subvert, overthrow, and replace African governments that did not enjoy President Nkrumah's favor. This issue rapidly mushroomed into a major confrontation between OCAM and the OAU. It took the form of a diplomatic offensive by the Ivory Coast, with Senghor playing a moderating role although he was more than sensitive to the complaints against Ghana.

The opening salvo was fired by the OCAM leaders at Nouakchott. The final communiqué condemned "with energy the action . . . of Ghana which welcomes subversion agents and organizes camps on her national territory." The communiqué, read to the press by Senghor, also announced an OCAM decision not to attend the forthcoming OAU summit to be held in Accra, capital city of Ghana, in protest over the alleged subversive activities.

An event—presumably fortuitous—took place in April, 1965, and quickened Houphouet-Boigny's determination to bring the subversion issue to a head. This was an attempt to assassinate Hamani Diori, president of Niger and close friend of the Ivory Coast leader. The evidence released by the Niger government suggests that terrorists, trained in Ghana, infiltrated the country. The assassination attempt followed a similar plot discovered by the Niger government in September, 1964, reportedly foiled through the watchfulness of villagers along the infiltration route. Since Ghana was known to have harbored several top leaders of an opposition party banned in Niger, it was widely believed that Nkrumah was guilty of complicity, and Houphouet-Boigny used the incident to dramatize his case against subversion. He called an extraordinary OCAM summit meeting in May, in

Abidjan. He indicted Ghana and declared the willingness of the Entente countries to present a dossier against Ghana to an OAU forum.

Although Houphouet-Boigny had solicited the support of African leaders through personal emissaries who pleaded for tolerance and mutual respect as the only viable modus vivendi for Africa, he was unable to convince many states to heed the call for a boycott of the next OAU summit. Senghor suggested a change of site for the summit and pointed out that such a boycott would threaten the very existence of the all-African organization, already weakened by internal disputes. The survival of the OAU in fact became the predominant issue, which overshadowed the one of subversion. In the end, eleven of the fourteen OCAM states—Senegal included—announced that they would not attend the OAU summit at Accra.[67] After long hesitations and negotiations, the OAU summit did take place in Accra. The OAU itself, as well as the government of Nigeria, played a mediatory role in the Houphouet-Boigny–Nkrumah dispute. Ghana did expel a number of Africans known to be connected with clandestine opposition parties elsewhere. Many African leaders came to Accra not so much because they wanted to do so but because of their fears lest the OAU disintegrate.

Ironically, the OAU got a new lease on life as a result of an event which tended to pull independent Africa closer together. This was the expected announcement of Rhodesia's independence from Great Britain, a move which tended to disenfranchise permanently the black majority in that country. The intensity of independent Africa's reaction to the Rhodesian government's decision, interpreted as a step backward in the decolonization process on the continent, rapidly displaced internal quarrels as the most important topic for OAU discussion.

The event is of particular importance here because it serves as an illustration of the connection between domestic and foreign policy in Senegal. During the December, 1965, OAU for-

---

67. Among OCAM leaders, opposition to the Houphouet-Boigny wing centered on admission of the Congo while Tshombe was prime minister, on the planned boycott, and on the drastic methods used by Houphouet-Boigny. Mauritania left OCAM the following month, although it still belongs to the nonpolitical specialized agencies.

eign ministers conference to formulate recommendations for the subsequent meeting of OAU heads of state, Senegal's foreign minister took a position diametrically opposed to that of President Senghor. He moved a resolution "deciding" to sever diplomatic relations with Great Britain should that country not prevent Rhodesian independence by December, 1965; Thiam, combining the passion and rational arguments at his command, reportedly convinced his colleagues, and the motion carried with at least solid majority support. As is well known, the vast majority of African heads of state rejected the foreign ministers' advice so that only five countries actually broke diplomatic ties with the British government. Thiam's role precipitated a crisis in Senegal which eventually led to his replacement as Senegal's foreign minister (he was appointed president of the country's Economic and Social Council but was later forced out for having criticized government policy).

President Senghor's position regarding the Rhodesian government's declaration of independence was similar in principle to that of his foreign minister. He regarded it as illegal and called on Britain to prevent independence, using force if necessary. Senghor argued that, if France was willing to use force against one million European settlers in Algeria, then Britain should also use force against some 220,000 European settlers in Rhodesia. France had brought about an "Algerian" Algeria; therefore Britain ought to bring about a "Rhodesian" Rhodesia. The two situations were, of course, not strictly comparable since the constitutional systems involved differed greatly and, more important in practice, since French forces in Algeria had been used chiefly against the nationalists. But both colonial powers had been sympathetic to the Africans' demands for independence and disposed to implement them. The real practical difference was that France had troops stationed in Algeria, whereas Britain had none in Rhodesia.

The foreign policy difference between Thiam and Senghor was in their public estimate of the usefulness of a diplomatic break with Britain. The foreign ministers apparently believed that such a break, possibly combined with an African economic boycott, could either pressure the British government into military intervention in Rhodesia or shame that government into

using strong diplomatic and other pressures to get Rhodesia's
white leaders to rescind their illegal act. Senghor apparently believed that such a break was not likely to secure the support of
a majority of African states, that it would yield only negligible
results, and that it was contrary to the African vocation of
dialogue in international affairs since it would shut off communications with Britain and tend to deprive African states of possible subsequent diplomatic leverage.

But Senegalese domestic politics were also an important factor
in bringing about the Senghor-Thiam disagreement. The evidence suggests that Thiam was not motivated only by foreign
policy considerations: he was in the process of solidifying an
independent power base in his native area of Louga, and consequently hoped to use his "radical" inter-African stance for that
purpose. Thiam was perhaps encouraged indirectly by his close
relationship to Senghor and by rumors of his becoming Senghor's eventual successor. Whereas Thiam owed his closeness to
Senghor in part to his reputation as a dispassionate analyst—
Senghor has a penchant for surrounding himself with technocrats—it seems clear that the former foreign minister is also
capable of inspired leadership bolstered by his analytic talents.

Functional cooperation

Between 1965 and 1968, the inter-African setting in which
OCAM operated lost some of the major political irritants which
had plagued it since 1960. There was a growing recognition that
the manipulation of strong emotions without necessary relation
to the actual influence of the OAU tended to weaken its legitimacy. One of the most outspoken "radical" Africans, Nkrumah, had suffered reverses within the OAU in connection with
his advocacy of a continental government and with his alleged
responsibility for subversion in sister African states; he was overthrown by Ghana's military in February, 1966. Moreover, the
OAU revealed itself to be relatively ineffectual in its response
to the general problem of southern Africa; no amount of resolutions could influence extra-African states to settle problems considered by them to be largely African.

To some extent, OCAM became a beneficiary of the OAU's

intrinsic weakness. Once the issue of subversion was more or less disposed of, OCAM leaders turned their attention again to their common welfare interests, carefully ignoring—at least officially—what political irritants tended to deflect the benefits of cooperation on practical matters. Senghor summed up the change by pointing out that "the UAM was too political, the UAMCE exclusively economic and social. . . . OCAM has an economic and social base, with a little politics." [68]

With a total population of about fifty-six million and an area only slightly smaller than that of the United States, OCAM reinforced its position as an international interest group of states seeking to promote their material welfare. The period after 1966 was auspicious for common action because it coincided with a number of international events of great consequence for OCAM states and with a renewed consciousness on their part of the advantages of common action. As discussed in the previous chapter, the problems of the deterioration of the terms of trade, and the renewal of the association with the EEC, helped to define areas of joint concern for the OCAM states.

Senegal contributed greatly to the articulation of a common front regarding these problems. In addition, OCAM endorsed President Senghor's suggestions for the organization of francophonie, a wider and looser grouping of French-language states throughout the world. There is some evidence that OCAM leaders' emphasis on economic and cultural cooperation was effective in propitiating an important component of the vertical dimension of Senegalese, as well as OCAM, foreign policy. An official of the French Cooperation Ministry, for example, sent a message to the OCAM leaders stating that "close cooperation between yourselves and with us means making a big contribution to world peace and African unity." [69]

To be sure, political problems among OCAM states continued to cause tensions. The military takeovers in Upper Volta, Dahomey, and the Central African Republic led OCAM leaders to postpone a summit meeting in 1966. Relations between the first

68. *L'Unité africaine* (June 20, 1966).
69. *West Africa*, no. 2536 (January 8, 1966), p. 47.

two states and the Ivory Coast were tense for a while; but co-operation resumed in 1967. Tensions also arose between the Ivory Coast and Guinea, mainly the result of Guinean sensitivities regarding a possible coup d'état in, or the abduction of Nkrumah from, that country. Further, there were frictions between the Kinshasa-Congo and Rwanda over the disposition of white mercenaries.

Nonetheless, as the result of a determination to concentrate on mutually beneficial economic and cultural cooperation, and the consequent effort to overlook, if not ignore, political tensions, OCAM was able to serve its members without serious disruption. The seriousness of purpose underlying OCAM was reflected in the joint sugar agreement (discussed in the previous chapter) and in plans for developing further OCAM markets for meat and livestock, cotton, and peanuts and peanut products, conceived as a general effort to help stabilize and reorient the flow of tropical agricultural materials.

POLICY CASE STUDIES

The three following brief case studies of Senegal's foreign policy behavior illustrate, more specifically than does the above discussion, some of the forces responsible for policy decisions. The first two—regarding the Provisional Algerian Government in 1960, and Portugal and Portuguese Guinea—demonstrate conditions under which Senegal has shifted her preference of method for the resolution of the decolonization issue. The third—concerning the 1967 Middle East crisis—shows the impact of potential regional economic development on her policy toward neighboring countries.

The importance of self-maintenance as a territorial goal of Senegal's foreign policy is obvious and needs no elaboration. Senegal's policy has not wavered from this fundamental commitment and was expressed clearly on a number of occasions which involved the territorial integrity of a state. Regarding the Kinshasa-Congo, for example, Senegalese foreign affairs spokesmen have upheld the right of the Congolese people to select and send abroad as their representatives whomever they choose regardless of the personality of the incumbent. Likewise, Senegal is opposed to the violation of a state's sovereignty under the guise of subversion and other similar techniques. Her position and behavior, in fact, suggest the hypothesis that the new African states' first foreign relations priority is the maintenance of territorial integrity unless their "revolutionary," ideological commitments may justify external intervention. This is evidently not the case in Senegal, whose commitment to territorial integrity is greater than that concerning the substance of another state's policy.

Algeria—1960

A few months after becoming independent, Senegal became embroiled in a dispute between the leaders of France and those of the Provisional Algerian Government (PAG) over the question of a cease-fire and of the organization of a referendum in Algeria suggested by France to settle the "self-government" issue. In the process, Senegal became the target of criticism for what some interpreted as a pro-French stand. Senegalese initiatives were largely responsible for the policy declaration made by the eleven French-language states at Brazzaville in December, 1960, and Senegalese delegates acted as spokesmen for the fledgling Brazzaville group at a number of United Nations debates on the Algerian issue. A brief examination of the motivations of Senegalese leaders, and of the policy followed on that issue, thus serves the dual purpose of highlighting fundamental aspects of Senegal's foreign policy and of assessing that policy in the light of past criticism.

To begin with, there can be no doubt about the Senegalese leaders' commitment to continued decolonization. Shortly after independence, Senegal began to withdraw her soldiers from Algeria and asked for the liberation of Ahmed Ben Bella and other Algerian leaders incarcerated in French prisons. Senegal also consistently reaffirmed her belief that "French" Algeria was a fiction and suggested national independence, majority rule, and respect for minority rights as the only possible outcome of the struggle. As Prime Minister Mamadou Dia declared,

Our position has been very clear from the beginning. We have not ceased to affirm that the only solution for Algeria was that that country enjoy . . . its rights to self-determination.

We do not misjudge the complexity of the problem. We know that it is much less simple than that posed by the decolonization of the former territories of French Africa. Nonetheless we must do everything, with our African sister countries, . . . to facilitate the reestablishment of a dialogue . . . to end in peace. We are ready to make any contact, to answer any initiative that could lead out of the impasse.[70]

This declaration contains a second, subsidiary commitment on the part of the Senegalese government: to peaceful means for settling the dispute and to mediation. Another principle of Senegal's foreign policy outlook which came to light during the discussions, implicit in the priority assigned to independence for Algeria, is that justice is a goal more important than peace. "Peace is not an end in itself," said Mamadou Dia, "it is second in relation to justice." [71] Justice was interpreted by Senegal as the self-determination and territorial integrity of the Algerians.

The purpose of mediation was to bring about a climate of understanding enabling the antagonists to reach a settlement through direct, bilateral negotiations. As Senghor put it,

Negotiation will be possible only if both sides substitute, for ultimatums and imposed solutions, the search for agreement and . . . of the compromise which, in a question as complex as the Algerian conflict, will allow an exit from the infernal cycle.

Embedded in the notion of compromise and mediation was the belief that the detached counsel of the mediators would

70. Senegal, *Journal officiel de la République du Sénégal: Débats parlementaires*, September 22, 1960, p. 37.

71. This discussion is based mostly on a pamphlet issued by Senegal, *La Paix en Algérie par la négociation: La Position du Sénégal à l'O.N.U. dans le débat algérien* (Tangiers: E.M.I., 1961), and on conversations with Senegalese officials. Quotations in this section are from *ibid.*

contribute to a peaceful solution after having "defused" the respective views of the antagonists. Similarly, the expectation of compromise suggests that either Senegal was not making a moral judgment on the relative merits of the antagonists' position or that she held that the best method to resolve the conflict was negotiation rather than armed conflict. Inasmuch as her moral commitment to justice was clear, the suggestion of compromise clearly reflected a choice of methods rather than substance.

The specific issue in which Senegal became involved, and about which French and PAG representatives could not agree at the time, was that of a United Nations role in supervising a referendum in Algeria. The French government opposed such United Nations intervention, whereas the leaders of the PAG insisted on it as a condition for a cease-fire. Senegal, in contrast to France, recognized that the issue had already been internationalized. But the Senegalese position also differed from that of the PAG. In principle, Senegal argued that a United Nations role was acceptable but interposed a practical question: Would a United Nations insistence on a role in supervising the election have a reasonable chance of succeeding? Mamadou Dia clarified his country's policy as follows:

> United Nations intervention . . . is entirely legitimate and necessary. But only on condition that it be guided by the democratic principles of the Charter, that is, contribute to the solution of difficulties instead of exacerbating them.

In view of France's refusal to agree to a supervisory function by the United Nations, there was no point in making matters worse by passing an unenforceable resolution. Moreover, Senegal feared that any such United Nations action might tend to inject the cold war into the African continent at a time when the United Nations appeared to be dominated by cold war pressures, when the United Nations peace-keeping force in the former Belgian Congo was becoming a target for East-West rivalries, and when Africa needed isolation from such pressures in order to adjust to the postindependence transition period. The Soviet veto of the admission of the Islamic Republic of Mauritania to

the United Nations was a fresh reminder of the cold war imping-
ing on Africa.

The Senegalese leaders therefore actively sought a compromise
agreeable to both antagonists which could lead to an end of the
fighting. Mamadou Dia, along with the presidents of Niger and
Cameroun, contacted the leader of the Algerian Liberation
Movement, Ferhat Abbas, in Tunis in November, 1960; other
contacts followed elsewhere. According to the Senegalese government, their efforts were successful and the informal contacts yielded an agreement acceptable to both sides. The Algerian leaders made no public comment at that time in view of
their official insistence on a United Nations role in the referendum. But they accepted the Senegalese proposal that the referendum be supervised by official observers from black African
states.

At the United Nations, the issue involved a Senegalese
amendment to a resolution calling for United Nations supervision, to the effect that international guarantees in the form of
an African ad hoc observation committee during the referendum
be the agreed procedure. According to Senegalese sources, the
Algerian leaders and France agreed to support the amendment.

It was only after the PAG suddenly changed tactics and persisted in seeking to use the United Nations as a means of pressure on France, repudiated its previous agreement, and demanded that all African states support its new tactics, that the
issue became critical from the point of view of relations between
the Algerians, on one hand, and Senegal and other African states,
on the other. No doubt the Algerians' abrupt reversal irked the
Senegalese, who thought they had finally found a way out of the
impasse. But what Senegal found difficult to accept was not so
much the change of tactics, brusque as it was; rather, it was the
Algerians' insistence that the Brazzaville states support it. Senghor stated that he supported Algerian independence uncondi-
tionally, but that this did not imply unconditional support for
all Algerian methods. Senegal, he explained, welcomed support
for her own goals but could not and would not equate lack of
support with ill will, or accuse nonsupporters of being colonialist
stooges. Judging others as either "traitors" or "friends" merely

on the basis of tactical differences, Senghor responded, "appears to be the same procedure about which the Khrushchev report itself revealed that it did the greatest damage . . . to the revolutionary movement."

Critics of Senegal's position on this issue have suggested that she supported France and abandoned Algeria. They are correct in pointing out that Senegal may have indirectly discouraged an Algerian "victory" by arms; but this was an Algerian, not a Senegalese, commitment. Hence, that criticism is directed at a method to resolve the conflict rather than at its substance. It may well be that Senegal's insistence on peaceful methods was influenced by her own decolonization experience; but the French had also reinforced Senegal's preference by agreeing to a referendum that would open the way to a peaceful resolution.

Critics have also suggested that Senegal yielded to French pressures on that issue and thus strayed from the path of genuine nonalignment. French pressures are not apparent in the record, although it may be assumed that they were exerted. But there was also Algerian pressure on the Senegalese, and the latter pressured the French by pointing out the consequences of another mistake such as that following the independence of Guinea in 1958. The existence of such influence in joint discussions cannot be a valid criterion for nonalignment; and neither can nonalignment be judged simply on the strength of agreement or disagreement. It does seem that Senegal's policy on this issue flowed from her conviction that a referndum supervised by the United Nations rather than by African states would tend to exacerbate, rather than solve, the dispute.

Portugal and Portuguese Guinea—1960–1965

The changes in Senegal's policy toward Portugal and the African contiguous territory of Portuguese Guinea reveals the influence of three perceptions: that regarding decolonization prospects; that regarding the effectiveness of the nationalists; and a continuing concern about possible separatism in the south. After independence, Senegal expected that the Portuguese government would respond to the challenge of decolonization in a manner similar to that of France and Great Britain. Senghor believed that Portugal was ready to initiate a process beginning with the gradual devolution of political authority to the African majority and culminating in eventual independence for the Portuguese colonies. Hence, Senegal opened an embassy in Lisbon and a consulate-general in Bissau, the capital city of Portuguese Guinea, in 1960. In view of the intransigence of the Portuguese government, however, Senegal had to recognize that Lisbon remained apparently immune to diplomatic pressures. Consequently, the two diplomatic missions were phased out as useless, beginning in mid-1961. As one government official explained, Senegal "has taken this step because it is now convinced that the Portuguese government refuses to examine realistically the problems . . . as they exist in 1961." [72]

When Senegal changed her perception of the prospects for a peaceful and gradual withdrawal of Portugal, her policy became one of increased diplomatic pressure on Portugal and of covert and overt assistance to the African nationalists in Portuguese Guinea. She has repeatedly protested Portuguese violations of her sovereignty on land and in the air. President Senghor asked independent African states to mount a symbolic blockade of Portuguese Guinea, and the foreign minister supported successful moves to bar Portugal from meetings of international organizations. For security reasons, Senegalese military officers head administrative districts bordering on Portuguese Guinea. At the same time, Senegal remains cautious since it wants to avoid an armed clash between her armed forces and those of Portugal—rumors of such encounters are quickly and emphatically denied by official sources.

Senegal's policy toward the Portuguese Guinea nationalists has shifted from verbal support for one group, based on ideological and ethnic affinities, to overt assistance and budgetary appropriations to another group. Caution is still reflected in the difference between official and actual policy. Some Senegalese officials maintain that the country has no official policy except one of humanitarian help, whereas others point to Senegal's increas-

---

72. Information Minister Obeye Diop, quoted in *West Africa*, no. 2305 (August 5, 1961), p. 855. Senegal subsequently barred Portuguese citizens from entering, and planes from violating, her national territory.

ing involvement, which could not take place without official knowledge and sanction. Government policy toward the nationalists at first supported one of the two major movements, Frente de Luta pela Independência National da Guiné (FLING). Many of the FLING leaders are French-speaking, some of them Senegalese, and ideologically oriented toward Senegal in addition to belonging to ethnic groups straddling the Senegal–Portuguese Guinea border. In the early stages of the nationalists' struggle, refugees seeking sanctuary in Senegal required little or no government assistance. They belonged to ethnic groups which shared traditional ties and customs with their counterparts in Senegal. The farmers in the Casamance, the southern district of Senegal, simply took care of their relatives.

In 1964, Senegal shifted and subsequently increased her support to FLING's rival, the Partido Africano da Independência da Guiné e Cabo Verde (PAIGC), headed by Amilcar Cabral. This policy change resulted from two developments. First, the PAIGC had emerged as the most effective nationalist fighting force in Portuguese Guinea, and it gained the approval and support of the OAU Liberation Committee. It had engaged in several successful skirmishes with Portuguese troops, secured the support of populations in densely forested areas, and forced Portugal to increase its defense expenditures. According to President Senghor:

> The fundamental position of Senegal is that FLING and PAIGC should agree to a common front. But our experience of both movements forces us to say at present that the movement of Amilcar Cabral appears to us to be provided with the best means. And this is why I have received Mr. Cabral and shall receive him whenever he wishes.[73]

Second, increasingly successful nationalist activities raised the prospect of a new independent neighbor. Given the economic,

73. *L'Unité africaine* (July 9, 1964).

social, and geographic isolation of the Casamance district of Senegal—all but separated from the country by The Gambia— and its common border with the future state, there is some concern in Dakar lest an independent Guinea become a pole of attraction for some of the Casamance population. Hence, Senegal moved to insure good relations with the nationalist movement which appeared most likely to lead Portuguese Guinea to independence.

Senegal has, moreover, become involved because of the increasing numbers of refugees in Casamance. Senegalese authorities estimate that there were some six thousand refugees in Senegal in March, 1964, but that by July of that year they numbered thirty thousand, and that in mid-1967, Portuguese Guinea refugees in Senegal totaled sixty-two thousand, including some fifteen hundred living in Dakar. This sudden influx of over sixty thousand people in Casamance required government assistance since the local population was unable to care for them. The Senegalese government therefore allocated funds administered by a high commissioner on refugees and appealed to the United Nations for further assistance. The refugees are now being resettled, chiefly in Casamance but also in other areas of Senegal, with the help of the Senegalese government and international welfare agencies.

Moreover, Senegal's support for the nationalists was publicly acknowledged by 1966. Cabral is a frequent visitor in Dakar and has direct access to President Senghor. Senegal allows arms, ammunition, and medical supplies in transit from Mali and Guinea through its territory on the way to Portuguese Guinea; some of the materiel and supplies are kept in special depots in Senegal. In Casamance, there is a specially constructed hospital at Ziguinchor and a rest center for wounded nationalist guerrillas, whose presence there in uniform is a common sight. Some officials affirm privately that Senegalese arms, clothing, and other supplies find their way easily across the border. There are continuous reports of nationalist guerrilla activities prepared and launched from Senegalese soil, although these are promptly denied by official sources. Moreover, nationalists cooperate with Senegalese authorities in detecting Portuguese agents and in the surveillance of Portuguese activities in The Gambia. Finally, Radio Senegal beams daily broadcasts toward Portuguese Guinea in African tongues as well as in Portuguese.

And yet, Senegal appears to oscillate between more or less overt support for Portuguese Guinea freedom fighters and extreme caution lest she become involved in armed conflict with Portuguese forces. Some younger Senegalese army officers are known to welcome such an engagement, but are carefully muffled by the government. After the Portuguese bombing of Samine in Casamance in December, 1969, official Senegalese policy shifted again and circumscribed the freedom fighters' activities inside Senegal. This was probably the objective of the Portuguese bombing, which illustrates both the vulnerability of a country like Senegal and the excessive fears of her leaders of external armed conflict with a colonial power.

The Middle East—1967

Another illustration of the dynamics of Senegal's foreign policy is the government's official response to the Middle East crisis of June, 1967. The policy statements issued by the information minister and subsequently by Senghor emphasized the following points: (1) the crisis was largely the responsibility of the great powers, which had created the unstable situation without the agreement of all parties concerned and subsequently neglected to contribute to its solution; (2) the Middle East must not become a cold war theater through armed clashes by proxy; (3) the antagonists must agree to a cease-fire; (4) they must use peaceful methods to settle the fundamental problems involved with the help and guarantee of the great powers; and (5) whereas Senegal did not question the existence of Israel, that country must nonetheless restore the status quo ante June, 1967, by withdrawing her troops from occupied territory, prior to negotiations. Senegal's stand on this issue was, then, generally neutral but leaning on the Arab side, later lamely justified by Senghor as simply taking the side of the "weaker" Arab states.

In an attempt to explain the motivation underlying Senegal's position in the 1967 Middle East crisis, domestic factors come to mind most readily. First, a country with a large Muslim majority can ill afford to take positions at great variance with that of Arab Muslim countries, especially on issues which directly affect their national security interests. But many Senegalese Muslims sympathized with Israel on the grounds that Israeli skills are useful to Africa, that the Israelis deserve recognition for their achievements in developing their country, and, at least in private conversations, that the Israeli action was essentially defensive. When it is remembered also that other predominantly Muslim, black African countries—such as Niger and Chad—refused to condemn Israel, then it becomes more difficult to evaluate the potency of this particular domestic variable; it does not seem to have played a major role in determining Senegal's stand on this issue.

A second domestic factor is the sizable resident communities of foreigners, especially, in this case, of Moroccans, Mauritanians, Guineans, and Lebanese. The issue, on which "home" government took a determined stand, may be expected to have aroused strong pro-Arab sympathies. Whereas there is no evidence that resident Guineans, Mauritanians, or Moroccans were unusually restless when they learned of the Arab military defeat, the same cannot be said of the Lebanese.

Members of that community displayed strong hostility toward Israel, attempted to organize demonstrations, were allegedly responsible for trying to set the Israeli embassy on fire, and issued a call for a boycott of local resident Jewish business firms. Moreover, Dakar University students painted university streets with anti-Israel and pro-Arab signs, and the painted message "Yankee Protectors" appeared overnight on the sidewalk in front of the United States embassy.

The Senegalese government was clearly concerned about possible trouble by some elements of the foreign Muslim community and took discreet but firm precautionary measures. It defined the limits of free speech by warning Senegalese would-be troublemakers that they would face prosecution, and foreigners that unlawful acts would result in their expulsion (some Lebanese were subsequently asked to leave Senegal). Moreover, small police units were stationed at strategic points in Dakar to act as a deterrent, and no clashes were reported. Whatever action some resident foreigners may have taken in Senegal had they been free to do so, serious problems were avoided by government measures designed to maintain law and order.

Another domestic factor may be traced to Senegal's weakness and to the general policy attitude which flows therefrom. This was reflected in the references to the cold war, to the responsibility of the great powers, and to the call for peaceful methods to resolve the crisis. In addition, Senegal's stress on the withdrawal of Israeli troops reflected concern for territorial integrity, which rests to a large extent on domestic considerations: fears of possible secession.

A second category of factors, arising from Senghor's personal commitments and values, probably had some effect on the content of the government's policy statements. One is Senghor's commitment to dialogue among antagonists as a means of arriving at agreement. Another was his consciousness that, as a Roman Catholic president representing only a small minority of his country's religious population, he is highly sensitive to the need for avoiding any action which can be misconstrued as directed against the Muslim majority. Some of his friends, in fact, claim that he tends to bend over backward, at times unnecessarily, to avoid such charges. Another may be Senegal's insistence that, this time, a solution of the Middle East crisis ought to rest on an examination of the fundamental issues involved, including the situation of the Palestinian refugees and free navigation in the straits of Tiran and the Gulf of Aqaba (Senegal did not, however, mention the Suez Canal). The reference to "fundamental" problems may have reflected Senghor's personal commitment to the need for taking into consideration all—or nearly all—the relevant factors before a decision can be reached.

But the most important influences which shaped Senegal's response were external. Paramount among these was the priority of the development of the Senegal River valley, entailing close cooperation with the three neighboring states of Mauritania, Mali, and Guinea. At the time, no particular problem clouded relations with Mauritania. Relations with Mali were improving,

and Senghor's frequent intercessions with the French government were bearing fruit: a Mali-French rapprochement was being worked out. By contrast, relations with Guinea were at their
worst, and it was therefore important not to antagonize Guinea
lest hopes for future collaboration suffer further setbacks. Given
the resounding pro-Arab position taken almost instantaneously
by these three important neighbors of Senegal, it would have
been insensitive and counterproductive to take a stand too divergent from that of the other three states. "We cannot," explained Senegal's foreign minister, "always act differently from
Guinea, Mali, and Mauritania on all problems. That is impossible." [74]

A second, less potent external factor was the country's role as
a cosponsor of the UNCTAD conference in New Delhi, and
her work on behalf of the preliminary Algiers meeting of the
poor nations. It may be assumed that Senegal's role in connection with these events has required some caution lest she alienate
some of the developing countries by taking too neutral a stand
on an issue of this magnitude.

A third external factor was influential in Senegal's response.
This was the coordination effort made by the OCAM states to
harmonize their policy. The crisis began on June 5, and Hamani
Diori, president of Niger and of OCAM, initiated telephone
consultations with member states. Largely similar policy statements were issued officially on the following day by all OCAM
states. Just how much Diori's proposals, or elements of a common OCAM policy, helped to determine Senegal's response is
impossible to say. But OCAM cooperation was very much in
the mind of member states at the time the Middle East crisis
was being discussed in the United Nations.

At the end of July, 1967, President Diori, in his capacity of
OCAM president, asked the Algerian government not to extra-
dite Moise Tshombe since this would mean certain death for an
African leader, resulting from an illegal and distasteful violation
of international norms. Moreover, Senghor suggested that
OCAM could be of assistance in solving the Middle East crisis.

74. Taped interview with Doudou Thiam, August 4, 1967.

What is significant in this suggestion is not so much that the OCAM states were split on the issue in their voting in the United Nations, and that it was therefore questionable that the organization could have been effective in any mediatory role. It is, rather, that Senghor did not mention the OAU. This was an illustration that OCAM at times looms larger in the mind of Senghor—and in that of OCAM leaders—than does the OAU as a referent in attempts to solve inter-African disputes.

One final external factor which may have played a role in determining Senegal's response was an earlier policy decision. This was the attempt by Senghor to work toward closer relations among Senegal and North Africa and the United Arab Republic—the latter dating officially from his 1967 speech at Cairo University, in which he defined his views on the cultural bases of inter-African cooperation. It is likely that taking a stand on the Middle East crisis, which would have antagonized the UAR or the rest of North Africa, could have at least embarrassed his cooperation efforts.

In the case of the 1967 Middle East crisis, the two most potent factors which underlay Senegal's policy were the external one of the priority of the Senegal River development scheme and the domestic one of the Lebanese resident community in Dakar. Inasmuch as the government was able to cope with the Lebanese-generated unrest, it seems clear that the external factor just mentioned was the most potent.

The preceding brief review of several policy decisions by Senegal suggests a number of generalizations regarding her foreign relations behavior. First, the use of force, instead of peaceful negotiation, is legitimate only in some instances of the decolonization process. If the colonial power is refractory and if the integrity of Senegal's territory may become involved, then Senegal will facilitate and assist the use of force by African nationalists. Second, if the colonial power appears sympathetic to nationalist aspirations, then the dispute should be settled by peaceful means. Third, if an African colonial territory is dominated by a resident European minority, then the colonial power is responsible for dislodging that minority. And, fourth, if tensions arise between high-priority economic development schemes and strictly practical nonalignment, then Senegal will adjust her policy pronouncement so as to propitiate the partners on whom economic gains depend.[75]

75. There may be a link between actual pressure by Senegal River states and Senegal's policy adjustment. During the height of the Rhodesian crisis, President Touré of Guinea took Senghor to task for allegedly reneging on a commitment to consider his country at war with a European Rhodesian regime, although no specific measures to implement that decision were mentioned. Touré told Senghor that support for an unspecified, hostile policy toward Rhodesia would determine Guinea's readiness to cooperate in the development of the Senegal River valley. It may well be that the Guinean threat was a factor in determining Senegal's subsequent response to the Middle East crisis.

CHAPTER FIVE

Conclusions

THE CONCEPTUAL POVERTY OF NONALIGNMENT

Nonalignment is a loose analytical concept. It covers too much territory and consequently is imprecise. The distinction between theoretical and practical nonalignment is useful because it isolates a psychological component of foreign relations behavior. But practical nonalignment can be interpreted to mean either of three policy orientations. First, there is autarchy, a purely theoretical possibility to which no African state subscribes. Second, there is an orientation intended to maintain its distance from (or proximity to) general nonalignment expectations. This would include distance from extra-African influences such as the cold war, or it could be judged by distance from inter-African commitments and expected behavior on particular issues. Although questions like these may encourage agreement in principle, there is no agreement concerning desired intensity of commitment or specific policy decisions. And, third, practical nonalignment can be taken to mean the pursuit of the state's national interest, regardless of whether it conforms to someone's expectations of what nonaligned behavior should be. For most African states, this third orientation usually comes closest to a description of actual behavior.

It is true that the concept of nonalignment has become widely accepted as legitimate. But this must be attributed chiefly to two factors. The first is the emergence of what has been called the new political multipolarity. This in turn resulted from a combination of the aftermath of the Second World War (which sapped the strength and will of European powers to maintain their former empires), the ability of African leaders to convince their erstwhile European mentors of the legitimacy of their claims for autonomy and independence, and the deadlock between the superpowers fearing mutual annihilation.

It has been suggested that the cold war, in effect, was the single most important environmental factor accounting for the successful adoption of a nonalignment stance. But such an interpretation is superficial. It tends to reflect a cold war mentality which does not, in explaining international affairs, look beyond the American-Russian struggle for influence and, more important, overlooks the fact that recognition of a nonalignment posture as legitimate dates from the adoption of peaceful coexistence as a modus vivendi, tenuous though it may be, between the United States and the Soviet Union. Had the cold war been primarily responsible for the success of nonalignment, its legitimacy should have declined after the late nineteen-fifties. It was precisely the emergence of an international environment moving away from bipolarity which facilitated trends toward regionalism and nonalignment.

The second major factor responsible for the gradual acceptance of nonalignment was a self-fulfilling prophecy. Africans benefited from Asian and other forerunners of today's nonalignment. When states like Senegal became independent, a nonalignment stance was almost de rigueur along the trails blazed by other Third World countries. The African states have since reinforced their nonalignment claims by declaring their intentions to refuse to join alliances or blocs as a matter of permanent policy. By helping to keep interbloc competition more or

less at arm's length, they have increased their freedom of ma-
neuver in an era which encouraged just such a course.

An assessment of nonalignment with the use of "distance" criteria yields some general observations. In theoretical nonalignment, such an assessment would involve a search for the distance
between the decision-making process and direct external influence. It is useful to conceive of two kinds of such influence,
using the ability of the process to resist what it considers un-
warranted encroachments on sovereignty as the distinguishing
mark. No country is, of course, entirely free from such influence.
One kind of external influence may originate inside a country,
as in resident foreigners having direct access to foreign affairs
decision-makers, or, in Senegal specifically, with a French-run
chamber of commerce or French advisers. Another kind of external influence may be assumed to be present in multilateral or
bilateral discussions between, say, President Senghor or his
foreign minister and their counterparts in and from other
countries. It can be further assumed that the first kind of external influence can be overruled with relative ease, whereas the
second kind may be too strong and require compromises.

But such assumptions do not enable one to measure influence,
or even to know with any degree of certainty if external advice
or pressure had much effect on the perceptions of the prime
foreign affairs decision-maker in Senegal. Such advice could, for
example, merely have reinforced his convictions and thus have
had little or no effect on decisions. Moreover, inasmuch as the
content of such discussions is not made public, this leaves only
circumstantial evidence and speculation; as more information
becomes available, speculation may or may not turn into hard
evidence. In the absence of concrete evidence, however, countries like Senegal may be assumed to be theoretically nonaligned.

It is not enough to view nonalignment as reflecting a broad
conception of African nationalism, primarily because such a
conception includes differing, and at times conflicting, elements.
Even the notion of practical nonalignment may be misleading
because the behavior to which it refers is, frequently, aligned
behavior. Such behavior can be understood in part by dividing
it into functional categories. In other words, practical nonalignment behavior, on closer inspection, tends to dissolve into be-

havior related to different issues (such as economics, defense, diplomacy, and ideology), each of which may exhibit more or less aligned behavior.

The nature and intensity of alignment in practice can also be understood through an examination of the level at which issues are being considered. The foreign relations behavior of African states is expressed at two distinct levels. The first concerns long-range issues such as exploitation, decolonization, and neocolonialism, issues believed capable of some manipulation and which command relatively unanimous agreement. But long-range issues tend toward abstraction and frequently indicate nothing more concrete than present and future trends in international relations. The second level concerns short-term issues and needs, related to economic intercourse and to security. It tends to reflect the more immediate and pressing problems of individual states, although it may also be expressed in collective policy statements and action. In this sense, all independent African countries are simultaneously conservative and revolutionary, and it would be misleading to classify them as either one or the other. As Vernon McKay has pointed out, all African states "are revisionist 'by necessity, not by ideology.'" [1] It may be added that they are also conservative by necessity, not by ideology.

The practical nonalignment behavior of African states may be conceptualized as taking place along a hypothetical spectrum whose extreme positions are conservative and revolutionary. Revolutionary behavior is intended to change the international environment or parts thereof and concerns mostly long-range issues. Conservative behavior is intended to benefit from the existing international environment or parts thereof and reflects short-run interests. The place of a country's foreign policy on that spectrum will vary with the issue, but most are near the revolutionary pole with respect to external exploitation in general, and near the conservative pole with respect to their more concrete and immediate needs.

There are, moreover, two additional factors which help determine a country's place on the spectrum: the intensity of

1. *African Diplomacy: Studies in the Determinants of Foreign Policy* (New York: Praeger, 1966), p. 22.

ideological commitment, and estimates of the need to transform the international environment. In some cases, ideological tenets close to the revolutionary end of the spectrum affect short-term behavior when the strength of such commitments dictates that short-term interests must be subordinated and sacrificed to long-range benefits. The substance of this kind of revolutionary ideology posits that, since African states are part of the downtrodden and oppressed international proletariat, they must therefore choose sides and align themselves with forces with which they share an overall commitment to weaken or destroy the exploiters. Examples of this type of spillover from the long range into the short term include approval of the 1968 Soviet-led military invasion of Czechoslovakia, unwillingness to recognize Moise Tshombe as the legal premier of the Kinshasa-Congo, severance of diplomatic relations with Great Britain over Rhodesia's independence, and material assistance to freedom fighters anywhere on the continent.

The other major factor which helps locate a country's position on the practical nonalignment spectrum is the foreign policy decision-maker's estimate of the need for or usefulness of mobilizing the international community to achieve the objectives. This factor is useful in understanding the Africans' widely divergent policies on such issues as the decolonization process. If one views that process from a historical perspective, as substantially completed, then achievement of the final objective seems to require only marginal effort; if, by contrast, the process is regarded as substantially incomplete and the forces at work as weak, then a much greater effort will be required. If, for example, Portuguese colonialism is viewed as an aberration and an anachronistic holdover, and if it is believed that it will have to yield to larger historical forces, then a constant, widespread, and forceful effort to reach the eventual goal of complete decolonization for Africa is not regarded as essential. Conversely, if Portugal's policy is believed to represent a powerful, dangerous, and persistent counteroffensive to the general decolonization process, then a much greater effort will be required. Views regarding the nature and direction of decolonization—and neocolonialism—also tend to affect African leaders' perceptions concerning ties with the former colonial metropole, and the speed and desirability of diplomatic and economic diversification and inter-African unity.

By using the categories just reviewed, it may be relatively easy to locate a country's general position on the practical non-alignment spectrum. But to pinpoint its location is a much more difficult undertaking. The reason seems clear: there are no satis-factory yardsticks. Because of the divergences mentioned above, there can be no such yardsticks, which presuppose agreement on measurement criteria. The utility of nonalignment as a tool for analysis frequently stops short at the gates of policy outcomes decided on by individual states.

It may be useful to plot elements of a country's practical non-alignment position (or simply its foreign affairs policy) on the spectrum and to compare it with that of others. All African countries may thus be called nonaligned, but some more than others. Taking into consideration the number of countries, one could then devise a mean or average position and use these points of reference as descriptive indicators. But a decision as to whether a country is nonaligned would still require the intro-duction of other criteria.

Even dividing foreign relations decisions into specific issues may not yield satisfactory measurements. Can we say that a country becomes nonaligned when less than a given percentage of its external trade takes place with the former metropole? Is 50 per cent of the total public and private foreign investment from one source a sufficient criterion? By the same token, does the mere existence of defense agreements constitute a violation of nonalignment? Is nonalignment the absence of foreign bases and troops from one's territory? Does nonalignment require a balance of diplomatic missions abroad according to some geo-graphic criterion? Or is a country nonaligned if it uses accepted ideological criteria in its recognition policy? Such criteria would still raise questions about the costs of policies in terms of eco-nomic growth and development, of the availability of alternative sources of foreign assistance, and of domestic aspects of na-tional integration and relative political stability. As indicated, differences based on such criteria, if viewed as indices of non-alignment, reveal policy expectations rooted in divergent esti-mates about the best method to achieve objectives. They may not be very different from striking poses without any relation to actual costs, benefits, and disadvantages.

These difficulties testify to the conceptual poverty of even the notion of practical nonalignment. The distinction between non-alignment and alignment in practice, when one brings to bear actual behavior on different issues, tends to use two different labels for essentially the same phenomenon. Moreover, if taken literally, the term nonalignment induces observers and practitioners to expect too much from it; behavior which does not conform to articulated principles invites misunderstanding, especially a kind of "alignment by association" verdict which obliterates the important distinction between orientation and policy. The cynic may argue that any behavior is permissible under the nonalignment cloak, provided that the requirements of theoretical nonalignment are met, and conclude that non-alignment is an intentionally loose concept invented by its adherents to impress observers into using a label which bear little or no resemblance to reality. Also, some of the confusion arises from semantics and is embedded in the true believer's conviction that anyone who differs from his own views and policies is therefore not "genuine." The bare notion of nonalignment yields only approximate insights at best. It can accommodate true believers and heretics, as well as its logical opposite of alignment, and may violate theoretical nonalignment by insisting that the right to make independent decisions be subordinate to prior agreement in practice on substantive issues.

ADAPTATION AND INNOVATION

Some writers have suggested that states, by their behavior in international affairs, be classified as either active or passive, revolutionary or tranquil. This kind of dichotomy does not, however, do justice to the foreign relations behavior of states like Senegal. It is more accurate to distinguish two simultaneous types of behavior in the pursuit of continuing objectives: adaptive and innovative. If these criteria are applied to Senegal, it becomes clear that there are elements of both adaptation and innovation in her behavior both before and after national independence.

In a sense, the preindependence foreign policy of Senegal consisted of a long series of adaptations to the French colonial and the inter-African federal environments. This emerges from a review of Senegal's political strategy in relation to the two major interrelated preindependence objectives: autonomy culminating in political independence, and inter-African economic breathing space.

With regard to the autonomy goal, adaptation was evident in several areas. First, it was evident in the pluralism of domestic politics, which required that national leaders be guided, at least to some extent, by the attachment of powerful religious leaders and of the urban bourgeoisie to at least continued close ties with France, if not to the status quo. Second, demands for autonomy were toned down considerably so as not to jeopardize French economic support regarding trade, public investment and technical assistance, and subsidies for agricultural products. Third, these demands were toned down also because of the African leaders' early conviction that they would benefit from serving a period of political apprenticeship before moving on to greater internal autonomy. Fourth, Senegalese leaders expected that French governments would invite Africans to participate to an increasing degree in the allocation of economic rewards if they would defer, or perhaps silence, their yearning for political self-determination. Fifth, demands for independence following the collapse of the French Fourth Republic were limited to the question of principle and expressed in the right to independence, to a large extent because of fears of serious economic consequences publicly announced by General de Gaulle. Other things being equal—meaning economic dependence and domestic obstacles—Senegal would have rejected the 1958 French constitution and chosen international sovereignty, if only because the French attitude was viewed as an obstacle on the road toward a gradual evolution which was all the more reasonable because it contrasted sharply with the French experience in Vietnam and in Algeria.

Adaptation, then, took the shape of accepting existing politi-

cal structures and reforms offered by the colonial power—
although such acceptance was accompanied by serious misgivings. Senegal accepted the relatively illiberal provisions of the
1946 French constitution, the 1956 enabling act, and the Community two years later because she viewed them as the best possible gains and because they did represent continuous—if slow
and hesitant—progress.

From the point of view of Senegal's relationship with AOF,
adaptation took the form of seeking to maintain her privileged
position as the federation's commercial entrepôt and exporter
of manufactured goods. This was reflected in her numerous attempts to bring about the unification of interterritorial parties.
Her most outstanding effort concerned the Mali Federation,
when Senegal agreed to a solidarity fund as an inducement to
a balanced, though unrealistic, constitutional relationship, to a
single party more tightly structured than the Union Progressiste
Sénégalaise, and to political independence from France. The
concessions made by Senegal's leaders, in fact, were limited only
by their concern for the country's persistence as an autonomous
national unit and for their domestic political base.

The other facet of Senegal's preindependence foreign relations
may be termed innovative. It consisted of efforts to revise existing conditions and structures or to alter the course of events.
Again, this can be demonstrated by looking at her policy toward
the same objectives of autonomy and inter-African economic
relations.

To preserve and increase her autonomy, Senegal sought to
avoid and eliminate the influence of foreign (French and African) political parties, as witness Senghor's break with the
French Socialists and his refusal to allow a local RDA branch
to take root. Further, Senegalese leaders changed the content
of the autonomy objective from federalism to active federalism,
and then to confederalism under the impact of French indifference, African frustrations, and their growing recognition that
political assimilation was an impossible dream and that, since
genuine federalism was not possible, some measure of separation
was the only possible eventual outcome.

In the pursuit of ever increasing autonomy, Senegal pressured France through verbal demands, the policies and plat-

forms of interterritorial African parties led by Senghor, the introduction of and participation in the drafting of legislation, and the use of moral arguments and veiled threats. Such pressures were, to a large extent, responsible for the 1956 enabling act, which increased local autonomy beyond the legal limit of the French constitution. Although Senghor's policy of gathering support for his African interterritorial alliance was motivated in part by the struggle against the RDA, it was also designed to influence the speed of the development toward political autonomy.

Senegal's revisionist goals were also concerned with the nature of her future economic ties with her AOF partners. This was especially evident in Senghor's skillful use of such slogans as balkanization and African unity, devised to prevent the dissolution of the federation, and indirectly to strengthen the IOM and weaken the RDA. Senegal subsequently used the issues of autonomy and independence to prevent the French government from allowing AOF to expire. Senghor was fully aware that what unity existed among the territories of French West Africa was traceable chiefly to the colonial imprint and that once the grid was removed, disunity would follow. Hence, the best— probably the only—chance for preventing AOF from succumbing to centrifugal pressures was to get the French to maintain existing unity for him. As discussed elsewhere, he also tried to address himself to inter-African solidarity after he saw that the French were not interested, but to no avail.

The same criteria can be applied to Senegal's policy since independence. The two issues of major importance to Senegal are the search for economic rewards and decolonization. The demands for material welfare require a fundamental adaptation to the country's economic dependence, a continuation of pre-independence policy. Senegal's adaptation is visible in her continued willingness to make use of existing economic structures; they already exist, work relatively well in the short run, and cannot be replaced rapidly by alternate choices.

The interpenetration of states, felt more by smaller and weaker states than by older and wealthier ones, effectively precludes the rapid realization of greater economic independence. The success of practical adaptation, especially in regard to economic ties, must be attributed largely to the readiness of the international environment to establish and maintain mutual cooperation. The motives of older states are many and include most prominently their search for prestige, humanitarianism, and welfare, as well as strategic goals. To a very large extent, the readiness of older states to cooperate with the new is an extra-African factor without which it would be almost impossible for the new states to pursue their own objectives with any assurance of success.

As already indicated, Senegal adapted to the new inter-African environment born of political independence by making a number of concessions to the incipient economic and political nationalism of other states. At the same time, her concessions to the Organization of African Unity with regard to economic cooperation were minimal. She preferred to retain the newly constructed framework of the French-language association of states, pending clear evidence that the OAU could offer like advantages. Moreover, Senegalese support for an OCAM sugar market, and for an eventual OCAM meat market, demonstrates her willingness to make additional concessions for the sake of present and future economic and technical benefits.

Adaptation is also evident in connection with the decolonization issue. Senegal altered her erstwhile attitude of benevolent neutrality toward the Portuguese Guinea nationalists because of stepped-up activity by the freedom fighters and the close proximity of that country. Inter-African norms and expectations are also related to Senegal's readiness to support the OAU Liberation Committee to the degree that she does. In another direction, occasional and pressing economic considerations have resulted in short-term adjustment of decolonization when it appears as a more recalcitrant and less urgent problem.

Time was also responsible for the adaptation of Senegalese policy in connection with decolonization. The change in her policy toward Portugal, for example, was the result of unrealistic expectations about the decolonization process and of the bitter lesson regarding the behavior of the Portuguese government. The contrast between Senegal's attitude toward the Algerian struggle in 1960 and that toward Portuguese Guinea in 1964 is striking: her attitude changed from an emphasis on talks and negotiations to one supporting armed struggle. The contrast between Senegal's initial discomfort at taking any position regarding the Arab-Israeli controversy and her open support of the Arabs in 1967 is even more striking; the latter was a direct response to the priority she attaches to cooperation with neighboring states to develop the Senegal River valley.

Much of Senegal's postindependence policy can also be understood from the point of view of a revisionist attitude, expressed in efforts to alter the environment or to prevent the occurrence of undesirable events. Her views concerning the decolonization issue have not changed. She remains committed to the completion of the liberation process, and her goal remains the political autonomy of Africans, based on majority rule. Decolonization is interpreted to include countries which are under direct rule by a European power, as well as countries dominated by white minorities, regardless of their international legal status. The operative criterion is not the locus of the effective decision-making authority; it is, rather, the nature and basis of that authority.

The other major postindependence issue concerning which Senegal's foreign relations behavior tends to be revisionist is economic welfare. In inter-African affairs, she took the initiative in 1960 to prevent the French-speaking ensemble from breaking up altogether and has since reiterated and demonstrated her commitment to functional and technical cooperation on numerous occasions. The notion of francophonie is designed in part to solicit help in the face of the probable decline of France's ability to provide technical assistance.

Of greater import was Senegal's initiative regarding the problem of the deterioration of the terms of trade. Once it was discovered that the specific nature of Senegal's dependence on extra-African economic forces was not inevitable, it was to be expected that the country would seek to influence these forces to her advantage. Senegal's participation in international economic intercourse, as a new element of the system, therefore gave way to demands that the system be altered to take her needs into account. Her demands for what she considers a more equitable distribution of the world's riches are concentrated into the one issue which, in collaboration with other Third

World countries, is capable of providing an effective impetus for altering the "traditional" East-West focus in international affairs. For the first time, the claims of Third World countries have compelled attention to an entirely different division, one based on welfare disparities rather than on ideological or other frictions among older, wealthier nations. As in the decolonization issue, long-range goals are sometimes adapted to short-term needs; Senegal and the OCAM states, simultaneously with their search for an international economic "New Deal," continue to emphasize the importance of their protective framework.

ISSUE-AREAS AND VARIABLES

One of the most provocative recent theoretical approaches to the study of foreign relations behavior is the "pretheory" of James N. Rosenau.[2] The pretheory is concerned with the achievement of greater precision in suggesting causal relationships between aspects of foreign relations behavior and the myriad factors which give rise to them. It is a useful orienting device if only because it forces the analyst to focus, among a possible universe of factors, on those explanatory categories which show the interrelationship between domestic and external factors. It tends to prevent the analyst from neglecting areas of explanation which he might otherwise not deem relevant or very influential.

The clusters of variables which Rosenau proposes as analytical guides are as follows: individual (or "idiosyncratic") variables, the "values, talents, and prior experiences" which distinguish one decision-maker from another; role variables, reflecting the role expectations of the society which decision-makers serve; governmental variables, which reflect the influence of structures; societal variables, arising from such factors as political culture

2. "Pre-Theories and Theories of Foreign Policy," in *Approaches to Comparative and International Politics*, ed. R. Barry Farrell (Evanston: Northwestern University Press, 1966).

and economic capabilities; and systemic variables, which refer to external influences.[3]

After identifying the variable clusters to be used as analytical tools, the next step in an attempt to find causal relationships is to assess their relative potency. Rosenau suggests that this be done on the basis of such distinctions as the size of a country, the state of its development, and the nature of its political system (open or closed). His experimental ranking of variables for a country like Senegal (a small, developing state with a relatively open political system), in order of descending importance, is (1) individual, (2) systemic, (3) role, (4) societal, and (5) governmental.

This hierarchy rests on several general propositions. Since developing countries have few organizational restraints on national decision-makers, he suggests, one could expect that idiosyncratic factors are more potent than in developed countries. Since societal, role, and governmental restraints are few and inarticulate, these variables can be expected to be less potent than idiosyncratic factors. And since the capabilities of developing countries are low, one should expect that systemic variables have a high degree of potency.

A few preliminary remarks are needed here to clarify my use of the Rosenau framework. His tentative ranking contains a number of difficulties from the point of view of developing countries. One such difficulty is inherent in the distinction between open and closed societies, to which Rosenau ascribes differences in the relative potency of societal and governmental variables. This seems to assume that officeholders, unrestrained by well-developed and entrenched bureaucracies, pressure groups, literate electorates, and widespread participation in the political process, necessarily indulge their own biases and idiosyncrasies. A further implicit assumption may be that idiosyncratic behavior by national leaders is, by definition, detrimental to the best interests of the country.

There seems to be no necessary relation, however, between such restraints and the potency of domestic variables on foreign

3. For a full description, see *ibid.*, p. 43.

relations behavior. In theory, there is no good a priori reason to suppose that decision-makers free from such restraints may not take into consideration and be influenced by external and internal conditions and factors as much as if these factors were made more widely explicit by intervening structures. It is possible to argue, in fact, that there is an inverse relationship between foreign policy decision-makers' freedom from domestic pressures and their ability to pursue the national interest. To dislike Rousseau's notion of the General Will is not the same as to deny that it has any operative relevance.

Since the number of decision-makers in developing countries is small, one may be encouraged to believe that individual factors invariably rank very high. But the number of decision-makers is not necessarily related to the potency of any given variable. The operating hypothesis that Senghor in reality makes all the important foreign relations decisions in Senegal is not an ipso facto demonstration of the high potency of individual variables. It could be argued that foreign policy determinations are primarily idiosyncratic if they are made by individuals in the absence of structural guidance from elements of the society which they serve. But these are structural, rather than functional, criteria. Functional analysis would seek to relate a comparative ranking of variable clusters not so much to structures as to the question of whether—and to what extent—a given individual decision-maker has actually taken domestic and external factors into consideration. This should be done irrespective of one's assessment of the merits of particular policy choices.

Another type of difficulty with the Rosenau experimental framework concerns the content of the variable clusters. The meshes of the five nets are so wide that it is frequently exceedingly difficult to know into which net the data properly belong. Economic dependence, for example, may be both a systemic and domestic factor, depending on one's point of view. Critics of neocolonialism, as well as students concerned primarily with the origins of dependence, may emphasize the potency of systemic variables; others may describe dependence from the inside in terms of the needs of the domestic economy and relations with the external world. Hence, the separation of data into variable clusters must, to an extent, be arbitrary.

This process is further complicated, in developing countries, by special difficulties in attempts to discriminate between societal, role, and governmental variables. Societal factors tend to be inarticulate or intermittent, governmental factors are controlled through centralization, and role factors are almost nonexistent, at least in comparison with developed countries. Consequently these three variables are here considered one, called "domestic" for the sake of simplicity.

The search for the relative potency of variable clusters may lead to or proceed from the assumption that one cluster must be more potent than others, that it must win a bid for influence among competitive clusters. Thus, if it could be shown that in some cases of behavior economic considerations loom larger than a commitment to decolonization, then it could be concluded that policy makers value economic rewards more highly than they do, say, the freedom of fellow-Africans still under colonial rule. This kind of conclusion certainly appears plausible when assessing Senegal's continued sales of raw materials to South Africa in spite of apartheid, or the continued use of the Benguela railroad to the port of Lobito in Portuguese Angola by Zambia and the Kinshasa-Congo.

But this kind of process assumes the search for an absolute image of foreign relations motivations. It implies a monistic view of reality in which one priority has—or should have—preeminence over all others, regardless of the issue.

In reality it is more accurate to think of the relative potency of variable clusters as being operative in their own discrete spheres of activity and relevance. These spheres of activity can be conceived as being parallel to one another, and coming into conflict only occasionally. The pursuit of decolonization can and does take place simultaneously with that of material welfare; they proceed along different paths and each has, in its own field, priority over others. To attempt to bring them under one conceptual roof would require highly idealistic, ideological, or utopian expectations about foreign relations behavior.

It is one of the merits of the Rosenau approach that it takes these distinctions into account. He suggests that they be handled with the concept of "issue-areas," defined as vertical political systems comprising interactions among national and international actors (as contrasted with horizontal, national political systems interacting with other national systems). Although this study is not concerned primarily with vertical systems, since it concentrates on the foreign relations behavior of one national actor, the concept, indicating discrete spheres of activity, is nonetheless useful in this context.

This section discusses Senegal's foreign relations behavior from the point of view of the four issue-areas suggested by Rosenau: the territorial, status, human resources, and nonhuman resources categories. Two specific issues illustrate the territorial issue-area—autonomy/independence and persistence—and one specific issue illustrates each of the other three areas —decolonization, diplomacy, and economic rewards, respectively.

Finally, an attempt is made to relate the relative potency of systemic, domestic, and individual variables to the samples of issue-areas selected for examination. Chart 2 recapitulates the findings to allow the reader an overview before proceeding to the discussion. It is immediately apparent that the findings presented here do not correspond to those suggested by Rosenau since they reflect actual behavior rather than an a priori experimental discussion.

Systemic variables are found to be most potent in three of the five examples, and domestic variables are most potent in the other two. Contrary to the expectations of the Rosenau model, idiosyncratic variables rank least in importance in each case. The potency of a given variable appears to vary in direct relation to the degree of actual or potential, direct or indirect, control over a given issue-area by Senegal's foreign policy decision-makers. This is particularly evident in the difference between the two samples of territorial issue-area: systemic variables are most potent in the case of the autonomy/independence issue, whereas domestic variables are most potent in the case of the persistence issue.

A few explanatory comments are in order concerning the choice of issue-areas, the comparative ranking of the potency of the variables, and the suggested causal links on which the ranking rests. First, the chart has an unintended static quality since it does not reflect differences in policy orientation or actual

CHART 2
RANKING OF VARIABLES BY ISSUE-AREA AND CAUSAL LINKS

	TERRITORIAL AUTONOMY/ INDEPENDENCE	PERSISTENCE	STATUS DECOLONIZATION	HUMAN DIPLOMACY	NONHUMAN ECONOMIC REWARDS
SYSTEMIC	*Inevitable Movement toward* Independence French Inflexibility Psychosis African Divergences	*Economic Rewards* Sovereignty Doctrine	*Geographic Proximity* African Norms African Capabilities	*Status and Rewards* Ideology and Religion	*Maintenance of Privileges* Economic Injustice * French Indifference * African Divergences * Ideological Hostility
DOMESTIC	Economic Dependence Political Forces Political Unification	Autonomous Entity Power Base Self-Determination Sovereignty Independence as an End	Weakness Economic Rewards Senegalese Experience	Central Decision-Making Senegalization Religion	Economic Dependence
IDIOSYN-CRATIC	Independence and Perspective		Historical Perspective	Dia Expertise Protégés	Culture

NOTE: The most potent variables are italicized.
* Refers to inter-African relations exclusively.

policy, either before or after political independence, or such
recent trends as the Senegalese leaders' greater understanding
of the complexity of the world economy and how this understanding may affect the primacy of a protective policy. Second,
both rankings and causal links may appear arbitrary, although
they are close enough to known reality to be plausible. Third,
other possible issue-areas are not shown, though they may be
relevant; but they overlap the areas shown and, more important,
tend to be subsidiary to them, as the African unity and OCAM
policy areas are largely subsidiary to the nonhuman category of
economic rewards. Finally, the issue-areas shown are not exhaus-
tive but appear to me to be the most relevant from the point
of view of this exercise.

The first territorial issue-area in Senegal's foreign relations
behavior reviewed here is that of autonomy and independence.
It is probable that the movement toward these objectives was
inevitable, whether one considers that the destination was
reached slowly or quickly. It was inevitable because of the
dynamics of modern political life implanted in the territories
and because of the growing gap between the kind of association
desired by the Africans and that offered and maintained by the
French. Once African leaders were conscious of France's foot-
dragging and inflexibility, disappointment led to frustration and
hence to demands for ever increasing autonomy.

Domestic variables pulled in two directions, one opposing
and one favoring autonomy and eventual independence. One
major domestic factor was the need to reconcile economic welfare and progress with political separation. These considerations
were so potent that they are discussed below as a separate issue-
area. Internal political forces led Senegal's leaders to tone down
their demands for autonomy. Most of the country's religious
leaders, and the urban bourgeoisie symbolized by Lamine Guèye,
were unsympathetic to any move tending to increase the distance between Dakar and Paris. Because of their close economic, political, and affective ties with France, they tended to
accept the colonial situation somewhat uncritically. Consequently, Senegalese leaders were careful not to move too fast
lest they run the considerable risk of being deprived of crucial
domestic support or invigorating dormant opposition in the
strategic urban centers. The three days of stormy discussion

leading to the last-minute decision to accept the 1958 French constitution, but to regard it as a step toward independence, underlined the potent domestic rift on that issue.

Domestic factors also pulled in the direction of autonomy and independence. Support came essentially from the younger, ideologically oriented cadres whom Senghor had recruited into his party over the years and who were responsible, in part, for his increasing militancy regarding the autonomy issue. Furthermore, the Senegalese government's control over the civil service after 1956, with the attendant leverage which could be translated into political support, militated for rather than against internal autonomy. Finally, the continuing political struggle between Lamine Guèye and Senghor oriented the latter toward an increment of separation from the colonial setting since the former was known for his unswerving French attachments.

Although domestic pressures could be kept from erupting, systemic factors proved nearly intractable on the autonomy question. Senegal's leaders, as a result, altered their early expectations about an African-French federation based on equality and came to favor complete internal autonomy short of actual political independence.

African impatience and frustration resulted from the inability of successive French governments to adapt to change as much as from the wide gap between noble promises and actual performance. French leaders could not bring themselves to abandon their traditional concept of a unitary French Union, with central controls located in Paris and manned chiefly by metropolitan Frenchmen. The immobilism and parochialism of French politics, the resilience of conservative forces (especially the colonial bureaucracy) looking askance at the prospects of decolonization, and the relatively ineffective support from French liberals—all these lay at the bottom of African disenchantment. As their hopes for a fraternal federation receded, men like Senghor reacted with plans for increasing decentralization. As the ideal political assimilation proved utopian, they opted for increasing political separation.

The logical conclusion of autonomy, political independence, was a step which AOF leaders—save one—were not prepared to take, not even when the advent of the French Fifth Repub-

lic made it theoretically possible because the constitution had
to be revised. The French continued to control the nature and
procedure of any change in political relations with Africa. And
in the short period of three months after May, 1958, the younger
militants of the interterritorial Parti du Regroupement Africain
led by Senghor pressured him into accepting eventual independence as a formal party objective. In the words of Lamine
Guèye, there was an "independence psychosis" among party
cadres everywhere which Senghor could not ignore.

His response was to ask that the new French government recognize at least the right to independence as inalienable, even
though he probably had no intention of making use of it at that
time. Again, factors external to Senegal—and to most AOF
states—carried the day. Not only was the decision-making role
of the French legislature vastly curbed, but the executive also
vetoed the new legislature's recommendations that the right to
independence be included in the proposed constitution. Although Senghor had marshaled impressive support among Africans with the help of the African unity issue, and although the
right to independence had become the minimum ideally acceptable to most African leaders, this was not enough to offset
French—and Ivoirien—insistence on freezing legal, constitutional African-French links. For Senegal, political independence
came later, not so much as a result of Senegal's leaders' actively
seeking it, but as a concession to the Soudanese for the sake of
the Mali Federation. Ironically, Senegal, having acceded to independence, not as a separate entity, but as part of a larger
political unit, claimed independence from that very unit when
her association yielded dangers to her political autonomy.

Senghor's own predispositions also influenced his views concerning political independence. In drawing the distinction between "real" independence, to be earned through ceaseless
domestic effort, and "nominal" independence, merely to be
written on paper, he was guided by the perspective which he
brings to an understanding of issues and by the primacy of
cultural considerations, which relegated political independence
to a secondary priority. He also sensed that international sovereignty, as such, would alter very little in the continued relations between the African states and France. But the potency

of this individual variable was clearly lower than that of systemic and domestic factors regarding formal independence. To the extent that his historical perspective and commitment to culture influenced his views, these yielded when confronted with the other influences mentioned.

The literature of international relations, and particularly that concerning Africa, occasionally singles out the efforts of given national leaders to perpetuate themselves in office or to maintain a particular regime, in the face of external threats, as one explanatory factor in their behavior. Frequently comments suggest that this type of behavior is justified only to the extent that the observer approves of the government or regime in question. This kind of argument is used in inter-African affairs, for example, by intensely ideologically committed leaders who seek to demonstrate that "conservative" behavior is reprehensible when indulged in by national leaders who happen to be the targets of ideological criticism. Thus, former president Nkrumah and others believe that some of their fellow presidents ought to be overthrown by internal and external pressures. But all national political leadership groups seek to insure the persistence of their countries' autonomy and of themselves as the ruling groups. Senegal is no exception. One of the issues with which Senegal's foreign relations behavior has been concerned is precisely the persistence of Senegal as an autonomous or independent political unit, especially in the face of external threats, perceived or real.

Senegal's "systems-persistence" behavior was evident before and after her national independence, since she existed as an incipient autonomous political unit in the context of the French Union. Prior to independence, Senegalese leaders resisted the potential and actual encroachments of the RDA led by the Ivory Coast's Houphouet-Boigny, just as Houphouet-Boigny himself, in the late 1940s, resisted what he considered Senegal's encroachment via the ephemeral CEFA organization. RDA encroachments on Senegal's political autonomy occurred in the form of efforts to use a local Senegalese branch of the interterritorial party and in the form of RDA conditions for a merger of interterritorial parties. In all such cases, Senegalese leaders resisted these attempts because they threatened, or were believed to threaten, the country's autonomy. The same can be said of her experience with the Mali Federation, when the activities of Soudanese leaders presented the danger of overwhelming Senegal within the new federal structure. The events surrounding these attempts confirm that incumbent national leadership groups will defend themselves against threats which appear to be directed at the seat of their political power and at the continued existence of the national entity which supplies their power base.

As may be expected, this kind of defensive behavior was reinforced after political independence. It is significant that the only example of Senegal's independent use of economic boycott arose from the alleged implication of one African country in a subversion attempt against the Senegalese government. More generally, however, the desire for the persistence of Senegal as an autonomous entity is responsible for the postindependence emphasis on limits to self-determination and on respect for sovereignty and territorial integrity.

The notion of self-determination originally gained acceptance as a procedure for the creation of new states. The operative criterion for self-determination has been the ability of a given people or leadership group to enforce their claims. Legal, historical, moral, and theoretical arguments have in practice served to reinforce, but not to lay the foundations for, claims for the self-determination of new states. Most African leaders remain unimpressed by ideological or other arguments and will oppose subnational groups within and without their borders seeking to enforce such claims. It is difficult to define operational limits for such concepts as national self-determination since it does not provide its own limitations and anyone can, in fact, invoke them. Practical limits are nonetheless required lest self-determination lead to fragmentation resting only on a desire for autonomy and totally unrelated to such practical problems as the optimum or best possible size or economic viability of a future political community. An abstract commitment to the right of self-determination may be good philosophy; but it is also bad politics since it does not solve—indeed may prevent the solution of—practical problems. National independence, once achieved within a given geographical framework, usually provides its own limitation on self-determination.

The commitment of such African states as Senegal to the sovereignty of their country is rooted in two major considerations. First, it derives in part from existing doctrine in international relations. That doctrine, like that of self-determination, was a response to the creation of new state units for the specific purpose of creating a new order. In time the doctrine has come to be regarded as an end in itself and as permanently entrenched. But since it has long been considered approved behavior, infringement carries with it the onus of an enfant terrible in interstate relations. Inasmuch as African leaders are demanding respect as equals with older, established nations, their use of the doctrine is conditioned in part by norms most likely to bring about such acceptance by others. Legal equality is most likely to be propitiated through adaptation to the existing norms that bestow equality.

In terms of international relations theory, such an outlook falls into the category of the "traditional" in the sense that it parallels, albeit unconsciously, the imutable and legalistic interpretation of the nature of the state and ignores recent changes in international relations which call the traditional interpretation into question. At this stage of nation building, it is understandable that African leaders should be preoccupied more with strengthening than with weakening the state.

The second major consideration underlying a commitment to sovereignty in the new states as they are is domestic. Any suggestion that present political entities are less than sacrosanct automatically raises the specter of domestic unrest; in Africa, this is complicated by overlapping ethnic boundaries, which tend to blur an already "irrational" boundary situation, and by latent opposition groups in search of a useful issue to garner popular support.

It is these domestic considerations that give rise to the intense commitments to maintaining existing political frontiers in other African states. The fear is that if Africans were to allow change in one country, then there could be little justification for preventing it in another. Hence, the sovereignty and territorial integrity of African states are held to be indivisible. This indivisibility is raised to the level of a principle whose fundamental purpose is the persistence of each new state.

For all that, it must not be thought that African leaders' concern for the political independence of their countries precludes legal, constitutional limits on their sovereignty. Their policy outlook toward sovereignty does not rest on well-organized or profound doctrine and consequently may appear to be inconsistent. The recent foreign relations behavior of such states as Senegal indicates that accession to political independence reinforced the commitment to systems-persistence, which in the process became a major objective in its own right: sovereign rights must be maintained and consolidated. The difference in behavior before and after international sovereignty indicates that persistence and sovereignty do not have the same content.

Prior to independence, political sovereignty was regarded as of relatively marginal practical utility. Senegal—as well as other AOF states—was content, as late as mid-1958, to ask for nothing more than recognition of the mere right to independence. She was ready to limit future political sovereignty by transferring some of its elements to multinational bodies. As indicated earlier, Senghor envisaged a political federation at first between Africa and France, then among African states themselves.

It is only since independence that Senegal has tended to regard sovereignty as an inalienable right incapable of admitting infraction. But the inconsistency is more apparent than real. This becomes clear with an examination of the two sets of factors which have determined her postindependence policy in that respect. Once international sovereignty was achieved, it tended to take on a life of its own and helped to prevent any limitation of newly achieved status. It was easier to agree to limit, defer, or give up sovereignty before independence—it was easier to give up something one did not yet possess.

A somewhat less potent set of factors included considerations of material benefit for Senegal. The country's preindependence willingness to limit political autonomy was chiefly a function of the economic rewards which could be expected from membership in a multinational political entity. Her attempts to bring about federal ensembles were clearly the result of expectations for material advantage. What is significant is that her readiness to limit her sovereignty after independence, through some of the cooperation agreements signed with France and, in principle, some of the provisions of the charter of the French-language association of states, conforms to the requirement that it not endanger persistence. Hopes for material rewards were the most potent factors in shaping her policy outlook toward the question of autonomy before independence, whereas persistence replaced economic rewards after independence as the most potent variable.

From the point of view of persistence, a status of international sovereignty is paramount in its effect on the nature of external relations. The implications of this point are of the greatest significance for an understanding of the future of inter-African integration efforts. Such integration can take place only if it allows for the persistence of the new states as separate entities, however these entities are defined.

Supranational political ties among African states can, other things being equal, be instrumental in furthering the welfare and prosperity of Africans. Beneath the official declaration regarding the sanctity of political sovereignty, there lies a profound recognition that it could—and perhaps should—be limited for a common purpose. In this sense the gap between the radical and moderate African leaders is not so great as may sometimes appear. But the crucial element is the question of whether a definition of common interests includes or excludes recognition of the right of African countries to persist as politically discrete entities. This right is the irreducible kernel of sovereignty. The error of men like Nkrumah on that issue was to believe or hope that this right, being an obstacle, can and must be abolished so that such common interests as economic benefits may be pursued more rationally and yield instant success. It was the merit of men like Senghor to have recognized that the right to persistence is fundamental and therefore cannot be denied or infringed on in the name of other priorities, important as these may be in their own right.

Senghor clearly expects that the refusal of some African leaders to recognize the potency of persistence will yield with the passing of time. His notion of regional and subregional cooperation, whose definition of mutual interests recognizes persistence, may provide the key to the future shape of inter-African relations.

The example of a status issue-area discussed here is that of the decolonization of Africa. This involves the end of the process culminating in political independence or autonomy for majorities ruled by extra-African powers or resident minorities; it involves the question of who shall control whose destinies. The specific subsidiary issues include Senegal's relations with southern and Portuguese Africa, relations with African nationalists in these areas, foreign trade, diplomatic measures, and national security.

Senegal's policy orientation and behavior toward these issues can easily be traced to systemic, domestic, and individual variables, in that order of importance. Idiosyncratic factors include Senghor's preference for evolutionary change; his belief that colonialism, if not entirely dead, is nonetheless moribund; and the perspective from which flows the distinction between adaptive and refractory colonial powers—France and Great Britain being examples of the former and Portugal of the latter.

Domestic factors were in evidence on repeated occasions, and their influence was undeniable on the general tenor and orientation of her policy. It goes without saying that Senegal supports the legitimacy of the struggle for freedom by nationalists in areas controlled by colonial powers or minorities. Moreover, Senegal's own decolonization experience at the hands of the French accounts for the misplaced optimism with which she expected Portugal to follow in France's footsteps and to initiate the decolonization process in her African colonies when African independence was in the air.

Senegal's internal weakness also influenced her policy outlook on the decolonization issue. That weakness was responsible for the tendency to hold colonial powers accountable for bringing about an end to colonialism; since she lacks the means to affect the outcome of this process significantly, she tends to expect— or demand—that colonial powers take appropriate measures, including the use of force if need be. Internal weakness also accounts for official concern to avoid the least military confrontation with Portugal over neighboring Portuguese Guinea.

Senegal sought to propitiate change from within in Portugal by suggesting that the moral onus of continued obduracy blackening that country's international status would contribute to the desired transformation. Finally, concern about the isolation and relative malintegration of the Casamance district, many of whose inhabitants belong to ethnic groups related to those in Portuguese Guinea rather than those of the rest of Senegal, led the government to take defensive measures and to establish sanctuaries for nationalists from across the border.

Domestic and idiosyncratic variables, then, were largely responsible for determining the general orientation of Senegal's policy toward the decolonization issue. But systemic variables were more potent in determining actual policy. The pressure of inter-African expectations resulted in behavioral norms demanding support for nationalists. Senegal has, especially since the creation of the OAU, been vocal in her condemnation of foreign rule in Africa; she has supported—at times initiated—the exclusion of recalcitrant regimes from international organizations, in obvious contradiction to her general belief regarding sovereignty; and she devoted, as a former member of the OAU Liberation Committee, substantial subsidies to that committee's operations. Her preference for using moral pressure as a means to achieve decolonization ends is related not only to her own weakness but more substantially to the weakness of recently independent Africa. Neither African military measures nor diplomatic sanctions against colonial powers are likely to have more effect than moral pressures.

By far the most important systemic variable affecting Senegal's policy concerning decolonization was the geographic proximity of a future independent African state. Her increasing militancy, and her readiness to support the nationalists in Portuguese Guinea, are designed to assure potential friendly relations with a contiguous state; this was made abundantly clear when the government shifted its support from those Portuguese Guinea nationalists with whom she had close ties of affinity to those who waged a more effective struggle and consequently appeared to become the likely leaders of the future state.

The discussion in chapter two provides some useful material for analyzing one example of a human resources issue-area.

Inasmuch as the government's control over the personnel of the Foreign Ministry is more complete than in other government agencies (only one French citizen being employed), it would seem logical to assume that domestic variables are paramount in that area. This seems to be borne out by the available evidence. Domestic factors include the centralization of foreign relations decision-making in the office of the president of the Republic; the (former) close personal relations between President Senghor and Thiam; the senegalization of recruitment and appointment criteria; the scarcity of available personnel; and the comparatively slow rewards of a foreign service career. Moreover, the existence of diplomatic missions in Saudi Arabia and in the Vatican are clearly related to aspects of domestic society.

Systemic variables appear to be less influential than domestic factors. Fiscal criteria for mission allocation are increasingly related to expectations of external status and economic rewards. In a few cases, the choice of top diplomatic personnel was a function of the desires of a host country, as was the status of a mission. Closing or opening missions was related, in some instances, to external political problems, and ideological or religious factors influenced the choice of a few ambassadors.

Finally, individual criteria were prominent in only a few cases. Former Premier Mamadou Dia, for example, tended to centralize economic foreign relations outside the Foreign Ministry as a result of his personal interest and expertise in this area. Senghor has introduced a few personal protégés, younger men with superior educational qualifications, into the foreign service; and his personal philosophy was a factor in opening an embassy in Brazil.

One final issue-area of overwhelming importance in most African states' foreign relations behavior concerns nonhuman resources, illustrated here by the pursuit of economic rewards in connection with the development and modernization of Senegal's economy. Senegal's policy in that respect was discussed in some detail in chapter three. This section reviews the relevant clusters of variables from the point of view of the Rosenau framework.

At first glance it seems difficult, if not impossible, to distinguish the potency of domestic from that of systemic variables. It could be argued that today's internal needs may be traced to the colonial period and hence to systemic forces which still tend to dominate or condition Senegal's economy. It could also be argued that it is the country's domestic needs and commitments which compel her orientation toward the outside. But these are merely two sides of the same coin. The importance of the product of monoculture for Senegal's welfare means that the country is linked to the external world as an individual's physical survival is linked to gastronomy. An intestinal view emphasizes external dependence, whereas a culinary view emphasizes the choices offered: the succulence and variety of a chef's creations available to all patrons. Granting that systemic forces are responsible for the present state of Senegal's economy and for her desire to modernize, what is relevant in this context is that the country's leaders are using foreign relations policies and techniques to achieve desirable domestic ends.

Senegal's pursuit of economic development and modernization have led her to adapt to, and to seek change in, the external environment. The specific objectives sought include the diversification and reorientation of agricultural and industrial production and trade, the continuation of foreign assistance, and the reduction of dependence through lower trade deficits and increasing self-sufficiency in foodstuffs. The importance of external factors, then, could be said to follow the dictates of internal need. Economic progress depends not only on Senegal's desires and goals but more so on the readiness of external forces to provide the help required. As indicated elsewhere, the ability of Senegal to secure such benefits was tailored to the external conditions deemed most useful or desirable to achieve domestic aims. Hence, systemic factors were more influential than domestic variables in the foreign relations aspect of the drive toward economic modernization.

In inter-African economic relations, Senegal has sought to maintain the privileges of the colonial situation and, when this proved not entirely feasible, adapted herself to the new environment of independent states. A combination of individual and systemic variables was most potent before independence. In the defense of his country's economic interests, Senghor made remarkably skillful use of his ability to manipulate ideas. At first he tried to influence the French-dominated political system in which the African territories operated. Fully aware of the lack of solidarity among the territories of AOF beneath the surface of the French-instituted quasi-federation, he pressured French decision-making circles into maintaining it. When this failed, he manipulated inter-African public and elite opinion through the myth of African unity, which, he sensed, could be endowed with a nearly irresistible appeal. In the process he launched what was, other things being equal, one of his most successful political campaigns to alter the inter-African environment; he reinforced the structural strength of the interterritorial party of which he was the acknowledged leader, split the ranks of the rival RDA, isolated the Ivory Coast as the only African territory adamantly opposed to African political unification, and secured at least theoretical concurrence of former foe and friend alike in the name of African dignity expressed in an African primary federation. His campaign was, in retrospect, a brilliant manipulation of a strongly emotional issue in the defense of Senegal's material and moral interests.

As noted earlier, his attempts failed essentially because of the greater potency of systemic variables which he could not overcome: French indifference, and the lack of active, well-articulated, common inter-African economic goals.

Systemic variables became more potent around independence. It was in deference to the new environment that Senegal overnight abandoned the objective of political unification and accepted instead the loose functional and economic cooperation scheme favored by her newly sovereign former AOF partners. In the development of natural resources, priority was given to the Senegal River basin; Senegal sought to handle or benefit from such external variables as ideological hostility, weak and nonconvertible currencies in the case of two states, Guinea's diplomatic isolation, pressures by the Bamako business community, and French contacts. In the area of wider economic relations, Senegal was able, in a relatively short period, to end her diplomatic isolation, to become one of the leaders of the French-language association of states, and to make up for the loss of the AOF economic hinterland with a reasonable degree of success.

Senegal's policy toward the larger extra-African environment was the opposite of that toward inter-African economic relations, a testimony of the conceptual flexibility of her foreign relations decision-making. Her extra-African policy was, at first, to adapt to the "givens" of that environment. After the first hesitant steps of political independence, she accepted fully the protective framework of the former colonial power: the fiscal, trade, and aid arrangements of the franc zone enlarged through the participation of the EEC.

But once Senegalese leaders evolved what they believed was a clearer conception of the relationship between her economy and that of the world, their early, relatively uncritical, adaptation made room for a desire to change some fundamental aspects of the world economic system. In the short run, Senegal has attempted to maintain the present advantages of the protective framework, while at the same time pressing for longer-run transformations. To this end, Senghor once again placed his mastery of ideas at the disposal of Senegal's material and moral interests by appealing to the conscience of the world and by helping to mobilize Third World public and official opinion in the name of justice and equity. Both adaptation and change, then, appear largely as responses to threats emanating from, and as a search for opportunities inherent in, the international environment.

LÉOPOLD SENGHOR'S PERSONALITY

The relative potency of individual variables may be attributed in part, as suggested earlier, to the lack of intermediate, well-articulated bureaucratic and other group pressures in the developing countries. But since this study came to the conclusion that, in Senegal, the effect of the personal attributes of Senghor was not nearly so pronounced as expected, this raises additional questions about the conditions in which idiosyncratic variables achieve a high degree of influence.

The case of Senegal suggests that the answer lies not so much in the nature of a political system as in the specific content of individual variables themselves. The absence of a "complex" political system may be a condition, but it is not a sufficient condition, for the relative potency of such variables. It would seem that individuals holding, for example, manichaeistic views of international affairs channel these into foreign relations behavior with greater zest, consistency, and drive than do leaders whose philosophy recognizes more subtle distinctions. This explanation certainly seems plausible if one compares the philosophy and behavior of Senghor and Houphouet-Boigny, on one hand, with those of Touré and Nkrumah, on the other.[4]

The material on which this discussion is based was presented earlier in some detail, especially in chapter four. For present purposes, two types of personal factors may be distinguished: elements of President Senghor's personal philosophy, and the influence of his French experience.

The first type of personal factor includes his views on the importance of culture, his general philosophy and theory of history, his penchant toward conciliation, his occasional single-mindedness of purpose, and the depth and perspective of his beliefs. The most salient are probably his perspective and his tendency toward conciliation.

Because of his belief in the primacy of man's cultural life and objectives, his thought emphasizes the construction of cross-cultural bridges, in Africa and elsewhere. Men should, according to Senghor, extract the common heritage of mankind from the myriad and puzzling facets of international interaction and look for common interests above geographic, racial, cultural, and other divisions. Since cross-cultural bridge-building accommodates the Africans' desire for recognition as equals, one important ingredient of this design is a high degree of sensitivity toward and opposition to cultural imperialism and arrogance.

Senghor's preference for conciliation in international affairs is related to the relative security of his early personal experiences, which demonstrated to him that hard work—rather than harsh words—got the best results and also caused fewer dislocations. No doubt his ability to transform certain aspects of French cultural imperialism into support for such crucial objectives as the

4. For a discussion of the political thought of Nkrumah and Touré, consult W. A. E. Skurnik, ed., *African Political Thought: Lumumba, Nkrumah, and Touré*, Monograph Series, nos. 3, 4 (Denver: University of Denver, 1968).

recovery of black peoples' dignity and pride also conditioned and strengthened his conciliatory bent. Moreover, that bent was reinforced by his reading of the historical process leading to "greatness"; it would be absurd for someone ascribing greatness to the peaceful, underlying dynamics of vigorous, effective cultural contact and mélanges to hold the view that constant conflict can accomplish much of lasting value.

As is true with most leaders of new states, Senghor's interpretation of contemporary historical trends in international relations may be classified as transformation theory.[5] Its roots are in philosophy and in a concern for man's condition, rather than in strict, systematic empirical observation. Its structural elements include assumptions about the forces at work—historical, irreversible laws of nature which may be discovered, adjusted to, and propitiated, but not opposed successfully.

The future-orientation of Senghor's postulates about the process of history makes it utopian. He speaks about a progressive evolution already under way, leading eventually to the harmonious cooperation of equals in mutual respect and for reciprocal benefit, to cultural diversity accompanied by an overarching unity, a nameless, divine symbiosis whose outstanding characteristic is the optimist's expectation of human brotherhood. Perfection of the human condition is to be achieved through improvements in man's environment. Improvement follows the emphasis of Saint Simon's physical and Teilhard de Chardin's moral changes. The expectation is that both technology and values will play their part in bringing about the desired end.

Another characteristic of Senghor's vision is that it presupposes neither manichaeistic nor dialectical clashes. The omega point, the ultimate objective, will come about not so much through brash and total victory over recalcitrant opponents as by means of responsible action, cooperation, and eventual global harmony among the world's civilizations. There is no specific prediction regarding the fate of state or nation; but the units expected to emerge are civilizations which transcend national boundaries. Neither is there any prediction about such categories

5. For a recent review of transformation theory, consult Charles L. Mc-Clelland, *Theory and the International System* (New York: Macmillan, 1968), chap. 2.

as capitalism or communism, although the new civilization will have left behind the exploitation of man.

Senghor sees opportunity and action rather than challenge and response. He leaves aside such interpretations as decline and decay, although it would be tempting to interpret the decline of the colonial era with the finality of a decay theory. Instead, he concentrates on the previous dormancy of African civilizations, and on their regeneration through renewed internal vitality and culture contact with others. Senghor thus uses the notion of culture not only to raise fundamental questions about the purpose of man but also as a cornerstone in the evolution toward mankind's ultimate goal. Culture provides one of the vehicles for progress since it points to the underlying unity of mankind.

There are elements of determinism in Senghor's theories as they affect international relations. His theory of history rests on postulates believed to be irreversible factors already in motion. His theories also posit a certain moving equilibrium among civilizations (rather than among nations) reminiscent of suggestions that geographic regions, rather than the Europe before World War II or the bipolarity of the American-Soviet cold war, will be the building blocks of the future international system. His future vision is rooted deeply in the humanitarian notion that the purpose of the unfolding of history is to enable man to achieve enough freedom, not to accumulate material goods, but to dedicate himself to the creation of works of art and culture.

As is usually true with deterministic postulates, the theory leaves room for human volition to supplement the forces of nature. A belief in a spreading world consciousness as a vehicle for progress does not stand in the way of actions by humans as free agents. Regarding the crucial and pressing problem of adjustments in the present inequities between the wealthy and the indigent, for example, Senghor believes in the usefulness of moral and institutional pressures. Neither the "free" economy of the world, nor the increasing consciousness of the rich nations, is enough to bring about agreement and action. Hence, Third World countries must intervene in order to nudge decision-makers, who may be conscious, but also reluctant, to draw the practical consequences of their consciousness. The progression from subsistence through takeoff to mass consumption thus seems something less than inevitable in the eyes of Senegalese leaders.

On a number of important occasions, Senghor has demonstrated that his commitments do not stand in the way of flexible adaptation. The most outstanding example of flexibility was the abrupt volte-face, following the end of the Mali Federation, regarding the type of policy best calculated to prevent the economic and political isolation of Senegal. To be sure, the advocacy of inter-African political ties evident since the mid-1950s was instrumental; it was designed as a method to maintain the economic benefits which Senegal enjoyed within AOF, and less directly to increase Senghor's inter-African political influence and to decrease that of Houphouet-Boigny in order to influence forthcoming decisions at the metropolitan center. But the unity issue, by 1960, had taken on a life of its own. Senegal's sudden reversal thus ran the considerable risk of mystifying or alienating the large number of Africans committed to the slogans of African unity and balkanization. Senegal's reversal, near the end of 1960, thus demonstrated that economic needs carried a higher priority than did such other considerations as loss of prestige and political influence. More generally, the entire preindependence period witnessed a series of compromises between desired and available goals. The Senegalese leaders' acceptance of the French Union in 1946, of the 1956 enabling act, of the 1958 French constitution, and of political independence was accompanied—and sometimes nearly overshadowed—by serious misgivings.

Another facet of Senghor's personality is the persistence of commitments once undertaken. Perhaps this trait is related to what other Africans sometimes refer to as his "professorial" manner. Having thought carefully about goals and methods, he tends to lecture to his audiences from systematically prepared speeches. Senghor occasionally refers to the utility, in public office, of pedagogical repetition to insure that he is being understood correctly. Be that as it may, Senghor at times displays a stubborn streak going beyond that of most other people. The point to which he carried his convictions—or hopes—for the success of the Mali Federation has already been alluded to. But there are other examples. What success the development of the Senegal River valley has achieved so far is in large measure the result of Senghor's patience in the face of initially unfavorable odds. Moreover, Senghor entertained long hopes—and worked toward the realization—of increased African involvement in the essentially French process of allocating economic benefits for Africa.

Senghor's optimism on these occasions was pitted against a number of significant obstacles. The attempt to enter into a political federation with the Soudanese faced profound ideological differences on such basic political questions as the purpose of the federation, economic policy, independence, and vastly different domestic political experiences and structures. In addition, Senghor's faith remained undiminished in the face of examples of Soudanese interference in Senegal's domestic politics. Senegal's early hopes for cooperation among the four states bordering on the Senegal River were long frustrated by the bitterness of Mali leaders after the federal attempt, by the profound ideological antipathies and many accusations of Guinean leaders (reinforced by fears of a coup d'état), and by Mauritania's relative indifference, all despite the concrete economic advantages which these states could expect to gain in due time.

With respect to African participation in deciding the nature and amount of French assistance, Senghor was clearly overly optimistic in his expectations that the French government would be willing to give up a share of its control over the well-being of the metropole. Finally, francophonie faces a number of significant obstacles. The issue of a world-wide French-language community, in the age of decolonization, attracts charges of neocolonialism, as witness the predictable official coolness of the French response and the reluctance of many other former French colonies to support, initially, more than relatively innocuous cultural ties. The formal presentation of the project was pervaded by a high degree of optimism in its expectation of support and cooperation by states whose ties with the African core are tenuous at best.

The persistence and faith which Senghor occasionally displays may be ascribed, also, to a more common trait described by many Africans as their belief in the potency of the spoken word.

This aspect of his behavior can certainly be explained easily with the help of either or both categories. In fact, one recent example was the mild verbal euphoria which accompanied the official creation, after long years of frustrated effort, of the Organisation des Etats Riverains du Fleuve Sénégal; other things being equal, one might have expected Senghor's public enthusiasm to be dampened by previous experiences with political unification in West Africa.

Finally, Senghor's personal philosophy reflects depth and perspective beyond the range of that of the average political leader. More than many other Africans, Senghor is free from the searing inferiority complex inculcated by the colonial situation. He presents to Africa and to the world beyond the vision of man as a creator of artistic expression transcending by far the deadening effect of science and material pursuits. He projects a future devoid of narrow nationalisms, in which men are judged as individuals according to their contributions regardless of the accidents of their origin. He proposes that Africans build their unity not on the ever shifting sands of political divergences, on the temporary and somewhat narrow conceptions of economic interests fenced in by present political divisions, or on the ephemeral emotions of personal differences among leaders, but on elements of common heritage, of shared economic opportunities.

Perhaps more than any other African leader, Senghor gazes beneath and beyond the verities and priorities of the day. To the psychological attraction of political independence, he adds the constraints and opportunities of interdependence. To the resentment against the colonial era and its sequels, he adds a historical perspective which seeks to discriminate between the useful and the objectionable. Beyond the burning resentment against erstwhile conquerors, he speaks of olive branches extended in the name of humanity. Hence, more is to be gained from glancing into the future than from dwelling on the past.

The influence of France on Senghor, as suggested in chapter four, has left a deep imprint. Perhaps that influence can be symbolized by the French-built statute still standing in front of the Senegalese National Assembly, depicting two soldiers, one black and one white, standing side by side as if working toward common goals, or by the annual celebration of Bastille Day as a national holiday in Senegal.

Beyond this superficial symbolism, there can be no question that France holds a special place in the mind of Senghor. France was, after all, a country which bestowed status and recognition on a young, struggling foreign student; it was the scene of intellectual excitement shared by personal friends both black and white, of the early battles of negritude, and of Africans' joint participation in legislative and executive work dedicated to the improvement of their lot. Despite its obvious and at times painful shortcomings, the French experience nonetheless reflected light through its encouragement of the quest for identity and pride, through a large measure of intellectual open-mindedness, and through fundamental concepts of freedom and equality which retain their relevance after formal independence.

President Senghor's preindependence political experience in France no doubt reinforced his predisposition toward gradualism. His participation in French politics during the Fourth Republic fostered an awareness that progress was possible and forthcoming in spite of African disenchantment with French hesitation, opposition, and bumbling. Africans had many friends among French political leaders, and men like Senghor were socialized into France's political culture at least to the extent that they tended to regard slow, at times painfully slow, progress as fairly legitimate.

African leaders' experience in France also reinforced their perception of the interdependence of nations—rather than separation and autarchy—as the essential and growing factor in international affairs. As "insiders," AOF leaders acquired perceptions leading to a readiness to cooperate within the French system toward the gradual acquisition of autonomy and the periodic revision of the timetable for it. If an old, well-established country like France had to rely on colonial ties and the international system, and especially on the United States from the time of the Marshall Plan, then there was little likelihood that new states like Senegal would be able to stand on their own feet overnight. This perception tempered Senghor's views on autonomy and independence and reinforced an awareness and tolerance for actual dependence not only on France but also on the international community.

As indicated earlier, Senghor can be critical, even caustic, in his assessment of things French. But since his French experience did not lead to total alienation, neither has it led to total rejection. The Senegalese president clearly believes in the existence of an especially close relationship between people at home in French culture and civilization; and there can be little doubt that this is continually reinforced by France's acknowledgment —and insistence—that such a relationship exists, a belief which was transformed through, but not abandoned by, the political decolonization process. What this amounts to is a determination of what people one is most comfortable with, and for Senghor, the answer includes both Africans and French-influenced people.

It is difficult to assess with precision what influence President Senghor has wielded on international affairs. He is not a firebrand orator whose audiences respond by spontaneously rising to their feet. But his talents nonetheless include a gift for articulating issues and inspiring enthusiasm; his influence takes place at the level of sophisticated discussion of issues of concern to elites more than to people at large. In international affairs, he is at his most eloquent when addressing himself to the rehabilitation of African culture, to the need for recognizing Africans as equals, and to the consequences of his country's economic isolation and of the inequities incrusted in international economic society.

Senghor's international reputation lends his country a luster which it could not otherwise have. In his own right, as a poet, philosopher, and humanist, he is known and appreciated more widely than is Senegal. When he travels abroad, he is not merely the representative of an African state; his reputation precedes and accompanies him. As an articulate spokesman for a black cultural nationalism and, intended or not, a founder of the negritude school of French-language African literature, he is assured of a reception which elicits intellectual anticipation and excitement. University and similar audiences are taken with the polished delivery and sophisticated—if somewhat mystical—content of his speeches. It is easy to imagine him as a distinguished professor in a university of world renown, a dedicated, imaginative, and conscientious scholar attracting students, peers, and citizens alike through the interdisciplinary breadth and depth of his interests.

Among African leaders, President Senghor tends to be regarded with some awe, perhaps because his achievements are so numerous and yet not always fully understood. Some display Senghor's works in their official waiting rooms, perhaps more for effect than out of a profound personal interest in their content. People are conscious that they owe respect and deference to the African star of negritude, but his relationship with many other African leaders does not appear to be as close as that, say, between Félix Houphouet-Boigny, Hamani Diori, and Hubert Maga (president of Niger and occasional president of Dahomey, respectively). In short, African leaders readily agree that Senghor is an outstanding African and an object of their pride; they may do so intuitively, and many would find it difficult to explain. But the Senegalese president is also one of the "deans" of the era of Africa's political liberation that followed World War II. In this context, he benefits from the seniority inherent in experience and longevity in office. As a result, other leaders frequently solicit his counsel and advice, and he is assured of at least a respectful hearing.

The idiosyncratic influence of President Senghor on the foreign relations behavior of Senegal lies more in a general orientation, flavor, and philosophical underpinning than in the contents of specific policies. He conditions that policy, but not at the expense of the national interest. Policy bears his unmistakable imprint, but not his arbitrary fiat. He may make all or most of the important decisions, but these reflect domestic conditions and needs as well as external circumstances. His role is that of an orchestra leader; he does not insist on playing each instrument. To the extent that he writes his own music, it is adapted to both orchestra and audience.

PENETRATION AND INTERDEPENDENCE

Discussions of Africa in world affairs are frequently cast in the framework of the morally just struggle for liberation from foreign influence, either before or after independence, or both. Many Africans themselves are comfortable with an interpretation of their foreign relations that leans heavily on such concepts as neocolonialism, imperialism, and intervention by others in the affairs of their newly sovereign states. And yet one of the chief characteristics of the international system as seen from the vantage point of the African states is that foreign influence is nearly omnipresent and likely to remain so for some time to come.

It is possible, however, to use concepts with much lower emotional content, quite apart from one's moral commitments. Concepts innocent of moral consideration are more likely, moreover, to yield an understanding of some of the basic conditions of the international environment which African states have joined. One of the most useful of such concepts is that of "penetration" suggested by Rosenau. Its great advantage over emotional terms is that it provides analytical clarity. Rosenau defines a penetrated society as one in which

> nonmembers of a national society participate directly and authoritatively, through actions taken jointly with the society's members, in either the allocation of values or the mobilization of support on behalf of its goals.[6]

Rosenau alludes to some of the difficulties involved in his penetration concept. He raises questions, for instance, about the proper definition of participation and its relation to penetration. The concept does raise the general problem of how to measure influence—the ability to get others to do something they would not otherwise do. Since that ability is a function of situational factors, the degree of overt influence required by, say, the French ambassador in Senegal is much smaller than that required of a Chinese envoy in order to qualify as penetration. Another question concerns the term *nonmember*. Is a native Frenchman who has become a Senegalese citizen a member of Senegalese society by virtue of his legal status? Or should he be considered a nonmember because his outlook is more modern and Western than that of other Senegalese with whom he works?

6. Rosenau, "Pre-Theories," p. 65.

These and other like difficulties aside, however, it is best to approach the question from the realization that there is no such thing as a fully sovereign state in today's world. This observation is valid irrespective of the geographic or national referent; it is as valid for Senegal as it is for the Soviet Union, although different in degree. If no contemporary state is fully sovereign, it follows that all states are penetrated to a greater or lesser degree. One would further expect that the degree of penetration is a function of the ability of a state to resist penetration by external forces. In view of the weak capabilities of the new states, it must be assumed that they are, given the international context, subject to a high degree of penetration. Seen from this perspective, penetration is a normal consequence of interstate relations, not necessarily of neocolonialist machinations.

Rosenau's definition of penetration leads directly to an examination of the many expatriate foreign advisers and technical assistants in countries like Senegal. The fifteen hundred Frenchmen who serve in Senegal are only a fraction of that country's thirty-five thousand civil servants. Their influence on Senegal's policies is, of course, not a function of numbers. It is a function of the simple need for qualified technicians not available on the spot, of their experience, of the rapport they are able to establish with formal Senegalese decision-makers, and of the length of their tenure in Senegal and their familiarity with the country's problems.

Their kind of penetration is "authoritative and direct" since they are there for that purpose. But it is also voluntary, welcome penetration since they are there at the invitation of the government of Senegal. In fact, there have been cases in which that government officially requested that individual Frenchmen be permitted to remain in their posts after their terms had expired, although French regulations required that they be transferred elsewhere. As may be expected, such individuals were widely respected for their extraordinary qualities and skills, and the Senegalese prized their service and expertise.

A prominent case was the employment of a Frenchman, Jean Rous, as political adviser to President Senghor, a post which he held from shortly after Senegal's independence to 1968. Rous has a wide circle of influential friends in Africa, Asia, and Europe. He shares Senghor's basic philosophic orientation and frequently acts as unofficial spokesman for the Presidency of the Republic, explaining, commenting upon, and popularizing Senghor's policy views. Rous attended, and gave Senghor a report on, the 1955 Bandung conference of nonaligned states, at a time when the future Senegalese president was a subcabinet official in a French government not overly concerned with that conference. Acting as Senghor's agent, he participated directly in both the allocation of values and the mobilization of internal and external support for Senegal's foreign relations objectives.[7]

Another clear case of penetration is that of the French resident business community. Their advice is authoritative since the institution to which they belong—the Chamber of Commerce, Agriculture, and Industry—is an official, public body of the Senegalese state. Their participation in national decisions is also direct because of their access, formal and informal, to deliberative and decision-making bodies. One effect of their participation seems to constitute an obstacle to the diversification of trade channels, even if the Senegalese are apparently willing to pay this price because of their dependence on continued French good will. Most important, the large firms which wield the greatest influence are subsidiaries of companies with headquarters in France; consequently their advice tends to follow, at least in part, extra-Senegalese criteria.

The locus of penetration need not be the territory of the penetrated society; it can be outside its borders. Thus, discussions among African heads of state, either during numerous state visits or at inter-African gatherings, may be examples of direct penetration. They would be authoritative, given the status of the officials involved. Discussions between Senegalese and French officials, in Dakar or in Paris, may be examples of such penetration if they involve a Senegalese decision which depends partly on French help.

African states' membership in international organizations may

7. Rous discusses such topics as Vietnam, the 1967 Middle East crisis, and the deterioration of the terms of trade for developing states more freely in his writings than does President Senghor in public. The media used include the weekly party paper of the Union Progressiste Sénégalaise, the weekly journal *Jeune afrique*, and various occasional French sources.

also involve penetration, which becomes routinized and institutionalized if it involves the voluntary abandonment of state sovereignty. The common bank which issues and controls the CFA franc may be said to allocate values authoritatively for Senegal since decisions are made jointly with nonmembers of that country's society. Very much the same can be said about bilateral and multilateral treaties and agreements entered into by Senegal. Senegal's readiness to enter into federal relations with other African states was another example of penetration; one of these ventures, the Mali Federation, opened the door to a degree of penetration judged excessive by Senegalese leaders.

The use of the concept of penetration could, in fact, be extended to encompass almost the entire sphere of the foreign relations of such countries as Senegal. It could include, for example, the activities of resident diplomats and special envoys who seek to alter other countries' policies. And it could include, in the case of the former French African territories, their penetration of French society. During the colonial period, Africans penetrated the French political system directly and authoritatively since they did participate, through legislative and executive action, in decisions made on behalf of France. This is no longer true; but indirect participation continues in the sense that Senegalese officials retain some influence on French decisions and have used that influence, after independence, to bend French policy on several occasions. This kind of indirect penetration, which for Senegal is reinforced by longtime personal friendships, is one of that country's trumps in her relations with the former colonial metropole.

For a full understanding of Senegal in international affairs, the concept of penetration must be complemented by that of interdependence. On the surface, there is something of a paradox in wanting to build nations—that is, to extol the virtues of nationalism—in an age when nationalism is on the decline, and to single out both the sanctity of the new national political boundaries and the interdependence of nations. The paradox is, however, more apparent than real. It can be reconciled by asking questions about the functions which these two emphases are expected to perform.

Present emphasis on the inviolability of political borders is rooted in domestic and systemic phenomena. First, it reflects the search for national integration as a reasonably effective way to provide a modicum of political stability, in the wishes of incumbent leadership groups to maintain themselves in office, in the psychological value of being master in one's own house, however built, and in the ability of the new, incipient national societies to persist. Second, it is grounded in a desire for recognition as equals, which happens to take the political shape of the boundaries delineated by the former colonial powers, and in resistance to anything resembling past colonial tutelage; the insistence, in inter-African affairs, on territorial integrity and sovereignty is rooted in the desire to achieve some order and stability which may be viewed as a transitory, short-term goal. It is designed to simplify, rather than complicate, the more general problem of the transfer of loyalties away from subnational traditional groups.

There is no reason to believe that a short-term sensitivity to political boundaries cannot accommodate long-term interdependence. An African state which simultaneously insists on respect for political sovereignty and appears to ignore it in connection with international trade or aid requirements is not, ipso facto, guilty of hypocrisy. That state is acting in the simultaneous pursuit of moral and material benefits, to be gained by different paths.

Such traditional functions of nation-states as providing for territorial defense and the people's material welfare are becoming increasingly difficult to perform for older nations, which are learning to lean on others as well as on the international community for the satisfaction of their wants. Chauvinism and jingoism may have had their place in the history of man, but they are fast becoming curious—if not outright pathetic—anachronisms. The thrust of African states is toward greater participation, toward greater interpenetration. As a result, the boundaries of political sovereignty are bound to become weakened further and thus open new doors for mutual influence.

Seen from this viewpoint, African nationalism is a transitory phenomenon, rooted in specific causes related chiefly to a concern for domestic stability and international recognition. The African nationalism of today will leave room for something larger once these demands have been satisfied. The major underlying foreign policy objective of such states as Senegal is to join the main stream of the international economy on bases more advantageous and equitable than present ones. The United Nations Conference on Trade and Aid is seeking to modify, not to abandon, the international economic order, the better to participate.

Senegal, almost from its inception as a geographic entity, has belonged to two different systems: the national, or Senegalese, domestic system, and the international, or multinational, system of the African-French ensemble. It is not surprising, therefore, that Senegal's conception of international affairs should be grounded in something larger than pure domestic considerations.

President Senghor has had a longtime interest in large-scale federalism transcending by far the political borders of existing states. This was reflected in his preindependence suggestions for altering the French Union and building wider, Eurafrican ties, and in his experimentation with federalism; it was reflected, after independence, in his proposal for a world-wide French-language ensemble, and in his characterization of the Senegal River development organization as a possible future model federation. Despite setbacks, Senegal has led the way in projecting her thought beyond narrow nationalism, old and new.

It can be argued, as Senghor does, that present developments in the international state system can be apprehended with the help of his transformation theory. Such developments as the diffusion of power, the integration and socialization of larger numbers of people, the increasing permeability of political borders, the increase in world population and the consequent pressures on sharing technology, the confrontation between poor and rich nations, the decolonization process, in short, the fluidity of the international state system, may all be perceived as contributing to closer cooperation among the political segments of the world community.

By the same token they can also be explained as *sui generis* developments without any relation to a theory of Senghor's historical sweep. The increasing interdependence of nations can be attributed primarily to technological development and to the ever growing need for apparently finite reserves of raw materials; the lack of violent conflict between the superpowers, to mutual fears of destruction; the dwindling of foreign assistance, to national parochialism; and the refractory response on the part of the rich nations to suggestions for altering the structure of the international economy, to egotism.

Although it would be difficult at best to establish causal links between the transformation of the international state system and Senghor's postulates, the utopian vision which he projects may nonetheless have some effect on the direction of that transformation. If it were widely accepted that a spreading consciousness of man's plight and the dysfunctional role of national and other parochialisms are making, or ought to make, political leaders more receptive to international cooperative ventures, then Senghor's vision would contribute to the realization of a world much like the one he foresees. To some extent, the nature and direction of change will be determined by changing values, and utopias are useful—Senghor would say necessary—devices to shift perceptions and hence alter behavior. Léopold Senghor's comments on these issues do not come out of a textbook on international relations. They bear the imprint of his experiences and, more profoundly, of his conviction that man is also a noble creature.

FUTURE DIRECTIONS

For students of Africa, their subject is a cemetery of predictions. This situation is related to three major factors. One may be their inability to understand African developments, especially if opportunities for prolonged field study and for contact were insufficient. Another may be their value commitments; Africans have long complained that too many foreign Africanists tend to look upon the continent as a laboratory for their own pet theories and models. The third, and probably most important, obstacle to predictions is the fluidity—and novelty—of many fundamental elements of the African experience.

I make no claim to immunity from any of these difficulties. It would nonetheless be of interest to attempt some educated guesses about the possible future direction of Senegal's foreign relations behavior, especially since President Senghor may plan to retire in the not too distant future.

Before turning to speculation about Senegal's foreign policy after Senghor, it may be useful to review briefly the chief characteristics of that policy during the first decade after political independence. First, Senegal's national priorities and objectives —economic rewards and decolonization—have not changed greatly since their gradual articulation during the preindependence period. Changes in the methods by which goals are pursued have occurred, related to changes in the international environment. Second, the country's style has been one of conciliation and gradualism; it has sought to avoid head-on confrontations in an attempt to prevent costly and unnecessary frictions.

A third major characteristic of Senegal's foreign relations has been a readiness to work within existing structures until dissatisfactions, real or perceived, made change unavoidable. One of Senghor's frequent remarks is that such structures have the advantage of existing; this suggests some reluctance to experiment with new departures, and perhaps that he places a higher premium on protection than on flexibility and initiative. This is not, of course, to suggest that countries like Senegal can remake the world, or to obscure the gap between capabilities and intentions.

A fourth characteristic has been a preference for building inter-African ties by starting at the bottom rather than at the top, reflected in Senegal's concept of regional African unity beginning with the development of the Senegal River valley. The country's leaders remain conscious of the many failures, before and after independence, of attempts at integration from the top. This aspect of policy tacitly recognizes that political frictions are not capable of being solved rapidly and assumes that closer cooperation calls for concentrating on mutual economic, technical, and cultural interests and on avoiding political irritants.

Another important characteristic has been the gradual, at times hesitant, adaptation of elements of foreign policy to systemic givens, and a correspondingly growing awareness of the interaction between national objectives and the international (especially inter-African) environment.

A sixth important aspect was her insistence on respect for the newly acquired political sovereignty and territorial integrity of African states. This is grounded in the conviction, in turn rooted in African experiments with political unification, that drastic attempts to change the political map of Africa tend to invite and precipitate greater domestic and external difficulties than already exist.

Finally, a seventh characteristic at a more abstract level has been Senghor's particular philosophy as it pertains to international affairs. It would be easy to exaggerate the impact this has made on the country's foreign relations behavior, since it expressed Senghor's personality and functioned as a more or less utopian guide for a future whose outline is barely discernible. Perhaps it could best be summarized as helping to lay foundations for the recognition by the external environment of Africa as a moral equal, and thus to operate at the psychological level of international relations. By definition, it is ahead of its political times to the extent that Africans are concerned with more pressing and immediate problems. If it is true that Senghor's philosophy, as distinct from practical policies, has hardly succeeded in coaxing harmony and cooperation out of international relations, it should nevertheless not be dismissed as mere aesthetic adornment. Senghor is a vocal and articulate critic of cultural and other types of arrogance, dedicated to the proposition that the various segments of humanity should be accepted for what they are rather than be shackled by extraneous judgments. It is not inconceivable that his convictions about the importance of cultural and historical affinities in international affairs will continue to be used after his retirement, both as an inspiration and as an instrument to accompany other elements of foreign policy.

It does not seem that the objectives and general orientation of Senegal's foreign relations will undergo any drastic change. The country's enormous dependence on the outside world, her attachments to those nations most able and willing to help, her emphasis on regional rather than continental cooperation within Africa, her opposition to minority rule in Africa, her insistence that political borders and sovereignty be respected, and her efforts to seek structural changes in the international economy will probably remain the most important concerns of her foreign policy.

What changes may take place with the retirement of President Senghor are likely to be changes of style and intensity rather than changes in substance. In an attempted forecast of what changes could be expected, it is useful to return to the distinction between domestic and external determinants of foreign policy decisions.

From the point of view of domestic politics, one may expect a slight shift to the left in foreign policy orientation once Senghor is no longer at the helm. The demise of at least two former close associates of President Senghor, directly and indirectly related to important foreign policy issues, indicates that prominent and capable Senegalese leaders are inclined to reorient elements of foreign relations policy, and that Senghor's views do not necessarily command unanimity.

Among the more or less latent factors in Senegal's society and polity, a number of incipient and possible pressures can be expected to affect the general issue of the speed of the socialization process, which is in turn related to aspects of foreign policy. Domestic factors most capable of affecting foreign relations include (1) younger technocrats' demand for a brighter place under the official sun, (2) indigenous merchants organizing for government support, (3) Casamance separatism, (4) reintegration of former Premier Mamadou Dia into the political system, (5) the separation of functions between the president of the Republic and the prime minister, and (6) the position of the armed forces.

Given the traditions of pluralism, compromise, cooptation, and fusion among contending and dissenting political forces, the absence of a skillful and respected national arbiter enjoying widespread political support could lead to the reinforcement of demands from a variety of sources and to a more collegial leadership group. This may well increase tensions and demands for continued cooperation and hence produce differences in political style. The reinstatement of Mamadou Dia, for example, has long been rumored as a distinct possibility; it may lead to more rapid efforts to transform social and economic conditions at the expense of the interests of Muslim religious leaders and of segments of the urban Senegalese and foreign bourgeoisie. Dia, in effect, could reemerge as a top national leader. He reportedly has spurned several overtures by Senghor and insisted that he is innocent of the charges for which he was convicted in 1962, and he has retained some popularity among technicians and elements of the intelligentsia. It is also likely that Dia would exert a somewhat more militant influence in international affairs and seek to diversify Senegal's aid and trade partners faster than the Senghor government has.

Recent government changes may not constitute a rejuvenation of Senegal's political system; it is nonetheless clear that younger people have been drawn more closely into the national decision-making process. It would be difficult, at best, to seek to reverse this trend in the future. The Senegalese sector of private commerce is beginning to organize and to assert itself as a pressure group; its interests are bound to conflict with those of the foreign resident business community, and this cannot fail to have important repercussions on the senegalization and diversification of external trade relations. In the government structure, the First Republic's division between prime minister and president of the Republic was used as a channel for fighting political battles and ended in a power struggle and the downfall of the system. It remains to be seen whether a repetition can be avoided in the Third Republic, especially after the departure of Senghor.

Finally, it is not impossible that the military, which in Senegal appears to be a privileged group even by "normal" African standards, may increase their demands on the political system, particularly if they thought that civilian leaders were not doing their job. Moreover, some officers are known to press for a more active military role in defending Senegal from Portuguese incursions. In view of the general concern over Senegal's future relations with an independent Portuguese Guinea to the south and over the dangers of separatism in the Casamance, arguments that more active support for the Portuguese Guinea nationalists is sound insurance may find more receptive ears.

Much of Senegal's foreign policy will continue to be affected by systemic forces. It is probable that future systemic developments will move Senegal toward greater adaptation and diversification in her relations with other countries. First, in inter-African affairs, the issue of the complete decolonization of the continent, and hence of what is widely regarded as white racism, may come to replace that of neocolonialism as paramount. African systemic pressures are therefore likely to grow in the form of demands for increasing support for black nationalists, particularly in southern Africa. These pressures may well reinforce domestic voices counseling greater Senegalese involvement in Portuguese Guinea.

Second, it is not likely that relations between rich and poor states will be altered drastically in the foreseeable future, or will be greatly affected by Senghor's retirement. Two kinds of motives underlie the rich nations' readiness to continue aid and trade. The first is a general conviction concerning humanitarian (and to some extent practical) values and an international sense of noblesse oblige; the second are more concrete assumptions related to interests, whether economic, strategic, or political. It may not be possible to predict the relative future importance of these two kinds of motivation, but the trend seems to favor greater weight to interests, without eclipsing humanitarianism. The combined pressures of the poor nations may well be able to arrest the decline of foreign aid, but they may not be able to increase the flow substantially so as to approximate the oft-declared norm of 1 per cent of Gross National Product. Economic assistance depends largely on the desire of donor nations to establish or maintain at least a presence, and at most an influence, in Africa. Indications are that their search for presence or influence will continue.

It is likely, by contrast, that trade relations can be further diversified as a result of the slowly increasing interest on the part of prospective trading partners other than former metropoles. At the same time, continued American insistence on a world of free trade tends to drive many African states into continuing the European preferences which they have enjoyed. Thus it is possible that international trade will, in the short run, be characterized more by protectionism than by liberalization. The signature of the second Yaoundé convention in 1969, renewing the relationship of the African Associated States and European Economic Community, structured that relationship for another five years. These ties may well become generalized for Africa with the inclusion of Britain—and several other European nations—followed by other African states admitted in a new associated status.

Third, should countries such as the Soviet Union and mainland China seek to expand their influence to the western tip of the African continent, it is likely that they would make overtures acceptable to any Senegalese government. If they can demonstrate, directly and indirectly through example elsewhere in Africa, their readiness to engage in cooperation and to respect Senegal's sovereignty, then there is no reason to believe that Senegal would not respond favorably. The Soviet Union, in fact, has already laid the groundwork for such cooperation with material help for the development of Senegal's fishing industry. Moreover, the Russians have demonstrated that they have become more sensitive to African states' sovereignty than they were in the early nineteen-sixties. The contrast between their unsuccessful bid for landing rights in Dakar during the Cuban missile crisis and the subsequent signature of a Senegalo-Soviet agreement for servicing regular commercial flights at Yoff international airport is instructive in this respect.

Finally, Senghor's departure is not likely to fundamentally affect French policy toward Senegal. It will almost certainly make Senegalo-French relations less harmonious. But France's attitude toward Senegal is based only in part on respect and admiration for Senghor; more important, the place of Senegal as a privileged state rests also on French political and strategic interests. It would be surprising if these interests would diminish greatly in the immediate future.

To sum up, Senegal's foreign relations will continue to be determined chiefly by the interplay between domestic and external factors, and both sets of factors indicate the likelihood of faster and greater diversification of relations with other states. Senghor's eventual departure from political leadership in Senegal will nonetheless be an irreplaceable loss. Léopold Sédar Senghor will go down in history as one of Africa's most illustrious leaders, whose message and vision extend far beyond the shores of his native country and continent.

Selected Bibliography

General Works

Adloff, Richard. *West Africa: The French-Speaking Nations*. New York: Holt, Rinehart and Winston, 1964.

Amin, Samir. *Le Monde des affaires sénégalais*. Paris: Minuit, 1969.

Ansprenger, Franz. *Politik im schwarzen Afrika*. Cologne and Opladen: Westdeutscher Verlag, 1960.

d'Arboussier, Gabriel. *L'Afrique vers l'unité*. Paris: Saint Paul, 1961.

————. *Le RDA est toujours anti-colonialiste*. Paris: Imprimerie pour le Commerce et l'Industrie, 1952.

Aurillac, J. *Régime politique et administratif de l'A.O.F.* Dakar: Gouvernement Général de l'A.O.F., 1949.

Battestini, Monique, and Battestini, Raymond. *Léopold Sédar Senghor*. Paris: Fernand Nathan, 1965.

Blanchet, André. *L'Itinéraire des partis africains depuis Bamako*. Paris: Plon, 1958.

Bonn, Gisela. *Léopold Sédar Senghor: Wegbereiter der Culture universelle*. Düsseldorf: Econ, 1968.

Borella, François. *L'Evolution politique et juridique de l'union française depuis 1946*. Paris: Librairie Générale de Droit et de Jurisprudence, 1958.

Bourcart, Robert. *Le Grand Conseil de l'Afrique occidentale française*. Paris: Encyclopédie d'Outre-Mer, 1956.

Brasseur, G. *L'A.O.F.* Dakar: Institut Français d'Afrique Noire, 1957.

Brigaud, Félix. *Histoire moderne et contemporaine du Sénégal*. Dakar: Grande Imprimerie Africaine, 1966.

————. *Histoire traditionnelle du Sénégal*. Dakar: Grande Imprimerie Africaine, 1962.

————. *Le Sénégal économique*. Saint-Louis: Centre de Recherche et de Documentation, 1967.

Camboulives, Marguerite. *L'Organisation coopérative au Sénégal*. Paris: Pédone, 1967.

Charles, Bernard. "Le Socialisme africain: Mythes et réalités." *Revue française de science politique*, Vol. XV, no. 5 (October, 1965).

Congrès constitutif du P.F.A. Paris: Présence Africaine, 1959.

Cowan, L. Gray. *Local Government in West Africa*. New York: Columbia University Press, 1958.

Crowder, Michael. *Senegal: A Study in French Assimilation Policy*. London: Oxford University Press, 1962.

Deschamps, Hubert. *Le Sénégal et la Gambie*. Paris: Presses Universitaires de France, 1964.

Dia, Mamadou. *Nations africaines et solidarité mondiale*. Paris: Presses Universitaires de France, 1960.

————. *Réflexions sur l'économie de l'Afrique noire*. Paris: Présence Africaine, 1960.

Diop, Ousmane Socé. *L'Afrique à l'heure de l'indépendance*. Paris: Nouvelles Editions Latines, 1963.

Doll, Peter. *Der Senegalesische Weg zum Afrikanischem Sozialismus*. Hamburg: Hamburger Gesellschaft für Völkerrecht und Auswärtige Politik, 1966.

Dugué, Gil. *Vers les Etats-Unis d'Afrique*. Dakar: Lettres Africaines, 1960.

L'Evolution économique du Sénégal. Paris: La Documentation Française, January 13, 1964. Note et Etude Documentaire 3,054.

Foltz, William J. *From French West Africa to the Mali Federation*. New Haven: Yale University Press, 1965.

Garnier, Christine. *Sénégal: Porte de l'Afrique*. Paris: Hachette, 1962.

Gonidec, P.-F. *Droit d'Outre-Mer: De l'empire colonial de la France à la Communauté.* Paris: Montchrestien, 1959.

———. *Droit d'Outre-Mer: Les Rapports actuels de la France et des pays d'Outre-Mer.* Paris: Montchrestien, 1960.

Guèye, Doudou. "Unité africaine et fédération." *Le Mali,* no. 11 (July, 1960).

Guèye, Lamine. *Etapes et perspectives de l'union française.* Paris: Union Française, 1955.

———. *Itinéraire africain.* Paris: Présence Africaine, 1966.

Guibert, Armand. *Léopold Sédar Senghor.* Paris: Seghers, 1961.

Hanf, Irmgard. *Léopold Sédar Senghor: Ein Afrikanischer Dichter Französischer Prägung.* Munich: Wilhelm Fink, 1968.

Hayter, Teresa. *French Aid.* London: Overseas Development Institute, 1966.

Julienne, Roland. "La Coopération entre la république française et les pays insuffisamment développés." *Revue de droit des pays d'Afrique* (Third Quarter, 1962).

Lavroff, Dmitri-Georges. *La République du Sénégal.* Paris: Librairie Générale de Droit et de Jurisprudence, 1966.

Leduc, Michel. *Les Institutions monétaires africaines: Pays francophones.* Paris: Pédone, 1965.

de Leusse, Hubert. *Léopold Sédar Senghor l'africain.* Paris: Hattier, 1967.

Lewis, William H., ed. *French-Speaking Africa: The Search for Identity.* New York: Walker, 1965.

Ligot, Maurice. *Les Accords de coopération entre la France et les états africains et malgache d'expression française.* Paris: La Documentation Française, 1964.

Lombard, J. *Géographie humaine.* Dakar: Grande Imprimerie Africaine, 1963.

de Lusignan, Guy. *French-Speaking Africa since Independence.* New York: Praeger, 1969.

Milcent, Ernest. *L'Afrique entre en scène.* Bibliothèque de l'Homme d'Action. Paris: Editions Témoignage Chrétien, 1958.

———. *Au Carrefour des options africaines: Le Sénégal.* Paris: Centurion, 1965.

———, and Sordet, Monique. *Léopold Sédar Senghor et la naissance de l'Afrique moderne.* Paris: Seghers, 1969.

Mortimer, Edward. *France and the Africans.* New York: Walker, 1969.

Peterec, Richard. *Dakar and West African Economic Development.* New York: Columbia University Press, 1967.

Piquion, René. *Les Trois Grands de la négritude.* Haiti: Deschamps, 1964.

Richard-Molard, Jacques. *Afrique occidentale française.* Paris: Berger-Levrault, 1956.

Rous, Jean. *Léopold Sédar Senghor: Un Président de l'Afrique nouvelle.* Paris: Didier, 1967.

Saint Marc, Michèle. *Commerce extérieur de développement: Le Cas de la zone franc.* Paris: Société d'Edition d'Enseignement Supérieur, 1968.

Senghor, Léopold Sédar. "The African Road to Socialism." *African Forum,* Vol. I, no. 3 (Winter, 1966).

———. *On African Socialism.* New York: Praeger, 1964.

———. "L'Avenir de la France dans l'Outre-Mer." *Politique étrangère,* XIX, no. 4 (October, 1954), 419–26.

———. "Défense de l'Afrique noire." *Esprit* (July, 1945).

———. "Eléments constructifs d'un civilisation d'inspiration négro-africaine." *Présence Africaine* (February–May, 1959).

———. "C'est Georges Pompidou qui m'a converti au socialisme." *Le Figaro littéraire* (May 12, 1962).

———. "Ce que l'homme noir apporte." In *L'Homme de couleur,* edited by Cardinal Verdier. Paris: Plon, 1939.

———. "Un Humanisme de l'union française." *Esprit* (July, 1949).

———. *Liberté I: Négritude et humanisme.* Paris: Editions du Seuil, 1964.

———. *Nation et voie africaine du socialisme.* Paris: Présence Africaine, 1961.

———. "Les Nationalismes d'Outre-Mer et les peuples de couleur." *Encyclopédie française,* Vol. XX (1959).

———. *Pierre Teilhard de Chardin et la politique africaine.* Paris: Editions du Seuil, 1962.

———. *Planification et tension morale: IVè Congrès national de l'union progressiste sénégalaise, les 10, 11, et 12 Octobre 1963.* Dakar: Grande Imprimerie Africaine, 1963.

———. "Recueil des interventions faites à l'assemblée nationale française par le Président Léopold Sédar Senghor de 1946 à 1958 en sa qualité de Député du Sénégal." Mimeographed. Dakar, n.d. [1967?].

———. "Some Thoughts on Africa: A Continent in Development." *International Affairs,* Vol. XXXVIII (April, 1962).

———. *Théorie et pratique du socialisme sénégalais.* Dakar: Grande Imprimerie Africaine, 1966.

———. "Vues sur l'Afrique noire: ou assimiler, non être assimilé."

In *La Communauté impériale française*, edited by Robert Lemaignen, Léopold Sédar Senghor, and Prince Sisowath Youtévong. Paris: Editions Alsatia, 1945.

————. "West Africa in Evolution." *Foreign Affairs*, Vol. XXXIX, no. 2 (January, 1961).

Thiam, Doudou. "Les Données économiques de la politique étrangère des états africains." *Communauté et continents*, Vol. XX (October–December, 1963).

————. *La Politique étrangère des états africains*. Paris: Presses Universitaires de France, 1963.

————. "Socialisme et politique internationale dans les états de l'Afrique noire." *Annales africaines*, Vol. I (1962).

Thompson, Virginia, and Adloff, Richard. *French West Africa*. Stanford: Stanford University Press, 1958.

Verdun, Louis-Georges. "Les Relations Sénégal-Gambie." *Revue juridique et politique: Indépendance et coopération*, no. 3 (July–September, 1966).

Welch, Claude E., Jr. *Dream of Unity: Pan-Africanism and Political Unification in West Africa*. Ithaca: Cornell University Press, 1966.

Zartman, I. William. *International Relations in the New Africa*. Englewood Cliffs, N.J.: Prentice-Hall, 1966.

Zolberg, Aristide R. *Creating Political Order: The Party-States of West Africa*. Chicago: Rand McNally, 1966.

Public Documents

Senegal

Commissariat à l'Information, à la Radiodiffusion et au Tourisme. *Voyage officiel aux Etats-Unis du Brésil de S. Exc. M. Léopold Sédar Senghor, Président de la République du Sénégal, 19 septembre–25 septembre 1964*. Dakar: Grande Imprimerie Africaine, 1964.

L'Economie du Sénégal. Dakar: Chambre de Commerce, d'Agriculture, et d'Industrie, 1965.

Ministère de l'Information, de la Presse et de Radiodiffusion. *Livre blanc sur le coup d'état manqué du 19 au 20 août 1960 et la Proclamation de l'indépendance du Sénégal*. Dakar: Grande Imprimerie Africaine, 1960.

————. *Sénégal d'hier . . . Sénégal d'aujourd'hui.* Casablanca: Imprimeries Réunies, 1961.

————. *Le Sénégal en marche.* Casablanca: Imprimeries Réunies, 1961.

Ministère de l'Interieur. *Livre blanc sur les élections présidentielles et législatives du 1 décembre 1963.* Dakar, 1963.

Ministère du Plan et du Développement. Service de la Statistique. "Commerce extérieur du Sénégal, 1957–1965." Mimeographed. Dakar, 1967.

————. "Comptes économiques, années 1963–1965." Mimeographed. Dakar, 1967.

————. *Situation économique du Sénégal (1965).* Dakar: Grande Imprimerie Africaine, 1966.

Ministère du Plan et de l'Industrie. Direction de la Statistique. *Bulletin statistique et économique mensuel.* Published monthly.

La Paix en Algérie par la négociation: La Position du Sénégal à l'O.N.U. dans le débat algérien. Tangiers: E.M.I., 1961.

Présidence de la République. *La Revue Esprit et nous.* Dakar: Grande Imprimerie Africaine, 1965.

Mali Federation

Procès verbaux des séances des 14 et 17 janvier 1959 de l'assemblée fédérale constituante. Dakar: Grande Imprimerie Africaine, 1959.

Séminaire organisé a l'occasion du congrès de l'union nationale de la jeunesse du Mali. Rufisque: Imprimerie Fédérale du Mali, 1960.

France

A.O.F. 1957. Paris: Haut Commissariat de la République en Afrique Occidentale Française, 1958.

La Conférence africaine française de Brazzaville (30 janvier 1944–8 février 1944). Algiers: Commissariat aux Colonies, 1944.

L'Equipment des territoires français d'Outre-Mer. Paris: Ministère de la France d'Outre-Mer, 1951.

Haut Commissariat-Général à Dakar. *Comptes économiques de l'Afrique occidentale française 1956, Rapport no. 6, échanges interterritoriaux.* Dakar: Service de Coordination des Affaires Economiques et du Plan, 1959.

Journal officiel de la république française—Communauté: Accords franco-maliens, July, 1960. Paris: Imprimerie des Journaux Officiels, 1960.

Secretariat d'Etat aux Affaires Etrangères Chargé de la Coopération. Direction de la coopération culturelle et technique. *Rapport d'activité 1964/65*. Paris, 1967.

Travaux préparatoires de la constitution: Avis et débats du comité consultatif constitutionnel. Paris: La Documentation Française, 1960.

Index

305